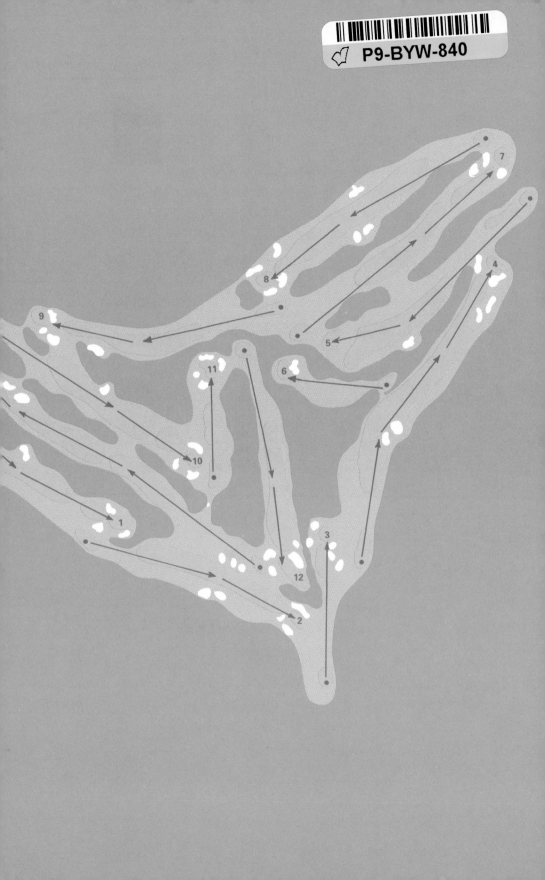

Heartbreak Hill

Heartbreak Hill

ANATOMY OF A RYDER CUP

TIM ROSAFORTE

St. Martin's Press ❧ New York

Design by Bonni Leon-Berman
Map illustrations © 1996 David Cain

Library of Congress Cataloging-in-Publication Data

Rosaforte, Tim.
    Heartbreak hill : anatomy of a Ryder Cup / by Tim Rosaforte : foreword by Lanny Wadkins ; photographs by David Cannon.
        p. cm.
    ISBN 0-312-14351-6
    1. Ryder Cup.   2. Oak Hill Country Club.   3. Golf—Tournaments—New York (State)—Rochester.   I. Title.
    GV970.R67   1996
    796.352'66—dc20
                                                            96-4377
                                                            CIP

First Edition: June 1996

10   9   8   7   6   5   4   3   2   1

DEDICATION

For Genevieve, Genna, Molly, Shirley, GiGi, Shirlyn, Sue, and Emma. The angels who have blessed my life.

And for Dad, who taught me the value of hard work and dedication to his family.

CONTENTS

FOREWORD
by Bernard Gallacher

There's something very special about the Ryder Cup. I think that was quite evident at Oak Hill. It's something that can't be copied. It was started the right way in 1927 and it's continuing the right way into the twenty-first century. I'm just happy to have been a part of it.

I have played in eight Ryder Cups and captained three, but this last one was the result I've always wanted. There was tremendous sportsmanship on both sides, and a thrilling ending. I'm proud of the way our team fought back on foreign soil, two points down going into the singles. Everybody doubted us, but I liked the pairings. I knew we had a very good chance. It's nice to go out with a win.

I just find it amazing how big the event has become. I couldn't attend the reception at Downing Street when your President was over here. But I know Bill Clinton is a big golf fan and he told Ken Schofield, the executive director of our tour, that he had watched the last two days of the matches and wanted to commend us for how tough our players played. I think that's a good indication of how much the Ryder Cup means to people.

The Ryder Cup has always meant a lot to me personally. Immediately after I turned pro my goal was to make the team. It was a barometer of your ability as a player. It gave you something to work for apart from the normal financial gains.

As a boy growing up in Scotland, my first memory of the Ryder Cup was Peter Allis holing putt across green at Birkdale in 1965 to beat Arnold Palmer. It was great to see Peter hole that putt, but in those days America was so dominant. My first Ryder Cup was 1969, and I remember it well. It was a very hostile environment. Our team was lucky to get a draw. It was such a magnanimous gesture by Jack Nicklaus, giving Tony Jacklin that three-foot putt on the final green. I was just hoping that if anything like that happened nowadays, I'd have the guts to walk on the green and say the matches were a draw and that was it—providing, of course, it was an eighteen-inch putt. I just hope some captain in the future will walk on the green and pick the ball up and call it a draw.

I don't know what would have happened if the matches at Oak Hill came down to that. Some of the British and Irish press decided we had the wrong team, the wrong selection process, and the wrong captain, and that we would be beaten. I was disappointed that they were predicting defeat before it had happened. I was under pressure on most fronts, but I did have the confidence of the players, and that was most important. The injury to José María Olazábal presented a problem. I wanted him to play badly because of his relationship with Seve Ballesteros. I figured he could hobble around and play one round a day, but when he pulled out, I was quite happy that Ian Woosnam would come in, and he rose to the occasion.

I've always been very confident going into the three Ryder Cups that I served as captain of the European team. The thing that concerned me was that my confidence level had been the same at Kiawah and the Belfry, and we were beaten there. I'm an optimistic person, but I was starting to feel not as confident as I should, especially when Lanny Wadkins had the Americans two points ahead on Friday night. I made a mistake in the pairings Friday afternoon by sending Bernhard Langer and Per-Ulrik Johansson out for the afternoon four-balls. I still hadn't put Woosnam and Philip Walton on the course yet. Although I was confident, I was wary of the out-come after what happened in the past. The players rallied and we had a good round of foursomes Saturday morning. If we didn't rally then, we would have found it irretrievable.

I disagree that the Ryder Cup would have been in trouble had we lost at Oak Hill. It's too important to golf to be en-dangered. At the end of the day, if you insist on thinking of that one putt on the final green at Kiawah, and a couple of matches that went the wrong way at the Belfry—if that's the way people want to look at it, it's sad. Certainly it was the wrong result from our point of view, but in both cases the matches couldn't have been any closer.

And I actually think the matches will get closer and closer. Everyone plays so much around the world that it will hardly matter whether the matches are home or away. The home ad-vantage won't be the same as it was in the past. That was proven at Oak Hill, a course that everyone said suited the Americans. Our boys adapted to it quite well.

Something I don't like is seeing the way the Ryder Cup has become such a media circus. I've always been more philosoph-ical when it comes to the Ryder Cup. I think the matches are really more than just about winning and losing. Since 1983, we've had such great matches—and it's done so much for golf—I think it's unfair for outside forces to put so much pres-sure on the teams. It's not fair that anyone should be blamed for losing Ryder Cups, whether it's the players, the captain, or the selection process. You win a Ryder Cup, you don't lose it. No matter what process you have, what players you want, in-evitably there are going to be errors made, errors that will influence the results of the matches. But these matches are more important than that. Thank goodness the players on both teams realize that. Some of the things that are written are endangering the Ryder Cup. Bernhard Langer has said, "I don't want to be the captain if you have to endure this hostility from the media. It's making your life too difficult." This is a solid, upstanding guy who would make a wonderful captain one day.

What I think our victory will do is make people realize that we have got a lot of good players in Europe, other than Seve Ballesteros, Nick Faldo, Bernhard Langer, Colin Montgomerie, José María Olazábal, Sam Torrance, and Ian Woosnam. It will inspire a lot of young players on our tour to get on the team. It will give them a lift, improve their standards, and more important, from now on our Ryder Cup teams will go in with the feeling that they can win, even without superstars.

The one downside to our victory was watching a terrific competitor like Lanny Wadkins lose. Our relationship goes back many years. I played against him in the Ryder Cup at the Greenbrier in 1979. Everybody had been beaten by Lanny, but they asked me to go out and play him and I got a result with him. One of the great things about Lanny is that he has an aura of being unbeatable. He's a tough guy who I had heard was uncompromising, but he wasn't the person that I was led to believe he was. Humble in defeat, he congratulated me, and ever since I've had the utmost respect for Lanny. He's a straight shooter. You get what you see with Lanny.

At the closing ceremonies, Lanny was so overcome with emotion that I had to help him out a little with his speech. He is so competitive and was so disappointed that he just couldn't get through it. He just couldn't believe his team could lose being two points up. I could see what was going through his mind. All the pressure of trying to win at home just got to him. I spontaneously jumped up and tried to make a joke of it. I think it helped him. He was quick to say you better look out for the Ryder Cup because I'm going to come back and fight like hell in two years time to win it back. That was typical Lanny again. He was already dismissing it, saying, "Well played, boys. Well played, Europe. Let's get down to training and get it back again." You could see competitiveness coming out. I told him he did such a good job, I'd like to see him back at Valderrama. He told me, "I don't want to be the captain, I want to be on the team."

Tom Kite is going to be a tough captain. He's well known over here, but he'll have a hard time being a playing captain. I've found there's just too much going on; captaining is a full-time job. Of course, we may have to deal with that over here if Seve is on the team. I think it would be great if they let Seve and Tom Kite fight it out to decide the Ryder Cup.

I've got to step back now. I'm out of this. They don't need me anymore. There're new guys coming forward. My wife and I want to attend and be big supporters, but it will be from the other side of the ropes. We won't even go inside the ropes, so people won't have to complain about us blocking their view.

I've seen the Ryder Cup close up eleven times. It will be nice to take a step back and enjoy it the way I did when I was a boy.

Wentworth, England
January 1, 1996

ACKNOWLEDGMENTS

I wrote my first book not knowing if my mother would ever get to read it. She was trying to beat cancer, and you know how that goes. My dad passed away in 1988. I hope that they have bookstores in heaven, because I know they'd be proud of their boy. I'd just like to thank them for giving me all the love they had. I wish all the children of this world could be as lucky.

I hope someday that my two daughters, Genna and Molly, can say the same thing about their parents. I'd also like to acknowledge that this book was really written by Tim and Genevieve Rosaforte, because without the reassurances of my loving wife, *Heartbreak Hill* would have never become reality.

The blueprint for *Heartbreak Hill* was John Feinstein's best-selling look behind the scenes of the PGA Tour, *A Good Walk Spoiled*. I thought John's best two chapters were about the 1993 Ryder Cup. I basically took that idea and expanded on it.

To do that, I needed the cooperation of Lanny Wadkins, the

U.S. Ryder Cup captain, and the U.S. team. I've been covering golf since 1980, so I knew all of the guys personally. When Europe won, it evolved into a book on both sides. Bernard Gallacher, Philip Walton, Sam Torrance, Mark James, and Per-Ulrik Johansson were especially helpful in offering their perspectives. Also giving insight on the European team were members of the AGW whom I lean on often for background, those being Renton Laidlaw, Mark Garrod, Michael McDonnell, Michael Williams, John Hopkins, Derek Lawrenson, Dai and Patricia Davies, Lewine Mair, Bill Blighton, and Lauren St. John.

It also helped to have a relationship with some of the caddies, and in that regard, Jim Mackay, Eric Schwarz, Joe LaCava, John (Cubby) Burke, Mark Love, Linn Strickler, and Andy Martinez were there to fill in some of the holes that players may have missed.

This book wouldn't have been written if Mark Mulvoy and Peter Carry hadn't given me permission at *Sports Illustrated.* As editors, Mark, Peter, Bill Colson, Joe Marshall, Jim Herre, and Mark Godich have pushed me at *SI* to become a better writer. They have stressed one thing, and I've learned it's the most important element in writing: that is, be a good reporter, deliver the material, and everything else will fall into place. That's what I've tried to do in *Heartbreak Hill.* I wanted to take the reader inside the Ryder Cup.

The PGA of America communications department has been extremely cooperative in helping me to do that, especially Joe Steranka, Julius Mason, Terry McSweeney, Jamie Roggero, Bob Denney, Sherry Major, and Kathy Jorden. The interview transcripts of Karen Schoeve were essential, as were the tapes provided by Jon Miller and Ed Markey of NBC and Dan Schoenberg of the USA Network.

And when it came to bouncing ideas off friends and colleagues, I was lucky to have a support group of Larry Dorman, Jaime Diaz, Rick Reilly, Reid Hanley, John Garrity, Dave Kindred, Matthew Rudy, Gene Wojiechowski, Geoff Russell,

Robinson Holloway, Kevin Murphy, Andy O'Brien, Don Greenberg, John Fragakis, George Stewart, Lynn Henning, Bob McFadden, Rick Goldsmith, Melanie Hauser, Bill Torrey, Sally Jenkins, and my attorney, Richard Paladino. They all made observations, had ideas, or provided guidance that inspired my career and led to the publishing of *Heartbreak Hill.* My heartfelt thanks to them.

Scott Waxman of the Literary Group sold the idea to St. Martin's Press. Shawn Coyne and Todd Keithley did what good editors are supposed to do by providing encouragement and editing the copy in a way that made it better. World-class photographer Dave Cannon of AllSport coordinated the pictures, and together I think we finished the job better than Lanny's team did at Oak Hill. In the final analysis, that Sunday collapse made it a better, more dramatic book. For the sake of Lanny, Curtis, and my countrymen on the U.S. team, I would have taken a one-point American victory. For the future of the Ryder Cup, it turned out better this way. Let's hope the sequel will be Victory at Valderrama!

Tim Rosaforte
West Palm Beach, Florida
December 1, 1995

INTRODUCTION

The American caddy was trying to get his yardage, but he couldn't find the plate. He was on the fifteenth tee at Oak Hill Country Club in Rochester, New York, Sunday afternoon during the height of the singles matches to determine the thirty-first Ryder Cup. There were media and officials crowding the area, and his player was getting impatient. He wanted to know what club to hit and he wanted his distance to the front of the green and then to the pin. The caddy needed the marker, so he could pace off the steps to the tee blocks and come up with two final figures. His juices were flowing. He had just seen a guy wearing a blue European team jacket standing on the yardage plate. He thought he was doing it on purpose.

"Look," he said, "get the hell off my marker right now!"

Embarrassed, the man moved aside. He was not trying to do anything funny. He just didn't know any better.

Both players hit their shots, and as they were walking off

the tee, down toward the par-three green, a man with a British accent stepped out and stopped the American caddy.

"Look here," he said. "You can't speak to the prince that way."

That man in the blue European windbreaker?

Prince Andrew, the Duke of York.

The Ryder Cup brings out the best—and worst—in people. The one played at Oak Hill was no different, but what made this one so special was the way it all turned around within a matter of an hour on Sunday afternoon. An anticlimax developed into another classic Ryder Cup cliffhanger, where heros would become labeled as chokers, losers would emerge as winners, and tears would flow with champagne. Tears of joy. Tears of sorrow. Enough tears to fill the cup they played for.

Saturday night, in the team room at Oak Hill Country Club, Tom Lehman was convinced the Ryder Cup was over. "And to be more honest," the big American from Minnesota said, "I thought it was going to be one of those seventeen-eleven routs, that there was no way they'd come close. I think that was the way most of the guys felt."

Across the hall, where the European team was trying to recover from Corey Pavin's dagger-to-the-heart chip-in for birdie at the eighteenth green, Ian Woosnam felt the same way. "Phone it in, mates," the Welshman said. "It's time to catch the Concorde home."

It felt as if there were fifty thousand spectators at Oak Hill that Saturday, and half of them had crammed around that eighteenth green dressed like American flags. The Euros could still hear the echoes of "COR-REY, COR-REY, COR-REY" as they tried to recover. Later that night, going down the lineup card, the British journalists who know golf and cover it—not the tabloid rottweilers—all predicted a heavy

European defeat. Some were calling Bernard Gallacher an idiot for conceiving such an order.

But Gallacher knew better. He *liked* the matchups, tossing them across the table at Ken Schofield, the European Tour's executive director, with a cock of the head. When the Scots cock their head at something, they are damn sure it's another day.

And it was.

Europe won seven and a half of the twelve points on offer Sunday to stun the heavily favored American team of Lanny Wadkins and win the thirty-first Ryder Cup. The Ryder Cup was saved.

The consensus among my colleagues was that a victory by the United States would have sent the Ryder Cup reeling back to where it was in the 1970s, before the rest of Europe joined Great Britain and Ireland, before the era of Seve Ballesteros, Nick Faldo, Bernhard Langer, Sandy Lyle, José María Olazábal, and Woosnam brought pride to the continent with victories in 1985 and 1987—and a tie to retain the trophy in 1989. Jaime Diaz wrote a "Teeing Off" column in the September 18 issue of *Sports Illustrated*'s *Golf Plus* section. The headline was "The Last Dance: If Europe Can't Win, the Ryder Cup Will Take a Giant Step Backward." Diaz's nut graph was this: Although nobody wants to talk about it, the possibility of a rout looms large at Oak Hill, and a blowout would severely damage the Ryder Cup's main hook—the possibility of a nerve-jangling photo finish. If Europe can't win, or come as stirringly close as it did in 1991 and 1993, the Ryder Cup will take a giant step backward to its former life as an exercise in goodwill, diplomacy, and butt-kicking.

Watching every shot on television from his home in Palm Beach Gardens, Florida, was Tony Jacklin, the man who defiantly led Europe to its resurgence, who talked Ballesteros into playing in 1983, who ripped Gallacher for the way he handled the Ryder Cup in 1991 and 1993. He was the first to send Gallacher a congratulatory telegram. "What happened only could have happened one in twenty times," said Jacklin. "But it happened. That's the beauty of match play."

Up in Dornoch, Scotland, a lone American was trying to hold off the Highland Horde. A friend of mine named Don Greenberg had a bet where he was paying a pound a point to every Scottie who could receive Sky TV. Saturday night, he was crowing and barking, counting his money, and enjoying the bragging rights for two more years. But Sunday night he was in the bar at Royal Dornoch Golf Club, turning out his pockets, saying things like "Yeah, everybody but Freddie took a dump on the eighteenth hole. Yeah, it was just like Muirfield Village. Right, that Walton. Gutty, real gutty. Yeah, that Gilford. Great putt."

I talked to Don from his home in Tampa on December 5. He was getting ready to go back to Dornoch for the holidays. "The worst part of it is that I've got two more years of it," he said. "Two more lo-o-ng years. Two more fork-filled years."

Diaz, the man whose analysis I respect the most in the golf-writing business, didn't think the European team had the depth to hang with the Americans. Larry Dorman of the *New York Times*, who is one of my best friends, now claims that the European victory didn't surprise him. But I doubt very seriously I could have coerced Larry into wagering on the Europeans Thursday night, no matter what the odds. I think we all came away from Oak Hill realizing that the Ryder Cup will always be close, no matter where it's played, no matter how the teams are stacked. We won't be sucked into thinking it will be anything but that ever again.

"It was as close as it gets," Dorman said in December, "which is what makes it so good."

Larry's right. This is the beauty of the event. The Ryder Cup has become so tight, so agonizing, so intense, that no

other golf event comes close to touching it. And what sepa-
rates it even more—even from golf's major championships—
is that it's so pure.

Even when Lehman lost the 1994 Masters to José María
Olazábal, you knew he still made $216,000. In the Ryder Cup,
the only money paid out is the lost bets like the one Greenberg
made up in the Scottish Highlands. This is for pride, and it's
amazing what torture these golfers go through for pride. It's
as Nick Faldo said: "You're just playing for a trophy, and you
end up lying on the floor shattered. It's quite amazing what
you go through."

This past Ryder Cup at Oak Hill had a little bit of everything going for it. The script included the excitement of seven
greenside hole-outs and two holes-in-one, but there was more
to this Ryder Cup than golf shots and a monumental comeback. It had the soap opera undercurrent of the Faldos—Nick
and Gill—dodging newspaper reports from London as if they
were Prince Charles and Lady Di. It had Fred Couples putting
a ring on the finger of Tawnya Dodd the night of the Gala
Dinner. It had the controversial captain's pick of Wadkins,
who took a two-time former U.S. Open champion in Curtis
Strange over a better player by today's standards in Lee
Janzen. It had Pavin, the U.S. Open champion, adding to his
legacy as the world's most clutch player by winning four of five
matches. It had Costantino Rocca emerging as the most lov-
able character in international golf. It had retribution for a
European captain who had lost eight Ryder Cups as a player
and two as a captain. It had a heartbreak ending for Wadkins,
who did everything right as captain except for the most important thing—he didn't win. And it had a bunch of no-names
emerging as heroes for Europe.

As a golf writer, I've been to every Ryder Cup since 1983 except for one. I missed Europe's first victory in twenty-eight
years at the Belfry in 1985. But I've covered six of them, and
I've never left the press tent on Sunday night feeling let down.
I have been to fourteen Masters, fourteen U.S. Opens, nine

British Opens, and fourteen PGA Championships. I've covered Super Bowls and World Series games, New Year's bowl games that decided national championships, Daytona 500s, and the 1984 Summer Olympics in Los Angeles. But nothing, nothing, generates as much theater as a Ryder Cup. It is the only sporting event in the world that consistently lives up to its hype.

The first time I saw this played out was in 1983 at PGA National. It was Sunday. The American team needed a halve in the eleventh of twelve singles matches. Lanny Wadkins was in the fairway, seventy-two yards from the hole. Jack Nicklaus, the American captain, was watching intently. Wadkins then hit the ultimate pressure shot, the ball flying through the air as a bolt of lightning flashed across the eastern sky, then coming down inside leather. Nicklaus went out and kissed the divot. And then he cried.

I didn't see Nicklaus cry when he won the Masters in 1986. I have never seen him cry except for that one day at PGA National, when Wadkins won the Ryder Cup for him. "It was probably the most nervous I've ever been, playing one shot," Wadkins said. "It was one of the most important shots I've ever hit."

This was back in the days when the Ryder Cup only meant something to the participants, before the American public discovered the Ryder Cup and it became the mega-event that it has become today. It was always big to the players. Now it's just as big to the golfing public.

"I'll never forget the first one I was involved in," said Curtis Strange, who was twenty-eight years old in 1983. "God, I had tears up my eyes and goose bumps—the whole bit. You felt like you wanted to come out fighting and swinging like Rocky."

The Ryder Cup at Oak Hill sold out 25,000 tickets in two days. The PGA easily could have sold twice as many tickets at roughly $250 per hologrammed admission pass. In 1989, the event received no network coverage in the United States. In 1995, NBC came on at 8:00 A.M. Saturday morning for four hours, came back after a Notre Dame–Texas football game for two more hours, then dedicated seven hours on Sunday, coming on at 9:00 A.M. and not rolling the credits until the closing ceremonies. The USA Network, sole carriers of the event in '89, broadcast ten straight hours on Friday, plus highlights shows.

And Curtis Strange came back as a forty-year-old veteran with the same tears and the same goose bumps. But this time, when he came out swinging like Rocky, he got knocked out.

Great champions get back up.

Just as the Europeans did on Sunday at Oak Hill.

Heartbreak Hill

RYDER CUP COMPETITION FORMAT

Most golf tournaments around the world are decided by medal, or stroke play, over the course of a seventy-two-hole tournament. It's quite simple. Add 'em up. Low score wins.

Match play is a different animal. Each hole is an individual battle. You win the hole. You lose the hole. Or you tie the hole, which is called a halve. Then you go on. It's the same game most golfers play at their clubs around the world. The match ends when one team is up by a number exceeding the number of holes left to play. For example, if one individual or team is 3 up with 2 holes to play, it is considered a 3 and 2 victory.

There are 28 matches in the modern-day Ryder Cup format. The first team to 14½ points wins. If there is a 14–14 tie, the team that holds the Cup gets to retain it. In that case, a tie may be like kissing your sister, but your sister is Cindy Crawford.

Sixteen two-man team matches are played on Friday and Saturday, four in the morning, four in the afternoon. The morning competition is the alternate-shot, or foursomes. The players on each team alternate shots until the ball is holed, or the hole is conceded. The strategy is for the captain to put together two players who are compatible, and then, by figuring out the pattern of holes, to have his best irons players hit into the par threes, or his best driver on the tee at the tough par fours.

The afternoon competition is the best ball, or fourballs. Again, this is two players vs. two players, but each golfer plays his own ball. More birdies are made in this format because it promotes aggressive play. The strategy here is to find two golfers who can make things happen.

On Saturday night, each captain fills out a lineup card trying to get the best matchups for the Sunday singles competition. There are twelve matches on Sunday, unless there is an injury. If such a case occurs, as it did in 1991 and 1993, a designated player from the opposing team is "put in the envelope" and must sit out. Each team then gets a half point.

The one other thing to know about match play is that not every putt needs to be holed out. Players can give putts, or concede holes. This can lead to controversy because it's up to interpretation as to what is a "gimme" putt. That tension is part of the psychology of match play. Sam Snead used to give short putts until the eighteenth hole, then make his opponents knock in a three-footer for the first time. Seve Ballesteros rarely gives a putt, no matter how short. It goes under the category of gamesmanship. Of course, Jack Nicklaus gave Tony Jacklin a three-foot putt in the 1969 Ryder Cup that may be the most gracious gesture of sportsmanship in golf history. That putt was well outside "gimme" range, but Nicklaus didn't want to give Jacklin the opportunity to miss it. While not popular in all quarters, it captured the Ryder Cup.

CHAPTER 1

Tears in the Sand

Over on the driving range, near the beach at Kiawah Island, close to where the helicopter for Vice President Dan Quayle was parked, Mark Calcavecchia was being treated by a paramedic. There were six matches still to be played in the 1991 Ryder Cup. But Calcavecchia wasn't thinking about that. All he could think about was the disastrous outcome of his own match with Colin Montgomerie. All he could think about was the way he let that match slip away, and it pushed him over the edge, first to tears and then hyperventilation. It reached the point where Calcavecchia nearly passed out unconscious in the grass.

Once he composed himself, Calcavecchia told his wife, Sheryl, that he didn't want to be a part of another Ryder Cup.

"It's obviously too much for me," he confessed. "Either I wasn't lucky enough or strong enough, I'm not sure which."

At the time, Calcavecchia had a reputation for being the toughest, most fearless American golfer. In the 1989 British Open at Royal Troon, he hit a searing 5-iron into the seventy-second green to set up what would be the tying birdie. Then, in a four-hole playoff with Wayne Grady and Greg Norman, Calcavecchia outdueled the two Australians to win his first major championship and become the first American to win and put his name on the Silver Claret Jug in six years.

But the Ryder Cup, Calcavecchia learned, was a different animal, and the one played at Kiawah Island was the mother of them all. In 1987, playing on his first Ryder Cup team, Calcavecchia played in only one match the first two days. When Jack Nicklaus told him on the driving range Saturday that he would not be playing in that day's matches, Calcavecchia burst into tears. On Sunday, determined to prove Nicklaus wrong, he defeated British Open champion Nick Faldo one up to lead an American rally that came up two points short. In 1989, at the Belfry, Calcavecchia played all four matches the first two days, and had captured two crucial points for an American team that trailed 9–7 going into the singles. Calcavecchia wanted this one bad. He was on record as saying he'd trade his major championship for a Ryder Cup.

On Sunday, he drew Ronan Rafferty of Northern Ireland. It was a bitter match. Calcavecchia didn't like Rafferty's attitude much, and the feeling was mutual. Rafferty had won three tournaments and led the Order of Merit that year. Calcavecchia had won the Phoenix and Los Angeles Opens before the British Open at Troon. The match reached the eighteenth hole. The American team had won three of the first four matches, but in group ahead of him, Payne Stewart had made a mess of the eighteenth, hitting his tee ball in the hazard, donning his rain suit, and taking slash after slash until it was clear the ball was staying in the marsh grass.

It was crucial for Calcavecchia to hit the fairway, but he did not. His first drive went in the water, and so did his second. His match, as Stewart's did against José María Olazábal, had ended in a concession. He walked to the green, sat down next to the team, pulled the visor over his eyes, and again cried.

Again, Calcavecchia was determined to make a Ryder Cup team. At Kiawah Island, he was 2-1-1 going into the singles. With Stewart as his partner, they had defeated Faldo and Ian Woosnam the first afternoon and on Saturday came back to win a hard-fought match against Steve Richardson and Mark James.

Buoyed by those victories, Calcavecchia went into his singles match loaded with confidence. At the turn, he was five up. With four holes to play, he was four up, meaning that Calcavecchia had Montgomerie dormie; he couldn't win the match. It looked like a sure point. All Calcavecchia had to do was close Montgomerie out and the United States would get its first win of the day. It was important that he do that, because David Feherty had knocked off Stewart and Faldo had done the same to Raymond Floyd in the first two singles matches of the day.

But Calcavecchia, as it turns out, was not up to it. The trouble began when he peeled off a tee shot into the ocean and made triple bogey seven at the fifteenth. That startled Calcavecchia, but did not panic him. It was just one bad swing. No big deal—he'd get Montgomerie at the next hole, a par five that ran along the beach. He hit a good drive, a good second, and what he thought was a good third, but his ball flew the green and ended in a footprint. A bad break, a bad bogey, and now his nerves were starting to unravel. Now the self-doubt was creeping in, and Calcavecchia was fighting it off as he walked to the seventeenth tee.

Seventeen at Kiawah Island is a par three of 197 yards. It

is one of those Pete Dye hellholes, and Montgomerie put his foot in it by rinsing his tee shot in the water. Here was an opening. All Calcavecchia had to do was blow a 2-iron into the gallery behind the green, make bogey, and the match was over.

Instead, he hit perhaps the ugliest pressure shot ever struck in Ryder Cup competition, a topped shank that did a Greg Louganis and dove in the pond a hundred yards short of its target. Calcavecchia was crushed. The moan of the gallery was heard on television sets all over the world.

"It was a shot I don't normally try to hit," Calcavecchia explained. "The last place I was going to hit it was let it get up in the wind and fade. I moved it further back in my stance than I normally do. I was going to hit it so low. . . . I told myself, 'Just hit it in the gallery. Just aim in the gallery and drill it, and if it fades, you're in the crowd and you can make four from there and it's over.' I played it so far back in my stance that I got ahead of it and it nose-dived."

Nose-diving with it was Calcavecchia, whose name in Italian means "old shoe." Here he was kicking himself to death in front of millions. The worst was yet to come. He still had a chance to put Montgomerie away by making a twenty-inch putt for double bogey. It was a putt he had made a million times in his life. It was a putt he normally backhands in, a putt he could make blindfolded nine out of ten times. But with Ryder Cup pressure filling his shoulders and arms and head, Mark Calcavecchia, British Open champion, couldn't even hit the hole.

On the eighteenth tee, his caddy, Drake Oddy, told him to forget about it, to purge it from his mind. "Just two more good swings," Oddy said, "and the match is over." Calcavecchia nodded. He busted a drive, his patented hard-boring cut to the fairway. It still left him a 3-iron, but he could handle that. From two hundred yards, Calcavecchia put one of the best swings of his life on that 3-iron. He hit it too well. Over-pured it, as the pros like to say. The ball flew the green and stopped in another bad lie. Under normal circumstances, it was a difficult chip. With a Ryder Cup match depending on it, it was impossible to get that chip close, even with Calcavecchia's routinely magical short game. When he was growing up, Calcavecchia would hit thousands of shots like this at North Palm Beach Country Club, inventing and imagining until it was dark. But it was never like this. It was never possible to imagine the feelings of a golfer who had just made a mess of three straight holes coming down the stretch of a Ryder Cup match that he had led by five at the turn, and by four with four holes to play. The chip came up twelve feet short.

Montgomerie was on the putting surface fifty feet away. He lagged up and tapped in for par. Calcavecchia now faced the twelve-footer. It he missed, Montgomerie would get out of the match with a halve. If he made the putt, Calcavecchia would escape with a victory and all would be forgotten.

"You know I'm going to make this," Calcavecchia said to Oddy.

Again, the putt never touched the hole.

Calcavecchia briskly shook Montgomerie's hand, and made his dash into oblivion.

An ambulance was there when Peter Kostis found them. Kostis was Calcavecchia's swing instructor but was working the Ryder Cup as an on-course commentator for the USA Network. "He was sick," Kostis said. "If he'd had any food in his stomach, he would have been throwing up. He was dehydrated and needed fluids. I'm not a doctor, but he was clinically in shock, there's no question about that. He could hardly talk, and to a certain extent, Sheryl was in shock as well, seeing Mark in that condition."

After Calcavecchia recovered, Kostis took him to the USA trailer in the television compound to watch the NBC network feed. Terry O'Neil, the executive producer for NBC, sent Roger Maltbie over twice for an interview. Both times, Kostis told Maltbie that Calcavecchia wasn't ready. Maltbie, a player himself, certainly understood. Part of him was embarrassed to ask. But it was his job, and Kostis, being in TV, understood that, too. Finally, Calcavecchia was well enough to want to join the rest of his teammates, who had been forging a comeback. Kostis commandeered a golf cart, and they drove out to the seventeenth green to watch the final match between Bernhard Langer of Germany and Hale Irwin. The gallery sitting behind the eighteenth green and fairway cheered Calcavecchia as he drove by. That made him feel a little better, but not much.

The matches came down to the final hole and a six-foot putt by Langer. Irwin, the three-time U.S. Open champion, later described the pressure as being so intense he couldn't feel his arms, couldn't even draw a breath. If Langer made the putt, the matches would end in a 16–16 tie and the Cup would return to Europe on the Concorde.

There were two spike marks in Langer's line. Peter Coleman, Langer's caddy, gave Langer the read. "Hit it first inside the left edge [of the cup]," he said. Tony Jacklin, who had captained Europe to two victories and a tie in the '80s, who had led his continent out of golf's dark ages, later said that no one had ever stood over a putt in the history of the game with more pressure on it than Langer's six-footer. "Nobody in the world could have made that putt," said Ballesteros. "Nobody."

Langer was two down with four holes to play against Irwin, but made four-foot putts at the sixteenth and seventeenth holes to draw even. At the eighteenth, Irwin was lucky to make bogey. His drive was headed for the tall grass when it hit Kathy Jorden of the PGA's communications department square in the back and kicked back into play. Now Irwin was on the green, helpless, as Langer bent over and took his unusual grip. The ball came off the putter of Europe's most respected player and looked like it was tracking to the hole. But it was a six-footer, not a four-footer, and the ball started drifting right and past its target. The look on Langer's face was excruciating, as if somebody had just stuck a knife in him. Irwin hugged Langer and later said, "There is no way that I would ever, ever wish what happened on the last hole to anyone."

Watching this scene from beside the green was Calcavecchia. The rest of his teammates were celebrating, popping champagne corks and spraying the crowd. Calcavecchia felt as if he were an outsider, even felt guilty that he had put Langer, his close friend at Bible study meetings, in that position. "It was sad that it came down to that," Calcavecchia said. "It's weird that it did, but it's sad. It almost doesn't seem right."

It wasn't until Stewart came by, his Hogan cap on backward and his clothes sprayed with champagne, that Calcavecchia snapped out of his funk. "Your half point won it for us, baby!" Stewart said, embracing Calcavecchia and pouring Korbel over his head.

At that moment, Mark Calcavecchia realized what a true friend he had in Stewart. He also realized what a burden had been lifted from his life. He would go away from Kiawah never the same, stronger in some ways, weaker in others, but always haunted by a ghost. "If we didn't win this thing, I wasn't playing golf for a long, long time," he said. "I was withdrawing from everything. I was just going into hibernation. As far as golf goes, that was as bad as it got."

Four years later, talking about it before the GTE Byron Nelson Classic at the TPC–Los Colinas in Irving, Texas, Calcavecchia reflected back on the 1991 Ryder Cup at Kiawah Island. He had gone from someone who would trade his major championship for a Ryder Cup in 1989 to a golfer who wanted no part of the Ryder Cup in 1993. It wasn't until 1995 that he was mentally prepared to be part of the Ryder Cup experience again.

"I had enough tension at Kiawah Island to last a lifetime," Calcavecchia said. "What happened to me was damaging in a way. It was something I'll never forget."

*   *   *

Sam Ryder never intended it to be this way. In 1926, the British seed merchant and mayor of St. Albans, England, attended an impromptu match at Wentworth Club near London between U.S. and British professionals prior to the Open Championship at Royal Lytham. Ryder so enjoyed the competition that in the bar afterward he said five words that in essence created the Ryder Cup: "We should do this again." Heads turned in his direction. Before Ryder knew it, he was investing £250 on what is now the most treasured trophy in professional golf. The golfing figure on the head of the cup is Abe Mitchell, a British professional who teamed with George Duncan that year at Wentworth to defeat Jim Barnes and Walter Hagen, 9 and 8. Mitchell was Ryder's personal golf coach, and he was scheduled to be Great Britain's first Ryder Cup captain but became ill and never made the trip across the Atlantic to Boston from Southampton, England, in 1927. The first matches were played at Worcester (Massachusetts) Country Club, with the United States winning 9½–2½. The British team, traveling in homburgs and dark gray overcoats, were treated in a way that amazed them.

"Everywhere we went, we were submerged by hospitality and kindness," said Arthur Havers, who was a member of that team. "Suddenly we were in a world of luxury and plenty—so different from home. It was something we had never expected. Even the clubhouses with deep-pile carpets, not like the run-down and shabby clubhouses at home."

Although they won in 1929 at Moortown in Leeds, England, and again in 1933 at Southport and Ainsdale, it was another twenty-four years before Sam Ryder's home team would prevail again. In 1969 at Royal Birkdale, one of golf's most sportsmanlike gestures occurred on the eighteenth green, when Jack Nicklaus conceded a two-foot putt to Tony Jacklin that meant a tie. Jack's words were, "Tony, I was sure you would hole the putt and was not prepared to see you miss."

Sam Ryder would have commended Nicklaus for protecting the spirit of the matches, but his teammates and captain were critical of his generosity. Sam Snead said he would not have given that putt to anybody, not even his mother. Billy Casper said, "The U.S. players had worked their tails off to get into that position and then Nicklaus gave them a tie. I think most of the players were very upset. I would like to have seen Jacklin hole the putt and earn it outright." Snead, the captain, concurred: "We went over there to win, not to be good ol' boys."

The matches became so lopsided in the 1970s that Nicklaus lobbied to open up the competition to the rest of Europe. In 1979, Ballesteros made his Ryder Cup debut. Two years later he was joined by Langer. But it wasn't until 1983 that the matches really and truly became competitive. That was the year Tony Jacklin became Europe's Ryder Cup captain. He insisted on first-class uniforms and accommodations, transportation on the Concorde, and the same treatment the Americans received. Nick Faldo, who at age twenty-six was already playing in this third Ryder Cup, noticed the immediate difference in attitude that Jacklin, the U.S. and British Open champion, had created. "That was the first time that half the team believed we could win," he said. "After that, the rest of the team believed we could win."

That Ryder Cup signaled the dawn of a new era in international golf, and the shifting of power across the ocean to Europe. On that team were the Big Five of Faldo, Ballesteros, Langer, Sandy Lyle, and Ian Woosnam. They came within a point of victory, but flew home from Florida with a new spirit. "I saw the whole team with their heads down a little bit because we lost," said Ballesteros. "I said, 'Hey, guys, this for us is like a victory, because for the first time we were close to a victory.'"

The breakthrough came in 1985 at the Belfry in Sutton Coldfield, England. Lee Trevino's team flew into a hostile environment and were ambushed. Whereas barely a thousand people watched the finals at PGA National in 1983, golf fans from all over Europe flocked to the British Midlands two years later to witness America's first Ryder Cup loss in twenty-eight years, since Lindrick in 1957. Lanny Wadkins, who had struck the winning shot in 1983, was soundly booed when introduced at the opening ceremonies. He turned to his teammates and said, "Don't you just love it." But in fact, most of them didn't and had a hard time handling the unruly crowds. It all worked against Trevino, who lost control of his team and was soundly defeated 16½–11½.

Two years later at Muirfield Village, Jack Nicklaus had a hard time getting American fans to be enthusiastic. He implored them to wear red, white, and blue and cheer for his team, but they were down 6–2 after the first day and 10½–5½ going into Sunday. The loss was the first by a U.S. team on American soil, and the European team and its fans turned the Muirfield Village pavilion into a beer-swilling party. The American team took offense at this, claiming that the Europeans didn't know how to win with dignity, that they were being shown up. Continental pride became overstated, and the singles match between Ballesteros and Paul Azinger in 1989 became a classic battle between two of the strongest personalities in world golf. Before the match, Curtis Strange told Azinger not to let Ballesteros pull anything on him, and when the Spaniard tried to take a ball out of play early in the match, the American refused. It was as if Ballesteros was testing Azinger. "All right, I can play that way," Ballesteros said. The rest of the match was played in stone-cold silence, with no putts conceded. It ended with Azinger winning with a bogey on the eighteenth hole, but not without a controversy. Ballesteros questioned whether Azinger took a proper drop after his drive hooked into a pond. Six years later, when they played a Shell's Wonderful World of Golf Match at St. Andrews, a supposedly lighthearted made-for-TV affair, Azinger and Ballesteros were still hardly speaking.

It all spilled over into 1991. The Europeans were omitted from a Ryder Cup highlight film, which they considered a snub. Several American players wore Desert Storm camouflage hats. Dave Stockton, the U.S. captain, seemed to want to win at all costs, and when the U.S. team did, it was the Europeans who went home with bad feelings. "We all agreed, the players, that the one at Kiawah Island was a mess," said Faldo. "Too many people felt it was life and death."

Tom Watson did his best in 1993 to restore the Ryder Cup to what Sam Ryder had intended it to be, and more than the American victory, that will be Watson's legacy as it relates to the matches. This year's competition, won by the Europeans, was called by Ben Crenshaw "the cleanest fight you could imagine." Other than a little gamesmanship by Ballesteros on Sunday and a hot-tempered exchange between Faldo and Tom Lehman in the first match the first day, the thirty-first Ryder Cup matches didn't give the tabloid writers much ammunition (they had plenty with Faldo's reported marriage breakup anyway). It's kind of gotten back to where it should be, but the Ryder Cup had to go through that boiling period to make it such a compelling event.

"The Europeans I didn't feel were that gracious when they were winning and they made the '89 tie out to be a win, so we took it personal," said Azinger, who was working the 1995 matches for NBC. "There were some hard feelings for a while. They rubbed our noses in it, from my perspective at least. Maybe there wasn't as much sportsmanship as there should have been in '91. It seems to be a lot more gracious now."

Tom Kite, who will captain the U.S. team at Valderrama in 1997, was on the losing teams of 1985 and 1987 and the team that tied in 1989. He was also on four winning teams, both before and after Europe's mid-'80s rise to power. He saw that wave coming, he rode it out, and he admits, quite begrudgingly, that it was good for golf and good for the matches for America to be knocked off its pedestal.

"We knew they had great players," Kite said. "We knew they had tremendous track records. We knew going in it would be a difficult task to keep the Ryder Cup or win it back, depending on the year we were playing. We got thumped, and in retrospect that was the best thing that could have happened. But being on those teams that got beat, I can assure you those players representing the United States were not thinking that was the best for golf."

After the U.S. team had won two straight in '91 and '93, there was the fear going into Oak Hill for the 1995 matches that the Ryder Cup was starting to lose its magic. The Europeans were supposedly getting old, with Faldo, Langer, Woosnam, and Ballesteros all approaching their late thirties. Lyle hadn't qualified for a team since 1987, and Ballesteros's game was a skeleton of what it once was. On top of that, Woosnam lost his putting stroke and José María Olazábal of Spain had to withdraw because of an injured toe.

Behind Europe's superstars, no generation seemed to be coming along behind to take the torch and run with it into the twenty-first century. Ronan Rafferty drifted after winning the Order of Merit and has not played another Ryder Cup match since defeating Calcavecchia in 1989. Steven Richardson, built strong and tall like Faldo, qualified for the team in 1991, but failed to do so in 1993 and 1995. Peter Baker, who starred at the Belfry in 1993 and was touted so strongly by Faldo, failed to qualify. So did Barry Lane, who had advanced to the finals and won the 1995 Andersen Consulting World Match Play Championships. Jesper Parnevik, the Swede who finished second in the 1994 British Open championship at Turnberry, was playing the U.S. Tour. So was Ireland's David Feherty, who qualified for the European team in 1991 and defeated Payne Stewart, the U.S. Open champion, in singles.

The team that Bernard Gallacher brought to Oak Hill looked totally outmanned. Think about it. When Tony Jacklin captained the team at Muirfield Village, he could send out the teams of Ballesteros and Olazábal, Faldo and Woosnam, and Langer and Lyle. A chimpanzee could make out that lineup card. Gallacher had Faldo and Colin Montgomerie, and beyond that, no other set team. He had to find a partner for Langer, then come up with two other pairs to face an American team that appeared deep in numbers and comfortable on the Open-style layout.

But all along, Gallacher was confident. He knew that Mark James and Howard Clark weren't highly respected in the United States, but that they had combined for twenty-nine victories in Europe. He knew about the bottle, the heart, of Per-Ulrik Johansson and Philip Walton. He knew he had a secret weapon in Costantino Rocca, and that Sam Torrance was determined to improve on his poor Ryder Cup record, the way Raymond Floyd was at the Belfry in 1993.

"I was one of the few people who felt we had a good chance to win," Gallacher said. "I was never going to write our team off. The Ryder Cup had always been close since 1983. Even though the American tour had bigger numbers, I knew our best twelve players would give America's best twelve players a good match. I was philosophical about 1991. It was a very even contest. America just deserved to win. In 1993, we had thrown it away. Being in a good position to win, I didn't think my decisions were completely to blame for the defeat. Even though the commentators were down on me, I was delighted with the support of the players, that they wanted to give me one more chance. Contrary to what everybody was saying, I felt that Oak Hill was a course that suited us well. That time of year, it climatically suited us. The thing that makes a U.S. Open course is the humidity and the hot weather. That's what makes it difficult for us to acclimatize. The U.S. Open is always a steam bath. Oak Hill is a very European-type course. It's the type of course that if our players kept their heads down, so to speak, they would do very well."

Nobody listened to Gallacher. Nobody listened except for the twelve players he brought to the United States on the Concorde on September 18, 1995.

CHAPTER 2

The Envelope

Davis Love III had to find Lanny Wadkins. He had just sunk a putt that would send the Ryder Cup back on the Concorde to the United States, but he had to find Lanny. It was 1993, on the eighteenth green at the Belfry, just seconds after Love closed out Italy's Costantino Rocca to ensure a 15–13 American victory. But before he celebrated, Love had to thank Wadkins for what was defined as the most unselfish move in golf history.

"That putt was for you," Love said.

Wadkins, this hard-edged Virginian, was weeping. What he did in the British Midlands that September Sunday was take one for the team. He volunteered to "go in the envelope," to sit out what was probably the last singles match in his illustrious Ryder Cup career.

It was a noble gesture, one never documented in the sixty-six-year history of the event. It was one Sam Ryder would have endorsed. It was, as captain Tom Watson kept repeating all week, "what the spirit of the Ryder Cup is all about."

"The envelope" is the Ryder Cup's answer to purgatory. It is usually a place reserved for the injured, or those not playing well. Wadkins was neither. He was just a true sportsman.

Golfers on this level of the sport are assumed to be selfish. They play a singular game for huge sums of money. At the Ryder Cup, they get paid nothing. They play for a piece of a trophy and a place in history.

Wadkins, forty-three, had already carved out his niche in the Ryder Cup record books. With two victories on Friday, he had moved into second place all-time with twenty Ryder Cup wins. His record of 20-11-2 was the best on the U.S. team that traveled to Sutton Coldfield, England, seeking to avenge the loss in '85 and the tie in '89 at that venue.

Leaving him out on Sunday raised a lot of eyebrows and even more questions about Watson's strategies. But it worked out. The American team rallied around Lanny and defended the Cup for the first time since 1983 at PGA National.

"That, to me, was one of the classiest acts I've ever seen," said Tom Kite, who was playing on his seventh team. "Lanny said he wasn't playing great, but you know he wanted to be out there. He's a great match-play player. He's got guts. Like Raymond [Floyd] said, 'When you go to war, you want Lanny on your team.'"

The Ryder Cup tradition of sitting out a team member in case of injury to the other team put Watson in a tough bind. Sam Torrance, the Scotsman who had sunk the winning putt for Europe in 1985, had what doctors called a "septic toe" and wasn't expected to play.

Floyd was out hitting balls on the practice ground. Watson didn't know what to do. He asked Wadkins for some help.

Lanny made it easy. He volunteered. "Raymond would have done the same thing," he said without hesitation. Watson was so moved his eyes watered up. Sunday morning, at the team breakfast, he gave his "Win one for Lanny" speech.

"Every match has a little bit of Lanny Wadkins in it," he said. "If your match is getting a little too tough for you, think about Lanny Wadkins, and what he did for you today."

Wadkins actually never figured not to play. He had played against Torrance for twenty years, and figured Torrance would be out there on crutches if he had to. They knew each other quite well. When Lanny was named to the team as one of Watson's wild-card picks, Sam was one of the first to make a congratulatory phone call. ˙

"I was just trying to make the decision easier for Tom," Wadkins said. "He has done everything for us this week."

Wadkins was also thinking of the younger players on the team. The rookies, Lee Janzen and John Cook, had only one match under their belts at the Belfry. Jim Gallagher, Jr., had only two. This was Wadkins's record-tying eighth Ryder Cup. He had played in thirty-three matches. He knew how much it hurt David Gilford to sit out the singles at Kiawah Island when Steve Pate couldn't play because of bruised ribs, suffered in a car accident on the way to the Gala Dinner in Charleston.

Lanny's thinking was, let the kids play. "It was already in the captain's agreement and is the same on both sides," Wadkins said. "It has been around for a long time and nobody has a problem with it. It's kind of a fluke to happen two Ryder Cups in a row."

Wadkins was scheduled to play Seve Ballesteros. Watson did not know that when he submitted his envelope and lineup to Bernard Gallacher on Saturday night. But Wadkins vs. Ballesteros is how it came up, and it made for one of the most anticipated singles matches in Ryder Cup history. Both are confrontational. Both have no backdown in them. It would come down to how Torrance felt in the morning.

"Last night I was getting ready to play Seve," Wadkins said. "I felt if there was any way Sam could play today, he would. I told Jim to play hard."

Wadkins watched, knowing he had delivered two points on Friday, knowing that his role had been reduced to cheerleading, knowing that for the U.S. team to win on European soil, it would take an inspired effort by Jim Gallagher, who was playing in his first Ryder Cup. Gallagher, who had been labeled a "lambchop" in *Golf World*, beat Ballesteros 3 and 2 to become the "Killer Lambchop."

"I told Lanny, 'I'm going to do it for you,'" Gallagher said. "You've got confidence in me and I'm going to do what I can for you."

This was the kind of team Watson had at the Belfry, and it produced the first Ryder Cup victory on European soil since the nine-point wipeout at Walton Heath in 1981. The bad blood that existed between the two teams at Kiawah Island was diffused by Watson, and there was no gut-wrenching drama over one putt deciding the match, as there was with Bernhard Langer. The last match between Paul Azinger and Nick Faldo did not even matter—except to Azinger, who wanted to play it out for pride. It ended with Faldo making a twelve-footer on the last hole to halve the match.

"Zinger got his wish," said Watson. "He said, 'Please make my match not count.'"

The half point culminated a frustrating week for Azinger. The PGA champion went 0-3-2. All week, he felt something funny in his left shoulder. Two months later it was diagnosed as lymphoma.

In the back of his mind, Azinger had that fear at the Belfry. Friday morning he was strapped with a limping Payne Stewart, and they suffered the worst first-morning loss since Arnold Palmer and Dave Marr were handled 6 and 5 by Dave Thomas and George Will. The 7-and-5 loss by Zinger and Stewart to Langer and Ian Woosnam set the tone for the first day and a half of competition. At lunch on Saturday, the Europeans had raced to a three-point lead. They were going into the Saturday-afternoon four-balls—notoriously the worst competition for the Americans—with all the momentum.

That's when the matches turned around. Watson, wanting to get Chip Beck and John Cook off the bench, sent them off first, figuring they would draw Faldo and Colin Montgomerie, Europe's strongest team, with a 2-0-1 record. Beck and Cook took them down with Cook's laser 4-iron into the eighteenth green triggering a 3–1 afternoon for the Americans. "I believe the heart of our victory was John Cook and Chip Beck winning their four-balls," Watson said.

That sent the Americans into Sunday on a high. Kite described the mood at the team dinner that night as being one of supreme confidence, and it reflected in a sweep of Langer, Seve Ballesteros, and José María Olazábal. The United States team won five of the last six matches, with Kite making three birdies and two eagles in one eight-hole stretch to shut down Langer. Fifty-one-year-old Raymond Floyd also concluded his last Ryder Cup by winning three of four matches, including his singles against Olazábal. "I was back there in the back end, and he put me in an area that really counts," Floyd said of Watson. "He told me, 'I'm putting you down there because if we need it, I think you can do it.' For him to have that confidence in me is something I'll never forget."

As a five-time British Open champion, Watson lobbied the PGA of America to be a Ryder Cup captain in England. He started the week by committing a social faux pas—refusing to sign Torrance's autograph at the Gala Dinner because he felt it would create a snowball effect on the eight hundred people in attendance at the Birmingham Metropole. Sometimes he struggled with the right words to explain his feelings, an example being his refusal to mention Langer when he was listing the world's best players. This gave the tabloids something more to write about. And when he sat Kite down Saturday afternoon and stuck with an uninspired Fred Couples, that raised the issue of whether he was making the right personnel decisions by being a self-proclaimed "captain by consensus."

But as it played out, Watson had clearly made the two biggest decisions his best ones by picking Floyd and Wadkins as his wild cards. By doing that, he surrounded himself with two lieutenants who had the "heart and guts" necessary for Ryder Cup combat.

Floyd, who captained the U.S. team to a tie at the Belfry in 1989, and Wadkins, who would lead the team at Oak Hill in 1995, gave the team a presence. There was no need for Watson to be out on the course looking at club selections and giving encouragement with Floyd and Wadkins on patrol. By the end of the week, Watson had commanded the respect of everyone—Americans and Europeans—not only for winning, but for winning with class and honor.

"It couldn't have happened to a greater man than Tom Watson," Gallagher said. "I'm proud to be on a team where he was captain."

It was a Ryder Cup that seemed to restore the Ryder Cup to what it was supposed to be. Putts were conceded when they probably shouldn't have been. Even Faldo and Azinger were seen with arms around each other's backs walking off the sixteenth. There were no knives in either player's hand.

"We had a great Ryder Cup. I've had a wonderful time," Faldo said. "This is just an unbelievable event. You just play so aggressive, you have to. The golf was spectacular on both sides. The best golf won in the end."

At the end of the day, that's what the Ryder Cup is all about. The War by the Shore/Battle of the Belfry sentiment that existed was laid to rest. The European fans still cheered when American shots went astray, but Watson had schooled them well. They were not as thin-skinned as the 1985 team. They actually fed off it.

"It's nothing we haven't heard before," Watson said.

At the closing ceremonies, Watson read a passage from

Theodore Roosevelt's famous and inspiring "Man in the Arena" speech and called the victory "the best feeling I've ever had in golf."

Two months later, at a news conference in Palm Beach Gardens, Florida, the PGA of America surprised no one by naming the man in the envelope, Jerry Lanston Wadkins, as captain of the 1995 U.S. Ryder Cup team.

CHAPTER 3

Dialed In

Lanny Wadkins first visited Oak Hill Country Club as Ryder Cup captain in late summer of 1994, one year before the matches. He had been to Oak Hill for the 1980 PGA and the 1989 U.S. Open, so when he drove through the gates off Kilbourne Road, it all came back to him. Out the left window of his courtesy car, he saw the eighth and ninth holes on the East Course, two long and narrow par fours. He could envision what they would look like with tight fairways, deep rough, fast greens and lined with U.S. golf fans, wearing their red-white-and-blue, cheering wildly for a Corey Pavin birdie. A smile worked its way on Wadkins's face. This was the classic American golf course, he thought, one that he would tweak until it looked and played every bit as hard as a PGA or a U.S. Open venue. This would be a huge home-course advantage for his United States Ryder Cup team when it arrived in Rochester, New York, the third week of September 1995. Wadkins could almost see himself raising the Cup during the closing ceremonies. He would go back to Texas a hero. "The Europeans," he said, "are used to playing more wide-open courses."

If only Wadkins could have seen Oak Hill seventy years ago when Donald Ross completed the design. The property was described as "barren, cheerless, and singularly lacking in beauty." It was as wide open as the Dornoch links Ross grew up on in the Scottish Highlands. Building golf courses on this property was like putting a tapestry on a blank canvas.

Upstate New York had been stripped of its oak forests in the 1700s to build the British fleets. It wasn't until Rochester physician John Williams came along after Ross that Oak Hill indeed became an Oak Hill. Williams planted acorns from around the world. Blessing the landscape of Oak Hill's 355 acres are descendants of the Shakespeare Oak at Stratford-on-Avon, England, and the black oaks that George Washington planted at Mount Vernon. Williams supervised the planting of 75,000 trees, some beech, some maple, some pine, too. "I do not like cemeteries," Williams once said when asked about his infatuation with trees. "I find stone markers cold and uninspiring. A living tree is a much better monument than a piece of granite."

The original design fee for both the East and West courses was $165,000, and the bill was written out on stationery from the old Seneca Hotel, where Ross was staying. Instead of bulldozers and backhoes, his work crew used horse-drawn slip pans and hand shovels. But Ross was quite prolific, designing at least 413 courses in the United States, Canada, and Cuba after moving to this country from Dornoch, Scotland, where he was a caddy, greenskeeper, and club professional. His most famous courses are Seminole, Pinehurst No. 2, Inverness, and Oakland Hills. Five of his courses hosted Ryder Cups including Worcester (Massachusetts) CC, site of the first Ryder Cup.

Ross believed that golf should be a pleasure, not a penance.

"It has been my good fortune to bring happiness and great trouble to many a man," Ross said during a testimonial for him in 1930.

The design work Ross did in the early 1920s has been altered over the years. Oak Hill is still a Donald Ross course, but changes in golf equipment required that it be lengthened and toughened to protect its dignity.

The first major championship played at Oak Hill was the 1949 U.S. Amateur. Charles Coe won by the second-most-lopsided score in Amateur history, defeating Rufus King 11 and 10 in the thirty-six-hole championship final. Coe would go on to win another Amateur and post a 7-4-2 record in six Walker Cup competitions. He doesn't remember having a three-putt all week, and today still recalls the huge rolling greens and the perfect putting surfaces that are synonymous with Oak Hill.

Robert Trent Jones did major redesign work after the USGA awarded Oak Hill the U.S. Open in 1956. Jones was a Rochester native who had followed Ross around during the construction of Oak Hill thirty years earlier. Jones put his imprint on seventeen holes, building seven new tees and putting his distinctive cookie-cutter shape on twenty-seven bunkers. Dr. Cary Middlecoff won the Open at seven-under 281 by one stroke over Ben Hogan and Julius Boros, but not until he had endured "golf's longest hour." That's how long Middlecoff had to sit in the clubhouse while Hogan and Boros completed their rounds. Boros lipped out a putt on eighteen. Hogan missed a twenty-eight-inch putt on the seventy-first hole that would have put him in a thirty-six-hole playoff, but seemed relieved that the torture was over. "I would hate to have to go back out there tomorrow," he said.

The Open didn't return to Oak Hill until 1968, when a colorful and quotable Mexican-American from Texas named Lee Buck Trevino shot four rounds in the 60s to tie the seventy-two-hole scoring record at 275.

This was back in the days when Trevino didn't have much money, so he took a free room in the Rochester home of Paul Kircher. Trevino figured the Kirchers thought he was going miss the cut anyway, and wouldn't be around for the weekend. "Barbara [Kircher] had no idea who I was," Trevino told the *Rochester Democrat & Chronicle*. "She just knew I was a Mexican-American. She had gone to the store and bought everything that had a Mexican name on it for food. She'd bought Old El Paso this and Old El Paso that. As far as I know, she still has 'em." He had a five-stroke lead with three holes to go and nursed it coming in for his first professional victory, winning by four over Nicklaus.

The Oak Hill members wouldn't stand for a relative unknown tearing up their golf course, so they voted to bring in the bulldozers again. This time the job went to George Fazio and his young nephew Tom. The members wanted "intimidating holes that offered the threat of double bogey." The Fazios gave them just that. Nicklaus was the only player in the field at the 1980 PGA Championship to break par. He won his twentieth major championship by a record margin of seven strokes over Andy Bean.

The 1984 Senior Open proved to be just as tough for the competitors. Nobody broke par, with Miller Barber finishing at six-over 286 for a two-stroke victory over Arnold Palmer. It was the second of three Senior Opens for Barber. Palmer is still kicking himself for the tap-in putt he whiffed on the fifteenth green.

There was no need to touch Oak Hill for the 1989 U.S. Open, but rains softened the course and sent the scores plummeting. Curtis Strange shot 64 in the second round, but Tom Kite led after fifty-four holes and was four strokes up with fourteen holes to play on Sunday when he drove into Rae's

Creek at the par-four fifth—one of the holes totally re-designed by the Fazios—and made triple bogey. Strange won his second straight Open, the first player to achieve that feat since Hogan did it in 1950 and 1951. He came in the press tent and his first words were, "Move over, Ben."

Oak Hill started lobbying for the Ryder Cup during the matches at Muirfield Village in 1987. An inquiry was made by Oak Hill member Bob Skipworth to Joe Black, a past PGA president.

"How the hell did Jack Nicklaus get the Ryder Cup here at Muirfield?" said Skipworth.

"It was easy, Bob," said Black, sounding like one of those investment commercials. "He asked for it."

The PGA of America had been criticized for some of its site selections for the Ryder Cup. In 1983, it went to PGA National as part of a contract clause with the developer. It had the same sort of arrangement in 1991 at Kiawah Island, which was actually a replacement for PGA West. That was part of a deal the PGA had with the Landmark Land Company.

PGA West was dropped because of the time difference between Palm Springs and the United Kingdom. Golf viewers in London would be watching the Ryder Cup in the middle of the night, and the results would never make deadline in the London and Glasgow newspapers.

Kiawah Island was announced as a substitute before the Ocean Course was even completed. The problem from a spectator standpoint was that the course was built in the South Carolina sand dunes, and the fans could never get close enough to the golfers, or had to walk great distances between greens and tees to follow the action. The players weren't particularly fond of it either. David Feherty of Ireland compared the landscape to Mars.

Learning from those mistakes, the PGA announced in the early 1990s that it was determined to take its big events back to the country's traditional golf courses. Oak Hill was a perfect fit.

Jim Awtrey, the PGA's CEO, made a secret visit to Rochester to meet with officials of the club one month before the Ryder Cup at Kiawah. "It was a very hush-hush thing," Skipworth told *Rochester Democrat & Chronicle* senior editor Jim Memmott. "We chatted and then Jim said, 'We're here to offer Oak Hill the Ryder Cup.' I said, 'Jim, you've made our year.'"

Oak Hill had four years to get dialed in. Rochester Gas and Electric installed a 4,000-foot cable aboveground on twenty-five utility poles to carry power from Allens Creek Road to Oak Hill. Nine temporary transformers supplemented the four already serving the Oak Hill area. Telephone cables were buried under the grass. NBC brought in 125 miles of television cable. Over five miles of temporary chain-link fence would be needed. Fifteen miles of rope and 3,000 steel stakes would cordon off the tees, fairways, and greens.

A commissary was built in a 5,000-square-foot portable kitchen constructed of five portable trailers. A dishwasher was installed that washed up to 350 racks of dishes per hour. The week of the tournament, approximately 50,000 hot dogs, 25,000 bags of potato chips, a ton of marinated vegetable salad, 1.5 tons of potato salad, 30,000 chicken breasts, 10,000 Italian sausages, 40,000 cookies, 25,000 brownies, and 15,000 danish pastries would be consumed. Three hundred and thirty-nine toilets were placed throughout the course, including a hundred portable individual toilets, sixteen rest-room trailers, and six handicap-accessible toilets. Plans were made for 13,000 thirty-three-gallon trash bags to be taken off the property every day.

The Transportation Committee hired 450 buses to transport people to and from the course. An additional 700 to 900 minivans, vans, limousines, and sedans were also put into service. Oldsmobile brought in 225 courtesy cars. A traffic flow plan was designed to get spectators in and out of the course. The European team would feel quite at home at Oak Hill, because once they passed through the front gate, they would be driving on the left side of the road.

Tickets went on sale in 1994, and sold out in forty-eight hours. Awtrey compared it to a Final Four. The PGA had no problem selling corporate hospitality. Forty-nine hospitality pavilions were sold at anywhere from $110,000 to $260,000. That was a record for a golf event and comparable to a Super Bowl.

Hotel rooms became harder and harder to find as it got closer to 1995. The PGA took up blocks in the downtown Hyatt, Radisson, and Holiday Inn. Spectators were told they would have to commute from Buffalo and Syracuse. Private-home rentals near the course were going for $10,000. Members of a volunteer force of three thousand were asked to pay $150 for their uniforms. The PGA paid $40,000 for two 38x20-foot Jumbotron scoreboards, one for the PGA Golf Experience at Genesee Valley Park downtown and one for the practice tee. Plans were made for the opening ceremonies, to include fifty-seven Scottish bagpipers, Chuck Mangione, and a flyover by four F-16 fighters from the New York Air National Guard.

Members were informed that the course would be closed three weeks prior to the Ryder Cup, and that they would be asked to use Softspikes on their golf shoes so as not to track up the greens. When a drought hit Rochester in the summer of 1995, the club deployed its grounds crew to hose the rough and make sure it grew to Wadkins's specifications.

When Wadkins arrived on Saturday, September 16, 1995, everything was perfect, just perfect. The captain thought he had it all wired.

CHAPTER 4

"The Biggest Putt of My Life"

Brad Faxon remembers the numbers on the digital clock next to his bed glowing like neon lights on Sunset Boulevard. It was probably the longest night of his life, a night that went on and on forever until he first saw the sun coming out from behind the curtains at the Loews in Santa Monica, California. Faxon first awoke at 2:14 A.M. Then it was 4-something. The wake-up call was scheduled for 7:00, but at 6:15 he quit tossing and turning and gave up on trying to sleep. He remembered seeing Lanny Wadkins on the green at Riviera the day before. Surrounded by reporters, Wadkins had casually asked Faxon how he was doing.

"I'm five under," Faxon said before teeing off.

"Oh, are you trying to make the team?" said Wadkins.

"Well, yeah, I'm trying to make the team," said Faxon.

"Well, go get 'em," was all Wadkins said.

That Saturday turned out to be a bust. Faxon shot even-par 71 to lose ground on the chase. Making the Ryder Cup team seemed to be an impossibility when he teed off Sunday in the final round of the PGA Championship. There were twenty players with better scores, and Faxon had to finish tied for fifth or better. He knew he had to make the team on points, because Wadkins wasn't going to select him—at least that was the impression. "He never told me that I had to play my way on the team," Faxon thought to himself. "He suggested it might be a good idea."

When Faxon reached the eighteenth green at Riviera that afternoon, he looked at the leaderboard, and down the nose of a fifteen-foot putt, knowing he had never faced a more important stroke in his life. It wasn't for the win, but it seemed as if it was for something far more important than that. It was to make the Ryder Cup team. It was to shoot 63 in the final round of the PGA, to equal the lowest score ever shot in a major championship. It was, as Faxon said later, "the biggest putt of my life, without question."

So much is now made of making a Ryder Cup team. It probably ranks right behind winning a major championship among the goals of a U.S. tour player. Faxon went into the PGA ranked fourteenth on the points table of American players. Only a miracle would put him on the United States team at Oak Hill. A miracle is shooting 63 on Sunday in major championship conditions.

A miracle is what Faxon got.

Faxon started with an eagle three at the first, then made birdies at the third, fifth, sixth, seventh, and ninth holes to shoot 28 going out. At the eleventh hole, he hit a 3-wood 288 yards downwind and two-putted for birdie from twenty feet. At that point, Faxon's gallery had swelled. People were yelling

"Fifty-nine!" and "Ryder Cup!" Every shot was coming flush off the clubface. At the fifteenth, he had a fifteen-footer for birdie but three-putted. That could have been devastating, but Faxon came back with a birdie at the par-three sixteenth.

"You know, I laughed on twelve when I had about an eight-footer," Faxon said. "Some guy said 'Fifty-nine' before I putted. And you know, I wasn't even thinking about that. I said, 'Oh, my God, now I've got to put this out of my mind.' I've never been real good at deciding what number I'm going to shoot and then go shoot it. I always get a kick out of guys that say they needed sixty-five after they shot it. I'm not good at predicting what my score's going to be before I play. But I know I needed to shoot a low score to have a chance to make the team."

Faxon deliberately didn't want to know what place he needed to finish. He talked about that before the tournament with Bob Rotella, his sports psychologist. He had already been putting too much pressure on himself to make the team. At St. Andrews, he was in position for a top-ten finish at the British Open but played poorly on the weekend. He returned home to the Ideon Classic, near his New England home of Barrington, Rhode Island, and had the fortune of being paired with Wadkins. "Nothing went right," Faxon remembered. "I wanted to play well so badly. That's as much pressure as I've ever put on myself. I was so worried about the results and the outcome that it took me out of my game. But how can you not think about the Ryder Cup? Every day you're home, you get a mailer from the PGA telling you what position you're in. The points table is posted on the walls of the locker room, right above the urinals. It's in your locker. It's in the paper. People are asking you months in advance for tickets, and you're not even on the team."

The PGA was the last chance to make it. Mark Calcavecchia and Kenny Perry were ranked ninth and tenth on the points table, sitting right on the bubble. On top of them were Corey Pavin, Tom Lehman, Davis Love III, Phil Mickelson, Jay

Haas, Loren Roberts, Ben Crenshaw, and Peter Jacobsen. The top ten after the PGA would get automatic berths. Lanny Wadkins, the United States captain, would name two wild-card selections the Monday morning after the tournament. For two years, since the season-opening 1994 Mercedes Championship, Ryder Cup points were accrued. Top-ten finishes were worth anywhere from five to seventy-five points in 1994 and from ten to one hundred fifty points in 1995. Points in major championships were worth double.

Pavin, the U.S. Open champion, had 1054.167 points to lead the team. He had clinched a spot before the PGA, as had Lehman and Love. Everybody else was uncertain. Mathematically, they could be passed and knocked off the team. Lee Janzen and Jim Gallagher, Jr., each had two victories in 1995 and had played on the victorious 1993 Ryder Cup team. Janzen had won the Players Championship and held off Pavin down the stretch at the Kemper Open. Gallagher won Greensboro and Memphis, was second to Mickelson at Tucson, and would have clinched a spot had he not shot 40 on the back at the Anheuser-Busch tournament when he held the lead on Sunday with nine holes to go.

Fuzzy Zoeller, who appeared to be a lock after the 1994 season, was playing for the first time since May in a last-ditch effort to make the team. Zoeller suffered a bulging disk in his back at Memphis. Back surgery had been scheduled but put off when Zoeller responded to traction and walking with a cane.

"Everybody enjoys making the Ryder Cup team," Zoeller said. "I've still got a shot at it. I've been practicing awfully hard, and playing pretty well right now, so who knows?"

Former Ryder Cuppers Payne Stewart and Mark McCumber were there, as was British Open champion John Daly. But the only player to make a move, other than Faxon, was one of the quietest, most unassuming players on the PGA Tour.

Jeff Maggert had eleven top-ten finishes in 1994 and five in 1995 prior to the PGA at Riviera, including a tie for second at the U.S. Open worth double points. His rounds of 66-69-65-69 placed him tied for third with Ernie Els, which was worth 160 Ryder Cup points and a jump from a tie for twelfth to sixth in the final standings. Maggert was actually sixteenth in the standings going into the U.S. Open at Shinnecock, but shot 64 in the final round to jump twenty-three players and tie for fourth. He earned 300 of his 601.500 points in the final two U.S. majors. "I'm a little disappointed about the tournament this week in not being able to win," he said. "I came up a little bit short, but the Ryder Cup is a good thing to take home this week."

It helped the players in positions four through eight on the point standings that three of the top four players at the PGA were foreigners, Steve Elkington of Australia, Colin Montgomerie of Scotland, and Ernie Els of South Africa. Knocked out were Calcavecchia and Perry, who finished eleventh in two straight tournaments going into the PGA. One stroke better at either the Ideon Classic or the Buick Open and Perry would have qualified. Calcavecchia, who won in May at Atlanta, didn't record a top-ten finish in six events since a tie for second at the Memorial Tournament. It illustrated the pressure and the preoccupation of making the Ryder Cup team.

Wadkins was happy with the way it turned out. Maggert may not be a riveting personality, but his fairways and greens style would work well at Oak Hill, where the rough was purposely grown U.S. Open deep. Faxon is one of the best putters on tour, and that is the single most important factor in match play. You need someone who can make putts, and Faxon is so reliable on the greens that his nickname is the Fax Machine.

"I'm excited for Brad," Wadkins said. "I think what he did is unbelievable. To stand there and make a putt on the eighteenth hole that he thinks is do or die for the Ryder Cup. The fact that he made it and poured it right in the middle showed me as much as anybody's shown in a long time. That was just a great putt and a great round of golf and I'm delighted for him."

Faxon's wife, Bonnie, was scheduled to give birth to their third child the week of the Ryder Cup. Doctors at Women's and Children's Hospital in Providence induced labor on September 10. For Faxon, waiting for the delivery of that child was much easier than sitting in the locker room at Riviera that last day, wondering if Mark O'Meara would finish third or better and bump him off the team. When O'Meara missed a birdie putt at the par-five seventeenth, it was almost assured. The only chance would be to hole out his second shot on the par-four eighteenth. Players were congratulating Faxon when the phone in the locker room rang. The attendant paged Faxon, who at first refused to take the call.

"It's Davis Love," said the attendant.

"Hey, Brad, this is Davis. Freddie [Couples] and I are doing laundry. How'd you play today?"

"Shot sixty-three."

"Oh yeah? That's great! Where's that put you on the Ryder Cup team?"

Love and Couples had a private plane waiting at the Van Nuys airport to take them to Freddie's tournament in Seattle. They finished early and started watching Faxon's scores being posted at Riviera. Five under. Six under. Seven under. Eight under.

"Hey, Freddie, Brad's going to make the team!"

They knew Faxon would be in the locker room, working the computer, trying to figure out his position. They knew he had to finish fifth, and that chances were O'Meara wasn't going to hole out. They ended up getting to Seattle three hours late. Couples missed the cocktail party for his own pro-am. "They had me going," Faxon said. "Right after that, I saw Jeff Maggert. You know, he's an emotionless sort of guy, but he walks by, buck naked, with a beer in his hand and he says in that Houston accent, 'Hey, partner!' I didn't hug him naked, but he was juiced."

The next day, Love and Faxon passed each other on adjacent fairways at Overlake Golf in Seattle. Love waited for his amateur partner to putt out, then announced, "Hey, every-body, let's congratulate Brad Faxon on making the Ryder Cup team."

Faxon bowed. Later he gave Love a box of expensive Cuban No. 1 cigars. He had delivered. So had Bonnie. They would all be together in Rochester with baby Sophie.

BERNARD Gallacher and Lanny Wadkins hold the most treasured trophy in golf, the Ryder Cup. (Stephen Munday, Allsport)

THE flyover at Thursday's opening ceremonies. (Simon Bruty, Allsport)

BERNHARD Langer *(left)* celebrates his monstrous fifty-foot birdie putt on the ninth green during Friday's foursomes. (Simon Bruty, Allsport)

OLD Wake Forest teammates Curtis Strange and Jay Haas *(above)* could never get hot on a cold Saturday morning.

(Simon Bruty, Allsport)

SEVE Ballesteros hugs David Gilford *(left)* on the thirteenth green after Gilford's putt from the fringe breaks like a half moon into the hole.

(Stephen Munday, Allsport)

JEFF Maggert was 2–0 on Friday, but had trouble off the tee in the Saturday foursomes.

(Stephen Munday, Allsport)

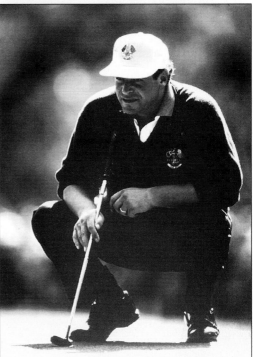

COSTANTINO Rocca had to line this one up, but he made a hole-in-one on the sixth hole Saturday morning, only the third ace in Ryder Cup history.

(David Cannon, Allsport)

COLIN Montgomerie took his shots by saying that the strength of the European team was the American team, but he didn't get his first point until Saturday morning and was a disappointing 2–3 in the matches. (David Cannon, Allsport)

BEN Crenshaw and Davis Love only made one birdie in their four-balls loss to Ian Woosnam and Sam Torrance.

(Simon Bruty, Allsport)

NICK Faldo had to deal with sand and dirt—and tabloid reports that his marriage was on the rocks. (Simon Bruty, Allsport)

U.S. Open champion Corey Pavin was the little man who came up big for the American side. (Stephen Munday, Allsport)

TOM Lehman thought his team would win in a rout and got the first point Sunday with a singles win over Seve Ballesteros. (David Cannon, Allsport)

PETER Jacobsen picked up his ball by mistake on Friday, came back with a big win on Saturday, but lost his singles match to Howard Clark, who had a hole in one, a chip-in for par, and a four-footer downhill to win at the eighteenth. (Stephen Munday, Allsport)

FRED Couples went 2-1-1, with a halve against Ian Woosnam on Sunday in a replay of their match that ended "all square" at the Belfry in 1993. (Stephen Munday, Allsport)

FORMER college teammates Per-Ulrik Johansson and Phil Mickelson went off last on Sunday, but their match was only for pride and bragging rights. (David Cannon, Allsport)

BERNARD Gallacher gets some hang time after Philip Walton clinches the victory. (J.D. Cuban, Allsport)

BERNARD Gallacher helps a choked-up Lanny Wadkins with his speech at the closing ceremonies. (Stephen Munday, Allsport)

IT turned out to be Heartbreak Hill for the U.S. team, especially Curtis Strange (face covered). (Stephen Munday, Allsport)

CHAPTER 5

"Welcome to the Team"

The movie title of 1995's PGA Championship should have been *Sleepless in Los Angeles*. Instead of Meg Ryan and Tom Hanks, it starred a cast that included Faxon, Calcavecchia, Perry, and Lanny Wadkins, the U.S. Ryder Cup captain. Wadkins had the unenviable task of making the two wild-card picks, and unlike his three predecessors, Wadkins had the toughest job.

Starting early in the week, he would awake at all hours of the morning and mull his options. His short list included Fred Couples, Jim Gallagher, Jr., Lee Janzen, Curtis Strange, and Tom Watson. He was leaning toward

Strange and Watson, because his U.S. team lacked Ryder Cup experience, but by doing that he would be leaving off Couples, who, when healthy, is the most talented American player.

But Wadkins was prepared to make that decision. All along, he was prepared to take the heat, because it was his team and, as he said, "my butt on the line." In 1993, Watson went for two veteran players in Wadkins and Floyd, and that worked out at the Belfry. Maybe Watson was having trouble with the putter, but he was still a presence, and the U.S. team needed a presence. That was also the thinking with Strange, who hadn't won in the United States since the 1989 U.S. Open at Oak Hill. It would be easier to justify picking Strange than Watson, simply because Strange didn't have the putting yips. As for Couples, Wadkins had an option. He would wait to see how he performed at the PGA, how his back stood up, and then make his decision accordingly. Gallagher and Janzen, the only two Americans with two victories in 1995, would almost have to play their way on the team at Riviera. Both were finishers, but they weren't at a point in their careers where they deserved being picked over Couples, Strange, or Watson. At least not in Lanny's mind.

Early in the week at Riviera, Gallagher and Janzen did their best to complicate the situation. Gallagher, who defeated Seve Ballesteros in his singles match at the Belfry in 1993, shot 64 in the opening round to trail Michael Bradley by one stroke. He didn't break par the remainder of the way and finished tied for forty-fourth. Janzen opened with a 66, but his putter went cold and he finished tied for twenty-third.

Three closing rounds of 68-68-68 convinced Wadkins that Strange would be one of his two picks. He had put the heat on Curtis to play well, and Curtis had responded. "I'm delighted to have Curtis," Wadkins said. "I needed somebody with some real heart and guts, and I just think that Curtis brings to the team what a Raymond Floyd or a Tom Watson would bring to the team. I need somebody like Curtis around."

Watson actually helped Wadkins make his most difficult decision. A month earlier, Wadkins had met Couples at Preston Trail Golf Club in Dallas. Couples hadn't played since the U.S. Open and was resting his back for the Western Open. Wadkins wanted to see for himself how Couples felt. They played thirty-six holes, with Mickey Mantle following them around in a golf cart. Mantle had just had liver replacement surgery. "I thought Fred was swinging the club as good as I'd ever seen him swing," Wadkins said. "At that point in time, it kind of changed my whole thinking a little bit, because I was looking at some of the other players. I didn't think Fred up to then was going to be healthy enough to play the Ryder Cup matches."

In the two weeks after their thirty-six holes at Preston Trail, neither did Couples. He went to the Western Open and was feeling fine until the back nine Saturday, when his back spasmed and he nearly had to crawl in. That forced him out of the British Open, which raised questions not only about his future on the Ryder Cup team but about his future as a dominant golfer.

But just by fate, Couples had played the third round at the Western Open with Don Pooley. Pooley had had a back injury so bad that at one point he could hardly walk. A trip to the Hughston Clinic in Columbus, Georgia, where he was treated by a physical therapist named Tom Boers, cured that. At first, Couples brushed Pooley off. "We were on the fifth hole," Couples said. "I said, 'Don, I can't feel any better than I'm feeling right now.'" Four days later, Couples was in Columbus visiting Boers. One month later, he was shooting 66 in the final round of the PGA and proclaiming himself a candidate for the team.

That left just Watson, who shot thirteen-under 128 in his two practice rounds at Riviera. Once the tournament started, it was a different Watson, or the struggling Watson we've seen battle his putter for the last five years. He shot even-par 274 and Saturday night ruled himself out, telling Wadkins to select Couples. Wadkins still gave Watson one more chance, but Watson closed with a 70 to finish tied for fifty-eighth.

On the practice putting green outside the clubhouse at Riviera, reporters tried to pry the answer out of Wadkins, but Wadkins didn't have an answer. He wanted to speak to Couples in the locker room, and to Strange after he completed his round. "I talked to Lanny at five o'clock," Strange said. "I thought he would know, and he said, 'I don't have a clue,' and that didn't sound good to me."

Later that night, Wadkins tracked down Strange and Couples in Seattle, where Couples was hosting his pro-am. It had been a long flight for Curtis. Both were obviously excited. "I think it's the most I've heard Fred talk," Wadkins said. "I couldn't get him off the phone." The conversation with Strange was especially emotional. Wadkins and Strange grew up junior golf rivals in Virginia and alumni at Wake Forest. Strange had honest misgivings about being selected. "I want to deserve it," Strange said. "The worst thing would be for me to go in there as a questionable pick and then mess up some crucial match. I understand chemistry and leadership and toughness, but the real question is, Do I bring the game? That's always the most important thing. But I told Lanny, 'If chosen, I will play my butt off.'"

Wadkins had consulted everybody from past Ryder Cup captains Raymond Floyd, Dave Stockton, and Jack Nicklaus to Greg Norman, the Australian who is the number one player in the world. In the weeks afterward, he received calls from Floyd, Paul Azinger, and Tom Kite supporting him on the picks. Janzen had made him look bad, winning the International in a shootout with Ernie Els. That gave him three victories and moved him past Greg Norman to the number one spot on the money list.

Afterward, Janzen wondered if what he did might cause the PGA to rethink the points system. He said, "I want to become the first player to win the money title and not be picked for the Ryder Cup."

Wadkins still liked his picks. What Janzen did was one week too late, and the modified Stableford format at the International wasn't a good indicator; had it been a stroke-play event, Janzen would have finished fifth. But now you had a guy with three wins not on the team, and in head-to-head, match-play situations, Janzen had joined Corey Pavin as America's best young closer. Around the country, golf fans were already starting to question Wadkins on sports call-in shows and in letters to the golf magazines. The Strange pick was the one most questioned. Wadkins was accused of letting the buddy system cloud his judgment. He and Strange were both Wake Forest graduates, and both grew up in Virginia. That's why it helped for Wadkins to get those calls from Floyd and Azinger. Kite told Wadkins personally, flying home from a corporate outing in Pittsburgh on a private plane.

"They just weren't blowin' smoke, either," Wadkins said. "It's nice to get support from your age-group peers."

The captain spent the five weeks before the Ryder Cup putting together some possible pairings. In a phone conversation, he learned that Phil Mickelson would like to play with Jay Haas. That was a pairing he hadn't put together, and the more Wadkins thought about it, the more he liked it—especially in better ball. In alternate shot, Wadkins thought Couples would complement Loren Roberts, since Couples's iron game was so strong and Roberts was one of the world's best putters; he would be there to cash in on the birdie opportunities.

First off on Friday morning, Wadkins liked the team of Pavin and Tom Lehman, since both were bulldogs and wouldn't be intimidated by what would probably be Europe's strongest pairing. The same way it worked for Couples and Roberts, he would arrange it so Lehman would hit into the greens and Pavin would make the putts. "I figured out if you tee off the first hole at Oak Hill in the matches, you're going to putt six times—if all the greens are hit in regulation. If you tee off on the even holes at Oak Hill and hit all the greens in regulation, you're going to putt on eight holes on the back and the first seven holes in a row. Obviously it sounds to me like for the back side, down in crunch time, you want your best putter hitting a majority of the first putts."

The last thing Wadkins had to worry about was the condition of Couples. When he left Riviera the Monday after the PGA, it was clear that Watson was the 2B choice should Couples's back flare up. But after the International, Watson called Wadkins and told him that Janzen should be the backup pick. That call changed Wadkins's thinking. He wanted to keep his options open. "At this point in time, I've got several 2Bs in mind," Wadkins said the week of the Canadian Open from his home in Dallas. "I want to look at who's playing well right up to the time of the matches."

Wadkins hoped he wouldn't have to make that decision. After the PGA, he played more practice rounds with Couples at Preston Trail, and he saw things in Fred that he had never seen before. "I'm making Fred a big part of my plans right now," Wadkins said. "He's playing good and his attitude is good and I think he feels a different responsibility as a captain's pick than when he made it on points. I can tell, he's got an excitement in his voice that I haven't heard in a long time. He's upbeat right now, and an upbeat good-playing Fred Couples is hard to beat."

With that, Wadkins slept well in the week leading up to Oak Hill.

CHAPTER 6

Taking the Blame

Bernard Gallacher was fed up, sick and tired of the Ryder Cup in 1993. He had played in eight of them, been second in command at three of them, but captaining two of them was Gallacher's breaking point. When his European team lost two matches to the Americans by three measly points, Gallacher unfairly took the blame. While he claimed to not treat it as life and death, said he didn't "really feel as bad about losing as a lot of people feel," it privately tortured him to the point where he wanted no more of the pressure and complexity. The life of club pro at Wentworth Club, in the leafy suburbs south of

London, while not as exciting, certainly wasn't as stressful as the Ryder Cup captaincy. But no other position in golf was. Gallacher had the thankless job of following Tony Jacklin, and every move he made was compared to what Jacklin would have done. Certainly, he was less effective—Jacklin was 2-1-1—and his players weren't motivated as much, but maybe those days in Europe were gone forever. Jacklin was golden, the man who saved the Ryder Cup for Europe. Gallacher was tarnished, the man who lost two straight.

In his defense, Gallacher claimed the torch should be passed on to players before their time had passed. He believed the Americans had it right, appointing a new captain for every match. "I am not giving up the captaincy because it will be a relief but because I feel it's right," Gallacher said. Still, those close to Gallacher knew he wanted no part of being the only captain in European Ryder Cup history to go 0–3. There was a stigma attached to that, and Gallacher had to answer for it.

In 1991, Gallacher was at the helm of a European team that lost by one point at Kiawah Island in what *Golf World* headlined as "The War by the Shore." U.S. players wore Desert Storm camouflage baseball hats and captain Dave Stockton turned into a replica of Norman Schwarzkopf. The PGA of America also snubbed the European team at the gala dinner, showing a Ryder Cup video that had just a small mention of the Europeans. "They were there to do or die," Nick Faldo said afterward in the London *Express*. "They had to win at all costs. They were so hyped up, they couldn't care less if we left there with a bad taste in our mouths . . . and a lot of us did. When they showed that video, our new boys looked at us with eyes as big as saucers, as if to say, 'What do we do now?' We were just sort of spitting blood. We had to bite our lips and say: 'Okay, guys, we'll accept that it's all part of it.' But it shouldn't be. The players were all right, it was out of their hands. It was very much officially oriented. The captain and offices were very much involved."

Behind the scenes, Gallacher was caught in the middle of a

fight between the European PGA Tour and the British PGA over control of the Ryder Cup. In 1975, the European Tour Players Division broke off from the PGA. Two years later, the Ryder Cup Committee voted to allow the rest of Europe to join Great Britain and Ireland to make the Ryder Cup more competitive. The British PGA resented this, and in 1988, under new executive director Ken Lindsay, it sought total control of the event. In truth, Sam Ryder did present the Ryder Cup trophy to the PGA, but without the players and the European Tour, Lindsay had nothing to work with.

At one point, Gallacher threatened to resign "to see how far the PGA want to take it." Gallacher felt that the PGA, and not the committee, would appoint its own captain. Ken Schofield, executive director of the European Tour, talked Gallacher out of it. It wasn't until November 1990, in a hotel at London's Heathrow Airport, that the two sides came together. Lindsay eventually resigned and was replaced by a more amenable Sandy Jones, but Gallacher felt the political infighting undermined the early stages of his captaincy.

The matches started with controversy and ended with controversy. On Sunday, Stockton elected to invoke the captain's privilege of declaring Steve Pate unable to play in the singles. Pate had injured his ribs in a limousine accident riding to the gala dinner on Wednesday night in Charleston, and he played in only one match the first two days. On Saturday night, each captain had to put a player in the envelope to sit out the Sunday singles in case of an injury to the other team. Stockton's choice was made for him. Gallacher went with David Gilford, a Ryder Cup rookie who had not played well in foursomes and four-balls paired with Europe's two best players, Nick Faldo and Colin Montgomerie.

The next morning, on the practice ground at Kiawah, Gallacher was told that Pate would not play. When Gilford found out, he collapsed in the locker room. "There's no question in my mind that they took half a point," Gallacher said in *Out of Bounds*, the book by Lauren St. John of the *Sunday Times*. "I mean, if Steve Pate plays, we don't know the outcome, but if he doesn't play, he gets half a point. I wasn't so concerned about the outcome of the Ryder Cup. I just felt sorry that David Gilford didn't get a chance to redeem himself in the singles."

Gallacher was emotionally wrung out from Kiawah, but promised to come back one more time—this time on his terms. "I don't think they played it completely fair," Gallacher said. "They raised the temperature both on and off the golf course. That had to be stopped, and we stopped it this time, but there was a certain coolness between me and the PGA of America." Maybe there would be vindication for that one-point loss in South Carolina. But there was no vindication in Sutton Coldfield, England, for Gallacher. Unlike Kiawah, the matches at the Belfry in 1993 were played in the spirit of the Ryder Cup, but it was Gallacher who took the blame for the loss.

When Seve Ballesteros and Bernhard Langer sat out four-balls matches Saturday afternoon, the European team was called rudderless. It was certainly not something Tony Jacklin would have allowed. As Europe's captain in 1983, 1985, 1987, and 1989, Jacklin never believed in ruling by committee. But as a past U.S. and British Open champion, Jacklin could stand up to Ballesteros and Langer. Gallacher, who was Jacklin's second-in-command, never had the playing record of his predecessor, and thus didn't have the credibility.

Gallacher grew up in Bathgate, a working-class town located halfway between Glasgow and Edinburgh in Scotland. As a player, he won eight times on the European Tour and was first on the Order of Merit in 1969, when he qualified for his first Ryder Cup team. That year he took on and defeated Lee Trevino, the 1968 U.S. Open champion, in singles at Royal Birkdale. Eight years later he was four up after four holes on Jack Nicklaus at Royal Lytham, and held on to win by holing an eighty-foot putt on the seventeenth. In 1979 at the Greenbrier, he pitched in to defeat Lanny Wadkins, his adversary at

Oak Hill. "Bernard's a dogged competitor," Wadkins said. "He reminds me a lot of Corey Pavin. He refuses to lose."

But as a captain, Gallacher came off as being too soft. Instead of being the bulldog he was as a player, the Scotsman bowed to his players' wishes. Up by three points at lunch on Saturday, the Europeans clearly had command of the matches' momentum. It was time to step on the Americans' throats, and not let them up. But Gallacher helped give them life. He took his foot off the jugular. Ballesteros asked to sit out, because his game had gone awry. On the fourteenth hole of an alternate-shot match with José María Olazábal against the American team of Tom Kite and Davis Love III, Ballesteros pulled Gallacher aside and asked to skip the afternoon four-balls. Gallacher tried to talk the Spaniard out of it, but Ballesteros insisted he was letting Olazábal down and needed time on the practice ground to straighten it out. Gallacher felt he owed it to Ballesteros to honor the request. That afternoon, Olazábal played with Joakim Haeggman and lost to Payne Stewart and Raymond Floyd 2–1.

Langer came to the Belfry having missed five straight weeks of tournament golf with a bad back. In his first three matches, paired with Ian Woosnam and Barry Lane, the German had gone 2–1. He and Woosie were unbeatable, destroying Payne Stewart and Fred Couples 7–5 Friday morning, and Paul Azinger and Couples 2–1 Saturday morning.

Jacklin was critical. On Sunday night at the Belfry, while the U.S. team celebrated their victory, Tony Jacklin approached George O'Grady, deputy executive director of the European Tour, and offered to captain the team at Oak Hill in 1995. He pointed out that Langer and Ballesteros often asked to be excused from the odd match, but Jacklin always told the German and the Spaniard that they were far too valuable to be left out. He concluded the absence of Langer and Ballesteros Saturday afternoon was too big a burden for the team to carry.

Jacklin wrote about it in the *Scotsman*. He talked about it in

Europe and America, where he made his new home. His rea-
soning was a mixture of personal and continental pride. It was
Jacklin who led Europe out of the Ryder Cup dark ages. Without a win in 1995 at Oak Hill, it would be a decade since Europe's last triumph. "I don't want to criticize Bernard,"
Jacklin said. "But some of the players can get a bit big for
their boots.

"One of the key things about the '80s was, when it came to
the Ryder Cup, egos had to be hung outside the door before
the players came to the team room."

This did not go over well with Faldo, Langer, Ballesteros, or
Mark James. They felt that Jacklin's ego had gotten too big,
that it was they who played the matches, not Jacklin. They
talked about the hardships on the European team: the toe injury that caused Sam Torrance to withdraw from the singles,
the scare young Peter Baker had one night when his young
daughter was rushed to a Birmingham hospital, the bad backs
of Ballesteros and Langer.

Letters were written to Gallacher, Schofield, Jones, and the
Ryder Cup Committee, urging Gallacher to return. Faldo
claimed that Jacklin was no longer in touch with today's European Tour, that he was going to America to play the Senior
Tour and would be in no position to evaluate talent from overseas. Gallacher was hurt that Jacklin would take those shots
at him, but his spirit, and his mind, changed with the support.
He agreed to return and captain the European team at Oak
Hill. "On the last two occasions, we have had one hand on
Sam Ryder's Cup," Gallacher said on August 28 in a news conference at European Tour headquarters. "And in three weeks'
time, we aim to have both hands on it."

CHAPTER 7

The Euro Side

Bernard Gallacher never tried to imitate Tony Jacklin. He was his own man and he brought to the role of captain his own qualities, first of which was an attention to detail. In his view, the role of Ryder Cup captain comes in organizing the week, which entailed the meals, the clothing, and, most important, the pairings. If he had his way, the twelve players who made the European Ryder Cup team would come off the Order of Merit. There would be no captain's selections.

In an interview with John Hopkins of the London *Times,* just before the 1995 German Open, Gallacher bristled when it was pointed out how much that diminished the art of the captaincy.

Hopkins wrote that "it is clear an exposed nerve has been struck. With a firmness bordering on brusqueness, Gallacher explains that he has had enough experience of selection by committee, when players have been included or excluded at the whim of selectors of captains, to avoid such selection techniques for the rest of his life."

This sentiment ran contrary to the belief of Europe's top players, who felt the European captain should have the option of making twelve selections, and who were angry that Gallacher would be making only two and not three picks in 1995. Gallacher himself triggered this reduction by lobbying with the European Tour to count money earned off the three American major championships, the Masters, U.S. Open, and PGA Championship, toward Ryder Cup points. His thinking was that if players were good enough to qualify for these events, they should not be penalized for it. The European Tour's thinking was that okay, we'll give you that, but we have to protect our tour, we have to keep our players from playing overseas. So because of that, the captain would get two picks, instead of the three he had had in 1985, 1987, 1989, and 1991.

A lobby was brewing to change that as late as the Buick Open, held in August, four weeks before the final European Ryder Cup event. Because of circumstances that were obviously leading toward Europe's not fielding its best team, Faldo suggested that the captain's picks be increased from two to four. "I think we have to move the goalposts," Faldo said. "For the good of the game, we need to field what we feel is the strongest team."

Gallacher was dealt two complicating factors, the first being that Faldo committed to play the U.S. Tour full-time in 1995. He did not win in Europe and had his worst year in major championship since 1986, the year before his British Open victory at Muirfield. The second was that José María Olazábal, who paired with Seve Ballesteros to create the vaunted Spanish Armada, was limping with a foot injury and was out of the top ten in the points table. At the International, Olazábal said he would suggest to Gallacher not to select him, because he wouldn't be able to go thirty-six holes a day Friday and Saturday.

At the end of the day, Gallacher had to go with Faldo and Olazábal, leaving out Ian Woosnam, Jesper Parnevik, and Barry Lane.

When Woosnam won the 1994 Dunhill Masters, the third counting event, Gallacher didn't think there would be any way the Welshman wouldn't qualify. But the putting problems that plagued Woosnam since 1991 continued, and he finished twelfth in the final accounting.

Parnevik jumped into contention based on his victory in the Scandinavian Masters. Like Faldo, he had been penalized by playing the U.S. Tour full-time. He was also being considered based on a second-place finish in the 1994 British Open at Turnberry.

Lane, who qualified for the 1993 Ryder Cup, had advanced to the finals of the 1995 Andersen Consulting World Match Play Championships, held on New Year's Eve. That technically made him Europe's best match-play player. To advance, he beat Bernhard Langer and Seve Ballesteros on the same day at the Oxfordshire in Thame, England.

Ideally, Europe's team would appear to be stronger with Woosnam, Parnevik, and Lane than it would with Howard Clark, Mark James, and Philip Walton, but those players had played their way on the team and Woosnam, Parnevik, and Lane hadn't. "I've said this all along, in fact there are arguments for having twelve automatic places and there are arguments for having more wild cards, but I think that any system might not be proved to be the best system," Gallacher said. "I think the way it was done from the very outset was framed around these better players, but I would have to say that even coming down the last few weeks, there is nobody that has proved to me they're good enough to oust José María out of the team, and that's really it. If you are going to feel sorry for anyone, it's someone like Miguel Angel Jiménez, who's actually in the eleventh spot. I mean, José María is actually going to finish twelfth in the table, and the thing that may have forced a change in my thinking would have been the exceptional performances in the last three weeks from players that have been on my short list and it didn't happen."

In the final accounting, the team Gallacher announced on August 28 would have made forty-nine Ryder Cup appearances and played in 190 matches. Seve Ballesteros and Nick Faldo would have played in more Ryder Cup matches (seventy) than the entire United States team (forty-seven). The Europeans would have two Ryder Cup rookies in Walton and Per-Ulrik Johansson to the Americans' five in Tom Lehman, Phil Mickelson, Loren Roberts, Jeff Maggert, and Brad Faxon. "I think we've got a very strong team," Gallacher said. "I think it's up to the players between now and the Ryder Cup to get their games into shape, and if they play well in Oak Hill we'll bring the trophy back. I am happy with my team."

Two weeks later, Olazábal pulled out and Gallacher replaced him with Woosnam, who had played in six straight Ryder Cups. Putting a positive spin on it, Gallacher said it spoke for the strength of the European Tour that he could replace one U.S. Masters champion with another, but Woosnam was just another member of the European team who came to Oak Hill trying to stave off putting woes.

On the seventeenth hole at Riviera, playing to make the cut on Friday, Woosie had a four-footer straight up the hill for birdie. Make it, and he would play on the weekend, and maybe pick up enough money to break into Europe's top ten. Twice he backed off the putt, then left it short, and missed the cut by one stroke.

Two weeks later, at the Volvo German Open, Woosnam resorted to using two putters in the same round. For putts outside three feet, he used his conventional putter. For the short putts, the ones he could yip, he used one of the longer broom-handled putters. It was a case of desperation. On Thursday at the British Masters, five days before flying to Rochester on the Concorde, he missed a putt of less than fourteen inches.

Three of Europe's players at Oak Hill, Mark James, Sam Torrance, and Philip Walton, used the broom-handle putter. Bernhard Langer had his own individual style, bracing the shaft to his left forearm, then locking it in place with his right hand. Nick Faldo gave up on his left-hand low grip at the PGA, saying, "I might as well look good while I'm missing the putts." Suppose it came down to one of these players needing to make a short putt to win a match. How would they handle it on Oak Hill's slick greens?

Faldo didn't appear to be worried. Two weeks before the Ryder Cup, he told correspondent Bill Blighton in a metaphor-filled stream of consciousness, "We shall *brush* aside all doubts, *handle* all adversity, and *sweep* to victory. If I go on any further, I will break into song."

The only European player who seemed to be putting well was Colin Montgomerie, who had struggled with his blade until August. At the PGA, Monty took fourteen more putts than Steve Elkington, but right after that, he won twice in three weeks on the European Tour. Asked at one point if he would ever go to the broom-handled putter, Montgomerie just scoffed. "No," he said. "Where do you go after that? Do you take up tennis? I don't want to be in the same room as one of them." And then he shuddered.

What Europe did have going into the Ryder Cup was players in proper form. In the Lancome Trophy, five of Europe's Ryder Cup team finished in the top six. The following week, Torrance won the British Masters to vault to number one on the Order of Merit.

Finally, there was the revenge factor. Europe hadn't held the Cup since 1991 and was tired of hearing how its side had supposedly slipped. Although their play wasn't up to standard,

Ballesteros and Faldo have a way of elevating themselves in the Ryder Cup, lifting their teammates with them. On paper, it may have looked like a blowout, but this was the Ryder Cup, so there were no favorites. "I think it's going to be a tough match and we will win," Gallacher said. "Our players are fed up and they want it back."

CHAPTER 8

Arrival

The British Airways Concorde made its first pass over the runway at 9:00 A.M. on Monday, September 19, looking and sounding more like a rocket ship than a passenger jet, and carrying with it the hopes and dreams of Europe's Ryder Cup team. The pilot, Colin Morris, made a flyover at Oak Hill, tilting the wings so the players on both sides of the cabin could see the course. There was an excitement on board. The Europeans were the decided underdog. They came to America with nothing to lose, but Sam Torrance liked that. "There's nothing wrong with being the underdog," he kept thinking. "We've got a lot of strong players and we're looking forward to the challenge."

It was Torrance who sank the decisive putt in Europe's victory at the Belfry in 1985. That win, the first for Europe in twenty-eight years, came at a time when the Ryder Cup was just gathering momentum. Now it had become a mega-event, golf's fifth major, broadcast on network television in the United States and over 120 countries around the world. In 1989, the U.S. PGA couldn't even get live network coverage of the event in the United States. NBC and the USA cable network would provide twenty-three hours of live coverage plus highlight shows over the three days. Yes, the Ryder Cup had come a long way since Torrance sank that winning putt on the eighteenth green at the Belfry a decade ago. "The Ryder Cup," Torrance would say, "is the ultimate competition in golf."

Pressed against the smoked glass windows at Rochester International Airport were an estimated two thousand people, some of whom had arisen at 4:30 A.M. and driven an hour just to witness this moment in Monroe County history. To some, this was as close as they would get to the Ryder Cup. "I heard about it last night and I said, 'Come on, we've got to go!'" said Janis Rawlings of Dansville. Next to her, Dorris Nash had been sitting in the airport's observatory since 5:00 A.M. Because of her height, Ms. Nash wanted a front-row seat. "We can't go to watch the team because we don't have tickets," she said. "I figured at least I would see them here, and I would see the Concorde up close."

On the floor below them, in the International Arrivals Concourse, PGA officials, the Rochester community welcome wagon, and some members of the television media had been waiting almost as long. Mary McCombs, an anchor-reporter for the ABC affiliate, had been at the airport since 5:45. The Concorde was scheduled to arrive at 8:10, and the parking garage was sure to fill up fast. Also waiting were Mitchell Platts, the press director for the European Tour, and Nick Faldo, who said he had been working on his game with David Leadbetter, the noted swing instructor, at Lake Nona Golf Club in Orlando.

Faldo reported that their twice-a-day sessions began in the steamy central Florida mornings and ended with the sun going down. He looked fit, fresh, and keen to play and was in good spirits, offering to carry a tray of finger sandwiches out onto the tarmac, then telling a story about his favorite Concorde landing.

"We were coming into Muirfield in 1987," Faldo said. "The pilot says, 'Do you want to see the golf course?' So we all said, 'Sure.' He dips the wing one way. Is that it? He dips the other wing. Is that it? Finally, Seve says, 'I think he better land this plane. It is not a yo-yo.'"

Television crews from the four Rochester and Buffalo affiliates had their trucks set up on the tarmac, taping the Concorde as it taxied to a stop. A helicopter circled overhead, carrying a photographer for the *Rochester Democrat & Chronicle*. A set of portable steps was rolled to the jet's doorway, and a red carpet was laid out on the cement. Bill Johnson, the mayor of Rochester, was there, and so was Jack Doyle, the chief executive from Monroe County. The PGA officers were wearing their burgundy cashmere blazers that U.S. captain Lanny Wadkins had picked out. Wadkins and his wife, Penny, were part of the greeting committee.

"I could never understand what the big deal was all about with the Concorde," Wadkins said on the tarmac. "When I flew in it, the inside needed renovating."

The big plus, of course, is the time factor. It took the Concorde four hours from gate to gate to make the Atlantic crossing, three hours and thirty-five minutes of flight time. Traveling at two and a half times the speed of sound, it took less time for the Concorde to fly London to Rochester than it did for *USA Today* golf writer Steve Hershey to travel from his home in New Smyrna Beach, Florida, to Rochester. Technically, the British team left the runway at Heathrow at 10:25 A.M. and pulled into the gate at Rochester at 9:30 A.M., so they picked up one hour on the day.

Torrance was first to deplane, the honor granted based on his victory less than twenty-four hours earlier at the British Masters. The Scotsman scorched a 3-wood to an island green on the last hole at Collingtree Park in Northampton, England, for a one-stroke victory over Michael Campbell of New Zealand. That victory moved Torrance to number one on the Order of Merit, ahead of his Ryder Cup teammates Colin Montgomerie, Costantino Rocca, and Bernhard Langer.

Following Torrance was his wife, Suzanne, a former actress. She was wearing black leather pants and a matching black leather jacket. One by one the Europeans and their wives walked down the steps and onto the red carpet. Montgomerie, the number one player in Europe in 1993 and 1994, was next to deplane, followed by Howard Clark and the always stoic Langer. Seve Ballesteros was the most striking in a dark double-breasted jacket. Without his hat, David Gilford looked like an accountant.

Faldo met his wife, Gill, put his arm on her shoulder, and walked toward the terminal. "Hello, darling," she said. The tabloid reporters approached. "Should we talk to them?" Nick whisked her away.

Next off was Ken Schofield, executive director for the European Tour, followed by Rocca, Mark James, Philip Walton, and Per-Ulrik Johansson. Last off was Ian Woosnam, who came hopping down the steps like a windup doll, followed by Bernard Gallacher. They looked confident, but not cocky, determined, but not tight. Inside the lounge, they drank Perrier and nibbled on sandwiches while Gallacher and Wadkins received keys to the city and the county, then faced a bank of television cameras.

"On the flyover, I looked down at all the cars and was just hoping there weren't any accidents from people gazing up instead of looking at the road," Gallacher said.

The news conference was mundane, except for one question thrown at Gallacher by a British reporter. On Monday, the London *Sun,* a tabloid, ran a front-page article delving into the supposed marital problems of Nick and Gill Faldo. Nothing like waiting until the Ryder Cup to run the story.

At the British Open, the *News and the World* was rumored to have a story accusing Faldo of having an affair with a member of the Arizona State golf team, but the piece never ran. The *Sun*'s headline was FALDO £10M DIVORCE SHOCKER, and inside was a two-page story with accompanying pictures of Faldo's homes in Surrey, England, and Orlando, Florida. All of this was there at the newsstands when Gill Faldo boarded the Concorde for upstate New York. She was quoted in the story as saying, "I have nothing to say about this. I am not getting a divorce."

At Heathrow, Gallacher and members of the European team addressed the rumors. "Gill's going on the plane and we're delighted she's going," said Gallacher.

"Don't worry about Nick Faldo," said Montgomerie. "There's more pressure in the cup than any other tournament, even the majors, and Nick handles pressure better than anyone I've seen."

Torrance wouldn't even acknowledge the question, telling the newsman, "Go play in traffic."

These distractions were the last thing Gallacher needed as he headed to Rochester. Faldo was perhaps the most integral part of his team, and a tabloid scandal four days before the Ryder Cup could be devastating. Most of the British writers who cover golf full-time were happy to be traveling when the story broke. Most elected to ignore it, but the tabloid writers are a bloodthirsty lot, and they feed on controversy by asking leading questions and twisting quotes into banner headlines. At one British Open, American Scott Hoch was not smart enough to see the trap being laid by the tabs, and the next day a story accompanying his interview was headlined WE ALL HATE NASTY NICK!

But Gallacher had plenty of experience dealing with London's "Beastie Boys," and he was prepared for the follow-up at Rochester International.

Reporter: "Do you think Nick Faldo's personal problems will hurt the morale of the team?"

Gallacher: "We're here to talk about the Ryder Cup."

It was clear, though, that the story would not die. The next day, stories ran in the tabloids picturing Nick with his arm around Gill's shoulder as they walked across the tarmac. Faldo's agent, John Simpson of the International Management Group, denied the story. At Oak Hill, Julius Mason, the PGA's director of public relations and media relations, began Faldo's news conference by requesting that no personal questions be asked. The story had clearly made the Faldos somewhat paranoid. When Gill lost her room key, she had visions of reporters from the *Daily Mirror* and the *Sun* hiding under her bed and in her closet. She had the locks changed and new keys issued, then discovered the key in her pocket.

The American team was free of controversy as it arrived in Rochester. Nine of them spent Sunday night behind a guarded gate at the Lodge at the Woodcliff Hotel in Fairport, fifteen minutes from Oak Hill. Couples, Faxon, Haas, Jacobsen, and their caddies rode a chartered bus from the B.C. Open in Endicott, New York, arriving in time to have dinner and watch the Dallas Cowboys beat the Minnesota Vikings in overtime. Wadkins went to bed at 11:00 P.M., while the players stayed up and talked about being together as a team for the first time. "One of the toughest things is to get the guys out of team room, have them quit joking, and go to bed," Wadkins said. "Sunday night, I went to bed about eleven, and there were still four or five guys just having a big time. At the Belfry, Tom Watson had to tell guys to go to bed. It would be midnight and we'd have to get up at six. It's like being back in college at a fraternity house."

Wadkins had it set up so the Faxons and the Lehmans had suites, so they could use the extra room for their newborn babies. Otherwise, there were no children on the floor. Everybody left his door open until it was time to go to bed. It was just like a college dormitory, and every night they would play Jenga and exchange gifts. The Stranges brought them all Wake Forest sweatshirts.

At Oak Hill on Monday, the players had the grounds and the course to themselves. The U.S. team was assigned the upstairs locker room, with each player allowed five lockers. Wadkins had brought in the two physical therapists who travel the tour for the Centinala Hospital in Los Angeles and had the training room equipped with an aquatherapy massage bed. "Putting our clubs in the Ryder Cup bags was neat," said Faxon. "Seeing a U.S. flag on a Ryder Cup bag with your name on it for the first time is something you'll never forget. Peter Jacobsen said he went to Arnold Palmer's once and saw his eight Ryder Cup bags on a shelf, displayed."

The Europeans were in the downstairs locker room, and the entire area was off-limits to everyone but players, their wives or girlfriends, caddies, and official members of the PGA and European Tour parties. This was totally unlike tournaments on either tour, where the media and equipment reps are allowed locker-room access. With over fifteen hundred media credentials issued, that would just create a zoo.

Gallacher wanted his team to spend the afternoon relaxing and unwinding at the Woodcliff, but most of them wanted to hit balls and see the course. Faldo, Montgomerie, Woosnam, James, and Rocca played nine holes. Langer, Ballesteros, and Per-Ulrik Johansson worked on the range. Torrance and Walton walked the course, since their clubs were on a commercial flight with excess baggage. The first American Torrance saw on the range was Bobby Wadkins, Lanny's brother, who was serving as the team's unofficial co-captain. Wadkins shook his hand and congratulated him on his victory and season.

The United States golfers had been practicing since the morning, but were still working on their games late in the afternoon. On the range, a huge Jumbotron screen stared blankly at the players, but later that night PGA officials and Oak Hill's grounds crew would eat pizza, drink beer, and watch *Monday Night Football* under the stars. Every player seemed to be accompanied by his instructor. Maybe a hundred spectators, most of them volunteers and tournament employees, watched this lazy, relaxed scene.

Any War by the Shore sentiment had been left behind two Ryder Cups ago. When Langer walked out to the practice green, Love played the role of ambassador and called out, "Bernhard, how do you feel?"

"Good, thanks," said the German, never breaking stride, but smiling ever so slightly to acknowledge the greeting. On the putting green, Rocca and James received high fives from Jacobsen, Couples, and Haas. Afterward, Faxon would say, "All the Europeans said hello to me except for Seve. He looked the other way."

With some time to kill, Couples and Faxon walked to the fourteenth tee carrying their wedges and putters. But first they made an escorted detour through the merchandise tent with Craig Harmon, the head professional at Oak Hill. Harmon wanted Couples and Faxon to meet his staff. Although the PGA had adopted a no-autograph policy to protect the players, Couples and Faxon both signed whatever was put in front of them. One man, wearing an Ashworth shirt, peeled off a sweatshirt for Couples to sign.

"Okay, let's go," Couples said. "Lanny's got a team meeting scheduled, followed by a cocktail hour and dinner."

Down the fourteenth fairway, about one hundred yards from the green on the short par-four, Couples and Faxon dropped a handful of balls and started tearing the first divots out of a pristine fairway. The course had been closed for a week, and the members had worn their Softspikes, so it was in absolutely mint condition. Wadkins had fretted that a dry August had not grown the rough to its specified length, but rains in the last week had accomplished that goal. Around the green, Faxon and Couples each lost a ball just wedging shots onto the putting surface. The day before, Wadkins and Love were playing the eighth hole when Love drove into a patch of rough between the fairway and a bunker. It took them four minutes to find the ball. This put a devilish grin on Wadkins's face. He wanted every home-course advantage he could get, and the Europeans were not used to playing out of the spinach week after week.

On the fifteenth tee, a par-three of 186 yards, Couples and Faxon decided to wedge down to the ladies' tee and then wedge onto the green. From one hundred yards, four balls hit their target, although one spun back into the rough and again was unfindable. Walking with them and carrying a video camera was Paul Marchand, Freddie's swing teacher from Houston. On the green, they were joined by two of the Harmon brothers, Craig and Dick, and Jay Haas.

"Freddie," Dick said, pointing at the corporate tents, "Craig wanted me to ask you if you wouldn't mind walking through there and signing a few thousand autographs."

Couples, who hates crowds, smiled sheepishly. "No problem," he said.

In the bunker, Faxon dropped a ball and turned to Haas. "All right, Jay, it's alternate shot, we're three up, and they've got a fifteen-footer." Faxon, who has one of the best short games in the world, picked a shot clean out of the sand, and the ball trickled down to within inches of going in. The Americans faked a celebration. "We win four and three," said Haas.

Finally, up on the eighteenth green, Craig Harmon asked Couples to pose with his brother, Dick. "You're his *former* teacher, aren't you?" he said.

On the putting surface, Faxon dropped a ball eighteen feet below the hole, and played the imaginary game all golfers play as youngsters.

"This is to close out Faldo," he said. The ball rolled up to the hole, took the six inches of break, and dropped into the cup on the last rotation. Faxon broke into a smile and raised his putter.

"Yes!" he said.

Couples was in a bunker, checking out the texture of the sand, not paying attention to Faxon.

"Who won NASCAR yesterday?" he said, knowing Faxon never missed a second of *SportsCenter.*

"Jeff Gordon," said Faxon, without a split second of hesitation.

That night, they were joined by Jeff Maggert, who flew in from Houston, Phil Mickelson, who arrived from Scottsdale, and Curtis Strange, who had played a charity tournament for Fuzzy Zoeller in Indiana. Finally, the U.S. team was together. While the Europeans went to bed early, they rode a bus to a restaurant in East Rochester and enjoyed a meal in a private room at the Northside Inn.

At the end of the evening a highlight video was shown that featured interviews from former Ryder Cup captains Byron Nelson, Sam Snead, Jackie Burke, and Dave Marr talking about what the Ryder Cup meant to them. In May, Wadkins and the PGA hosted a dinner at the Loews Anatole Hotel in Dallas for all the living U.S. Ryder Cup captains. Only four didn't show up. Jack Nicklaus was on vacation in Mexico. Lee Trevino was celebrating the birthday of his wife. Dow Finsterwald had a corporate commitment. Ben Hogan was undergoing cancer surgery that day in Forth Worth.

The dinner, held before the GTE Byron Nelson Classic in Irving, Texas, was an opportunity for Wadkins to pick the brains of his predecessors. "It's the first time I've been in a room with Arnold Palmer where I didn't notice every second he was there," Wadkins said. "It's hard to imagine being in a room where Arnold isn't the dominant figure. It was like, 'Hi, Arnold, how are you doing? Excuse me, I want to talk to Jackie. I want to talk to Sam. I want to talk to Byron.' The one sad part, actually, was that Hogan was scheduled to be there."

The U.S. team was just as captivated as Wadkins. They had goose bumps walking out of the Northside Inn on a crisp night in East Rochester. Captain Wadkins had requested that a copy of the tape be sent to the team room at the Woodcliff, where it could be shown throughout the week. "If that doesn't fire you up," he said, "nothing will."

CHAPTER 9

Hypertension

A t 10:00 A.M. Tuesday morning, Oak Hill had become a city teeming with restless anticipation, as in the minutes before a heavyweight prizefight—except there were three more days before the fighters would climb in the ring and start exchanging leather, or in this case, balata. The grandstands behind the driving range were packed. People were ten-deep behind the fences and crammed on the hillsides overlooking the practice ground. The Jumbotron screen carried a message in giant block letters:

Welcome
To
Oak Hill
and
The Ryder Cup

Finally. It was here. "On Monday, there were no spectators there," said Tom Lehman. "It was dead quiet. You get out there Tuesday, and look out of the locker room, and there were people everywhere. Then you realized—this is the Ryder Cup."

Corey Pavin was the first American player to walk down from the locker room to hit balls. He received a thunderous ovation, the type of ovation usually given to a champion as he walks up the eighteenth fairway on Sunday afternoon. The first match wasn't going to be played for three days, and the U.S. Open champion already had goose bumps. "I've never felt anything like that in my career," he said. Just to break the tension, Pavin purposely topped his second practice shot into the grass.

"Tuesday was like walking into Yankee Stadium at the World Series, like the Olympic torch was lit. It was a totally different deal," said Faxon. "I walked out on the practice tee and got the ovation Nicklaus or Palmer get walking up the eighteenth hole at a tournament. It was impossible not to get excited about it, and then it got almost ridiculously funny because of people going berserk."

One by one, the Americans made their way to the range, and it seemed they all had their swing teachers with them. David Leadbetter was with Faxon. Jim McLean was with Peter Jacobsen. Jim Flick was with Tom Lehman. Marchand and Dick Harmon were standing behind Couples. Rick Smith, who works with Lee Janzen, was looking at Ben Crenshaw. Dean Reinmuth was with Phil Mickelson. Also on the premises were Butch Harmon, who was working for Sky Sports as an analyst for the European broadcast, and Billy Harmon, the head professional at Newport Country Club and a former caddy for Haas.

"It's a big thrill to me because I know how much it means to Jay to be here on this team," Billy Harmon said. "This may be Jay's last team to make. Dave Marr was saying that the other night because Jay's the type of guy who's going to be spending more time with his family. I just hope he plays well. I owe everything to him."

Everybody on the American team looked sharp, including the caddies, who were wearing their Ryder Cup uniforms of khaki pants and blue shirts, with off-white sweaters or vests. The caddies alone each received six pairs of pants, six shirts, two vests, a sweater, two sweatshirts, a rainsuit, and two pairs of Nike sneakers, and five Oldsmobile courtesy cars to share among the twelve of them. They never get courtesy cars at a PGA Tour stop. "I can't thank Lanny enough," said Maggert's caddy, Brian Sullivan.

The players, of course, had it even better. It cost the PGA $12,000 per player to outfit the American team. This included two blazers for the opening and closing ceremonies and a Hickey Freeman tuxedo for the Gala Dinner on Wednesday night. Curtis Strange came out on Tuesday and said to Dick Harmon, "This is the best I've ever looked in my life." Privately, he told *Golf Magazine* editor George Peper, "If I ever get to be captain, I'm just gonna order seven days' worth of white shirts and khakis and say, 'Boys, go play.'"

It got so complicated that Ben Crenshaw and Tom Lehman would wear the wrong sweaters to the team photo session, so a quick change to blazers was required to get everybody in the same uniform. "There's not many tournaments where we play and come in three or four days beforehand where your clothes are laid out on your bed when you get there and your slacks are numbered and your shirts are numbered," Faxon said. "We had three guys wearing the wrong shirt or wrong sweater vests or something."

Some of it was nerves. The American team clearly did not expect the greeting it received during the practice rounds at Oak Hill. Jeff Rude of the *Dallas Morning News* noticed it watching the players warm up. "These guys are way too tight, way too tight," Rude said Tuesday morning. "Look at their faces. It looks like colon surgery. Pavin and Mickelson came out of the clubhouse and never made eye contact with anybody."

Standing next to Rude was Glenn Sheeley of the *Atlanta Journal-Constitution,* and Sheeley is always quick on the uptake—especially with an easy target like Rude, who is called Captain Intensity because he's always wound so tight. Nobody likes to go after Rude more than Wadkins, who would have been proud of Sheeley for taking a shot when it was there for the taking. "That's because they don't want to make eye contact with *you,*" Sheeley said. Rude scowled and headed for the putting green in search of quotes.

Jimmy Roberts of ESPN was out working the range, and he got Jacobsen to stop for an interview. Roberts trained under Howard Cosell, and his questions always seem to reflect it. Too many TV reporters say something probing like "Talk about the winning putt" and then put the microphone under a golfer's nose. Roberts is too strong a reporter. He remembered that Jacobsen was working on the other side of the microphone for the Ryder Cup at Kiawah Island, and was assigned to the match between Bernhard Langer and Hale Irwin that decided it. "It was the most dramatic, nerve-racking thing I've ever seen in my life."

"Do you wish it was you," Roberts said, "or do you not wish it was you?"

"I wished it was me," Jacobsen said, "and I hope it comes down to me this week."

The scene on the first tee looked and felt like a Sunday afternoon for the final group at a U.S. Open, with spectators lined down both sides of the 440-yard par-four, wrapping like two ribbons being tied at the grandstands behind the green.

Almost every hole on the front side at Oak Hill was like this. Wadkins wanted Strange playing with Pavin, to shepherd him around the golf course for the first time. There was nothing to these pairings. Mickelson was with Maggert and Jacobsen with Haas. In the second group, Love went out with Lehman and Strange with Pavin. The last group to tee off was Crenshaw with Couples and Roberts with Faxon. It didn't seem to matter who was a partner with whom.

"Wanna do something?" Couples said, looking for a game.

"Sure," said Crenshaw. "Wanna flip for partners?"

"Ten bucks?" said Couples, trying to establish a bet. "Lanny said he's putting up the money. Caddies want any of that action?"

The caddies, Joe LaCava for Couples, Linn Strickler for Crenshaw, John Burke for Faxon, and Dan Stojak for Roberts, were silent. The gallery was hushed.

"The players are playing for ten bucks," said Dick Harmon, trying to break the tension. "The caddies are betting a hundred."

That night the two teams dined at the Woodcliff, sitting at round tables with the wives and PGA officials. Faxon was the only player to go unescorted. His wife, Bonnie, was still home in Barrington, Rhode Island, with baby Sophie. At dinner, Faxon sat at a table with the Faldos, but there was no sign of any tension. "We saw the other side of Nick Faldo," Faxon said. "He was a riot."

This is what was so different about this Ryder Cup from the ones held in 1989 and 1991. With the exception of Ballesteros, and the little intimidation games he likes to play, the players on both sides considered themselves to be allies, not enemies. This wasn't a war, it was a summit. "I think what most of the people who watch golf fail to realize is we're friends with those guys," Wadkins said. "I've played with Sam Torrance and Bernard Gallacher and Seve Ballesteros and Bernhard Langer for twenty years. We've been to dinner together. Our wives are friends. The one thing about the pro tour compared to other sports is that very few guys have enemies. Number one, I've always taken the approach that I don't want to have any enemy because I don't want a personality interfering with me trying to win a golf tournament. Nobody's going to make me go to dinner with somebody, so if I don't care for them socially, I can at least be civil to them. I want to win as bad as anybody, but life's too short to be rude with people you play with all the time."

Practice on Wednesday looked like a symposium for the teachers and sports psychologists of *Golf Digest* and *Golf Magazine.* Standing on the first tee while both teams teed off was Leadbetter, the only instructor with players on opposing sides. Since 1986, Leadbetter had been associated with Faldo, but recently he had begun working with Faxon. "I'm split down the middle this week," Leadbetter said, drawing an imaginary line down his chest. "I'm wearing the Swiss flag."

A story appeared that morning in *USA Today* questioning the PGA's Ryder Cup selection process, and this had some members of the U.S. team fuming. Written by Steve Hershey, it pointed out that the last American player to produce a victory was Pavin at the U.S. Open, that Faxon, Mickelson, Strange, and Roberts each had only one top-ten finish since the spring, and that Crenshaw and Jacobsen hadn't had any. These were good points, but they struck a raw nerve that was first exposed in a Heat Index chart that accompanied a story Jaime Diaz wrote in the *Golf Plus* supplement of *Sports Illustrated.* Diaz had little to do with the chart, which was written by a committee of editors in New York, but he found himself taking the heat for it at the World Series of Golf.

The Heat Index was actually the creation of Jim Herre, the new senior editor of *Golf Plus,* who for six years had been the managing editor at *Golf World.* In 1991, it was Herre who came up with the "War by the Shore" headline that will forever be associated with Kiawah Island. Herre believes in "creating a buzz," and he certainly did that with the Heat Index. It had all the players—and their wives—talking not too kindly about *Sports Illustrated.*

The harshest evaluations were given to Jacobsen ("Nice guys finish last. Too soft to stick it to the likes of Seve"), Haas ("What's he doing here? Besides Curtis, only guy on team who hasn't won in two years"), Couples ("Heat sensitive. Most talented American, but makes Watson look like a good putter"), and Maggert ("Nice swing, no Sunday punch. Could be the weak link when things get tight").

The symbol for the Heat Index was a sun. Pavin got five for being a "Man of steel." Mickelson got four. Faxon, Love, and Strange got three and a half. Roberts got three. But Maggert got two, which indicated he was "half baked," Couples got one and a half, Haas only one ("Gooey mess"), and Jacobsen just a half. Some of the players ignored it, but when I spoke to Jacobsen three weeks later at his home in Portland he was still doing a slow burn.

"How ya doin', Peter?"

"Feelin' pretty gooey."

Pause.

"Because you got slimed?"

"Yeah, who the [expletive] is this Jim Herre, anyway?"

Herre's take-no-prisoners philosophy was well ingrained in the staff of *Golf World* when that magazine came out with its irreverent chart evaluating both teams. Most of the comments under "Defining Moment" were fair, but the one accompanying Jacobsen's crossed the line. The editors at *Golf World* wrote: "Needing to hit a three-quarter 6-iron to the last green of the 1988 Western Open to win, was momentarily distracted and hit full 6-iron over green into lake to lose." First of all, that was seven years ago. Second, Jacobsen rebounded in 1995 to win two tournaments back-to-back on the West Coast, the AT&T National Pro-Am at Pebble Beach and the Buick Invitational of California at Torrey Pines in San Diego.

As in the case of Diaz and the Heat Index, *Golf World* senior editor Gary Van Sickle unfairly took the blame because his by-line accompanied the story. Players don't always realize that writers don't make headlines or do charts. At the B.C. Open, Jacobsen confronted Van Sickle. Those watching in the press-room at En-Joie Country Club thought Jacobsen was mad enough to take a swing at Van Sickle.

A wire service account of their confrontation appeared in Sunday's *Rochester Democrat & Chronicle*. When Van Sickle asked Jacobsen if his concentration was improving as the Ryder Cup approached, Jacobsen responded sternly: "Gary, you're the expert on the Ryder Cup. You write what you want. You will anyway." Van Sickle tried to explain that his defining moment of Jacobsen was the time he tackled the streaker at the 1991 British Open, but Jacobsen saw no humor. "Articles like Gary's come out, very negative to the American players, which again I just had a hard time understanding why the negativism and pessimism come out from the American writers."

At Oak Hill, Jacobsen just wouldn't let it go. Van Sickle nominated him as captain of the BBC—the Big Baby Club. *Golf World* features editor Geoff Russell, a Herre protégé who contributed to "Defining Moments" items, offered to send a big box of diapers to the American team room.

Bob Rotella, the sports psychologist who works with Faxon and Love, thought this was the best possible way to deal with pressure. "It gives them something to prove," Rotella said. "It's the equivalent of a football coach putting something on a bulletin board. It gets their mind off home-course advantage, and because they feel underappreciated and undervalued, it gives them something to prove, a common goal."

Relations between the European team and the European press were just as strained. In a Wednesday news conference, Torrance was first asked about his less than spectacular Ryder Cup record (4-13-6), about whether the team was collectively too old, about whether the alleged marital difficulties of Nick Faldo were affecting morale, and about the untimely sniping of Jacklin. Torrance's temper finally boiled over when the "menu question" was asked. "Give us a break, will you?" the Scotsman said. "We're here to talk about golf. Not about marriages and not about autographs. This is quite enough." On the way out of the press tent, Torrance cursed the media. He later admitted, "This is a hypertension tournament, but we're here to allow for that and use it."

The traditional Gala Dinner that night seemed to break the tension—and Torrance was a big part of it. In 1993, it was Torrance who ignited a firestorm of tabloid controversy by asking members of the U.S. team to sign his menu during the Gala Dinner at the Metropole Hotel near the Belfry. U.S. captain Tom Watson, trying to protect his players, politely but firmly denied Torrance's request.

"You know what will happen if I sign, Sam," Watson said. "We'll spend the whole night signing."

Torrance pointed out that it was part of the event's tradition. Watson promised to sign at the victory dinner on Sunday, but Torrance was insulted at the snub. The tabloid rottweilers picked up on it and blew it out of proportion—"Fork off" was the best headline. Gallacher did the best job of diffusing the situation by telling the press he could forge Watson's signature for Torrance, but it was obviously still a sore point to the Scotsman when he was asked, quite simply, "Will you be asking anyone to sign a menu tonight?"

That issue was addressed after the two teams walked into the Rochester Riverside Convention Center, the men in tuxedos and the women in formal evening wear. Dick Enberg, the master of ceremonies, announced a no-autograph policy would be in effect. The evening was devoid of any long-winded speeches. Johnny Mathis provided the entertainment at the $350-a-plate dinner. The big news of the evening was the announcement that Couples had given Tawnya Dodd an engagement ring at the Woodcliff just before riding the team bus to the convention center. Couples began dating Tawnya in late 1992, just as the marriage to his first wife was falling apart.

He told friends it was more nerve-racking giving Tawnya the ring than playing in the Ryder Cup matches.

"I was walking out the door and he told me to close my eyes," Dodd said. "I thought it was a necklace, but when he put the ring on my finger I asked him what it meant. He said nothing. Finally, I got him to tell me it was an engagement ring. I told him, 'I've got to tell everybody!' He said, 'No, you can't, it's the Ryder Cup.' I told him that's why I should tell everybody. It was typical of Fred to do it that way."

Dodd stood up in front of the bus and tried using the driver's microphone, but her hands were shaking. Couples had walked to the back of the bus and was hiding in the seat behind the Loves, Davis and Robin. It was hard to hear what Dodd was saying, but when all the wives in front of the bus started screaming, the Loves picked up on the announcement.

"That was one of the neatest parts of the week to me," Davis Love said. "It made the dinner."

In between courses, Wadkins told a friend that he thought the matches would be over by Sunday morning. Publicly he concluded the evening by wishing the best to both teams. Of the Europeans, Wadkins said, "I hope they have a great week. Not too great, but just good enough." When the dinner ended, Nick and Gill Faldo walked out holding hands. The paparazzi were not there to record it.

By Thursday, the players were getting tired of the official dinners and the mandatory news conferences and the practice rounds. "This is more nervous than I am the day before a major championship," said Haas. "I need to get clotheslined by that middle linebacker. I need to get knocked on my ass."

Wadkins sensed the uneasiness and let Couples, Love, Strange, and Crenshaw take the morning off. "I think a couple of them are close to getting overbaked," Wadkins said.

Gallacher had his full team out and practicing. It had now become a guessing game between the two captains. Wadkins was almost sure that Gallacher would put his strongest team of Faldo and Montgomerie out first. To counter that, he had his two bulldogs of Pavin and Lehman. "I needed something to light a fire under Corey," Wadkins said as he rode in a golf cart to the media tent to announce the pairings. "He's been going through the motions."

Wadkins told Pavin and Lehman on the seventh tee. Pavin's reaction?

"Perfect."

In their respective press conferences, Gallacher was far more uptight than Wadkins. Maybe he had reason to be. Ballesteros was way off form, and for the first time in his Ryder Cup history, would not be in the lineup for the foursomes. Also sitting out was Woosnam. Gallacher put together Torrance and Rocca, sending them out second against Couples and Haas. The third pairing would be Europe's weakest, with Howard Clark paired with Mark James. Combined, they had a 1-9-0 foursomes record in Ryder Cup play. They would face a surprising pairing in Love and Maggert. Love talked Wadkins into this, and Maggert earned the start based on his play in the practice rounds. "I got to know Jeff a lot better at the Presidents Cup," Love said. "Kelly and Robin were also close. I knew he was a really really good player, I knew from how he hit the ball that it would be a good matchup in alternate shot. Plus, it would be a pairing they weren't expecting, and I kind of liked that, too. They were expecting me and Freddie." This showed the flexibility that Wadkins had and Gallacher didn't.

Last out, the European captain put Langer with Johansson, figuring the veteran would provide stability for the Swedish rookie. Wadkins sent out two major championship winners in Strange and Crenshaw. "Well, I think the pairings for us are kind of a combination of practice and ideas and discussions with both the players and basically of what we thought would work on this golf course," Wadkins said. "We're very pleased with our pairings and the way they're working out. I'm just out there watching these guys playing, and I don't have anybody out of twelve people approaching even playing mediocre right now. They're all playing really well. I'm just excited about the way they're playing. And the toughest thing is now playing the other four guys, because they're playing as good as the guys I've got in there, so it's a wonderful problem for me to have."

Wadkins explained the philosophy of his pairings. Rather than put two big hitters together in alternate shot, he split them up. That's why Couples and Love weren't together. They'd be hitting a lot of irons off tees and their strength would be negated. He also paired good iron players with good putters, as was the case with Strange and Crenshaw, and Lehman and Pavin. Finally, he considered personalities. But more than anything else, he listened. "I've been to eight Ryder Cups. I never had a captain that didn't," Wadkins said. "I think it would be foolish not to. These guys are experienced and know their own feelings and who they play with. They play with these guys week in and week out. The last thing I want to do is put two guys together who either have a personality problem or for some reason don't play well together. I want guys that get along. I like to have a guy that likes his partner's game. Like when I played with Corey last time at the Belfry. Corey liked my game with him and I liked Corey's game with me. So that made it go well together. These guys all like their partner's game and like it with them. That's important. That gives them a lot of confidence. They're not going out there unsure of what their partner's going to play. They're wound just perfect."

Rude asked Wadkins about his thoughts on the afternoon pairings.

"I'm not going to sit here and tell you that," said Wadkins.

"Well, we're alone here," Rude said in the crowded interview room. "You can trust me to keep it a secret."

Wadkins had the perfect opening to nail his hometown writer, and he did.

"That's usually the way it works with you, isn't it?" he said. "I bet that's what you tell your girlfriends, too. No, Jeff. I'll have any ideas about noon tomorrow."

This lighter moment was a great contrast to Gallacher's news conference, which he began by saying, "I really don't have anything. The comments are on the paper. The team—I like the team and I'm sure Lanny likes the matches. I think we're going to have a great match."

Gallacher's first question was about Ballesteros, as were his second, third, and fourth:

Writer: "Can you discuss why Seve is not in the opening round? Is that anything to do with injuries or your decision?"

Gallacher: "Seve's going to play an important part in the Ryder Cup, but it won't be in the opening-day foursomes."

Writer: "How did he take it, Bernard, when you told him?"

Gallacher: "How did he take what? Who?"

Writer: "Seve. That he wouldn't be playing."

Gallacher: "Seve agrees with the decision, agrees with the team."

Writer: "Bernard, why does he agree with you?"

Gallacher: "Why does he agree with me? Because we can't play Seve in every match. It's doubtful if we can play every player in every match the way I see fit for the benefit of the team."

It was clear which captain was feeling more pressure, which one had the 0–2 Ryder Cup record, which one had the most to lose. Gallacher's personality was best described by John Hopkins in the *Times* of London prior to the matches. "Gallacher's gift has always been perspiration, not inspiration," Hopkins wrote. "He worked harder than most. As a professional, he ground away for hours on the practice ground, overcoming a strong left-hand grip to win two tournaments and the Order of Merit in only his second season as a professional—and make the first of eight successive Ryder Cup appearances.

"There is an obvious grittiness about him, from the tilt of his head and the look in his eye to the edge in his voice. He has got where he is by hard work, and, pal, you had better know that. The demons that drive him on are stereotypically Scottish. Gallacher positively resounds with the ethics of Lord Reith and the frugality of John Knox. He personifies those Scottish adjectives, canny, pawky, conservative, and Calvinist.

"In this, he is unlike Tony Jacklin, his predecessor as Ryder Cup captain, with whom he is so often compared. If there is a touch of Arthur Daley about Jacklin, then Gallacher could be cast as a primary-school headmaster able to instill the basic principles of life into his charges. Jacklin would have been a consummate politician, wheeling and dealing, caressing and cajoling, imploring and flattering. Jacklin is a broad-brush merchant whereas Gallacher has a nose for the minutiae."

That in part explained the pricklish behavior. Even softball questions were handled as if they had some hidden meaning, as when Gallacher was asked if he was more confident after spending four days at Oak Hill with his team.

"I'm not more confident, no," he said. "I'm just the same. I'm just the same as I was before I got here. I'm just the same as I was when I announced the team. I'm not any more confident. I'm confident."

The opening ceremonies were held at 3:30 P.M. on the driving range, with the opening music provided by the Eastman School of Music Wind Ensemble. Inside their locker rooms, the players watched Chuck Mangione, a Rochester native, introduce his opening number. "This describes where we are, 'The Land of Make Believe.'" A lone bagpiper came out and played "Amazing Grace." This was followed by the Massed Upstate New York Pipe Band, fifty-six bagpipers representing pipe bands of the Feadan Or, Oran Or, and the Mohawk Valley Frasers. It was to this music that both teams made their way out of the clubhouse in alphabetical order, the Europeans in double-breasted blazers and the Americans in their maroon cashmere. It was Gallacher next to Wadkins, Ballesteros next to Couples, Clark next to Crenshaw, and finally Woosnam next to Strange, the last two captain's picks filing into the arena.

Sitting in the front rows below the stage were Dave Marr and John Jacobs, two former Ryder Cup captains who were amazed at just how big this event had become, how 100 million TV viewers would watch what had become the most anticipated and most compelling event in golf. "Who ever thought it would have gotten like this?" said Marr.

After the teams were introduced, the flags were raised and the national anthems played before the first-day pairings were announced. The players had their game faces on, anticipating the morning. Nobody's gut was churning more than Tom Lehman's. The Ryder Cup rookie would be hitting the first tee ball for the Americans.

CHAPTER 10

The Bulldogs

It was 7:30 A.M. on a dark, damp, and overcast morning at Oak Hill. The weather had changed from the late-summer warmth and sunshine at the opening ceremonies. Heavy rain was blowing in off Lake Ontario and was scheduled to hit Rochester before noon. The faces were grim and somber, sixteen nervous men warming up for the first day of the thirty-first Ryder Cup.

Tom Lehman had a wakeup call for 5:00 A.M., but was up at 4:00, tossing and turning. The Ryder Cup rookie was no worse than Ben Crenshaw, the forty-four-year-old veteran playing in his fourth Ryder Cup. "I have never in my life been as keyed up and as nervous as that first morning," he said. "Alternate shot has got you like this." He squeezed his hand together. "I've never felt that nervous, it was an anticipatory nervous. I couldn't wait to start, to get out into the rough. I couldn't draw a breath."

The Europeans were dressed in orange sweaters and vests, brown pants, and yellow shirts. The Americans were in black pants, green shirts, and gray sweaters or vests. Dick Harmon was standing behind Couples, Jim Flick behind Tom Lehman, and David Leadbetter behind Faldo. Smoking a cigarette, Bob Torrance was keeping an eye on Colin Montgomerie. Curtis Strange came out looking as if he hadn't had a good night's rest. The range was so crowded, he had to hit balls over the stage used for the opening ceremonies. Strange would be hitting the first tee ball for the Americans in the fourth and final match of the morning.

Lehman would be hitting the first ball in the first match, and in the back of his mind he thought back to the 1991 Ben Hogan Tour stop in El Paso, Texas. It was the same week as the Ryder Cup at Kiawah Island, and he remembered being one of the guys piling into the locker room at Coronado Country Club, screaming and hooting and hollering every time an American did something good and getting upset and cussing every time one did something bad. "Everybody in that room dreamt about what it would be like to be on that team," Lehman said. Now he was not only on the team, he was its leadoff hitter.

"I've always felt like this underdog," Lehman said, "because of where I come from. I've had to struggle to see myself as the guy who belongs. I go back and forth on that—do I belong, or don't I belong? Sometimes I feel like I do and other times, it's 'Wow, I'm here.'"

On Thursday night, Paul Azinger asked Lanny Wadkins if it was okay to address the U.S. team. Azinger had played in three Ryder Cups, but had not qualified for the 1995 matches because of his fight with lymphoma. He was at Oak Hill to make his television debut as an analyst for the USA Network and NBC Sports. His singles match against Seve Ballesteros at the Belfry in 1989 was a classic, with Azinger saving bogey from the woods at the eighteenth hole to win the match one up. In 1991, he and Chip Beck were involved in the controversy involving Ballesteros and José María Olazábal. In 1993, after the U.S. team had already clinched at least a tie to retain the Cup, Azinger refused to forfeit his match against Faldo. It may have been meaningless, but not to Azinger and his pride. He ended up getting a halve against Faldo for what was considered a moral victory. It also delivered a message. Two months later, he was diagnosed with cancer. "I told them I know the anxiety you're feeling because I've felt it myself," Azinger said. "You just have to remember that as nervous as you're feeling, just look in the eye of the other guy and know they're just as nervous. It's just you against them. Then I gave them a Chip Beckism. I told them, 'Positive thinking can overcome a mechanical breakdown.'"

At 7:55 A.M., Lehman and Pavin began their walk from the practice green to the first tee. Lehman's mother was waiting by the hospitality tent. "I want to say hi to my son! I want to say hi to my son!" she pleaded with a security guard. Pavin was calmly walking with his wife, Shannon, but Lehman was clearly feeling the adrenaline rush. He pumped his fist walking by the grandstands, and the roar grew louder. Faldo and Montgomerie made their entrances, their jaws set, their captain waiting. "I'm nervous and I'm not even playing," Gallacher said.

Among the 25,000 spectators at Oak Hill was Dottie Pepper, the LPGA star who led the U.S. team to a victory in the 1994 Solheim Cup. "I came here this morning waiting to see these guys throw up on the first tee the way I did last year," she said.

Gary Schaal, past PGA president and honorary chairman of the Ryder Cup, was in charge of making the introductions. The referee was Joe Black. "Europe has the honor," said Schaal. "Play away."

Montgomerie already had the head cover off his driver. He would hit the first ball of the 1995 Ryder Cup. He heard encouragement coming from a Scottish voice. "Let's go, Montee!" His drive was center cut, and the big man blew out a sigh of relief.

"Now playing for the United States," said Schaal, "Tom Lehman."

No other player on the United States team had come such a long way in a short time as Lehman. In 1990, he was driving around the country in a beat-up Volvo playing the Ben Hogan Tour. At one point, he was about ready to take the job of golf coach at his alma mater, the University of Minnesota. When the athletic director insisted that he rent cross-country skis out of the pro shop in the winter, Lehman turned the job down and became the Ben Hogan Tour Player of the Year. In 1994 he made Jack Nicklaus's Memorial Tournament his first PGA Tour victory. In 1995, he recorded his second victory at the Colonial National Invitation. But he had never faced a moment like this.

"I didn't feel like I practiced all that well. I wasn't sure of my swing. So it was a real honor to be put out first," Lehman said. "That gave me the sense of confidence that I belonged, that I could get the job done. I was nervous about it the night before, but by the time I got to the first tee Friday morning, I was so calm and relaxed, it was ridiculous."

The first hole at Oak Hill measures 440 yards. Ben Hogan called it the hardest opening hole in major championship golf. All Lehman did was take out a 3-wood and bomb it 290 yards down the sprinkler line, a good forty paces ahead of Montgomerie's tee ball. "I just ripped it," said Lehman.

That drive set the tone for the first five holes of the match. Lehman and Pavin won the first, second, third, and fifth holes to go four up on Europe's strongest team. At the second, Lehman had a little tap-in for par after the Europeans had made a mess of the hole. Faldo conceded the putt, but not loud enough for Lehman and Pavin to hear.

"I said it's good," Faldo finally said.

"We gotta hear it," said Pavin.

Afterward, Lehman explained he was keyed up but that Faldo has a tendency to mumble, which he didn't appreciate. "'He wasn't being really clear about it, and he made this overt gesture as if to say, 'Okay, you idiot, pick it up.' That made me mad. I wasn't going to take any crap from anybody. Good thing Corey went over and talked to him."

At the next hole, Lehman striped a 5-iron into the 210-yard par three and Faldo complimented him by saying, "Good shot"—something he rarely does—and the exchange was forgotten. The early turning point in the match came at the sixth hole, the little par three over Allen's Creek where four players made holes in one during the second round of the 1989 U.S. Open. Pavin hit a shot that pitched eighteen inches from the cup and released to the back of the green. Faldo blocked his iron, but caught the right corner of the green. Although Pavin's shot was much better than Faldo's, Lehman was away. He thought he'd made the twenty-footer, but the ball just turned left at the hole and lipped out. Montgomerie stepped up and holed from fifteen feet to give the Europeans their first glimmer of life. Normally emotionless this early in a match, Faldo slapped Monty on the back. They were only three down, with twelve holes left. At the next hole, the seventh, Lehman's trusty 3-wood let him down. He pushed his tee shot into the creek, behind a weeping willow. Faldo hit the green after Montgomerie's tee shot hit the fairway, and in less than fifteen minutes the Americans' four-up lead was cut in half.

Soon it would be down to one up. Pavin missed the fairway left at the eighth, and again the Europeans were on in regulation. Wadkins was standing on the ninth tee to settle his team down, but Lehman missed another fairway. "Basically, on this golf course, if you drive it in the rough, you're probably going to lose the hole," Lehman said. But at the ninth, with the first drops of rain beginning to fall, Pavin advanced it into the greenside bunker, Lehman hit from the sand to four feet, and

Pavin made the putt to stop the bleeding. Halving that hole was crucial.

"That putt was big, big, big," said Dick Enberg.

"Made it like the U.S. Open champ," said Johnny Miller, "which he is."

That seemed to calm Lehman down.

"I think the most difficult thing to do, in the alternate-shot format, is not get down on yourself for hitting a bad shot and putting your partner in a bad spot," Lehman said. "When I'm out there playing on my own and I hit a bad shot, I just chase it down and hit it again. I don't think about it. I don't worry about it. I don't punish myself for it. I just do it.

"When you're playing with your partner and your team-mates are following you, you hit a bad shot and you're kind of like, 'Why did I hit it over there? I'm letting Corey down.' That's the hardest part to overcome, and that's why I say play-ing with Corey is so good. Because to Corey it doesn't matter. Corey just came over to me and said, 'You just got to get com-mitted to the shot you want to hit and just swing the club. Don't worry where.'"

The rain was falling hard by the time the first group reached the tenth green. One of the spectators sitting in the grandstands was Mike Johantgen of Brockport, New York. He had been there since 6:15 A.M. "It was so dark, we needed flashlights to find our way down here," Johantgen said. This was an extremely dedicated group of golf fans. They were not about to get up and leave just because of a downpour. On the scoreboard, they could see that Torrance and Rocca were a surprising three up on Couples and Haas, but that Love and Maggert were comfortably ahead of Clark and James.

"Jeff was playing great," Love said. "You never would have known he was a rookie at this."

In the last match, Europe had gone one up early, but Cren-shaw and Strange had it back to all square. Down by the eleventh green, Wadkins had set up camp and was waiting for Pavin and Lehman to come through. "I'm not worried about them," he said. "They're two bulldogs. They'll be all right. All they have to do is win a hole."

Wadkins was getting reports on the walkie-talkie from his brother, Bobby. Couples wasn't playing well, but Haas's putter was keeping them in the match. Crenshaw was playing well, and Wadkins was ready for the Masters champion to play a lot of golf before the day was over. The captain was already thinking about his afternoon pairings for the four-balls. He had until noon to submit his teams to Kerry Haigh, the PGA's senior director of tournaments. In better ball, he was going to ignore the fact that Couples was playing poorly and pair him with Davis Love III. He would be a fool not to. They had won the last three World Cups. He had Faxon, Jacobsen, Roberts, and Mickelson on the bench. He would wait until the last minute, to see how the morning played out.

The first match was crucial, and the Europeans drew even on the par-five thirteenth hole, Oak Hill's famous Hill of Fame. They did it in a most unusual manner, after missing their first fairway. From 240 yards out, Montgomerie hit the green with a 3-wood and Faldo made a fist-pumping bomb from forty-five feet for birdie. The Europeans in the gallery of 25,000 were roaring when the group reached the fourteenth tee. Jacobsen, Faxon, and Roberts had come out to greet Lehman and Pavin. Jacobsen said something to break the tension and make them laugh.

"Nice putt, Nick," was all Lehman said to Faldo.

"Thank you, Tom," was the simple reply.

The match had quickly developed into a classic, one of the best in Ryder Cup history. On the fourteenth green, Pavin stepped up for the first time by making a thirty-five-footer up the hill to regain a one-up lead. But one hole later, Lehman was indecisive on his club selection and pulled a 5-iron left of the green. "I hit the wrong club. I knew it was the wrong club, but I kind of went with Corey's feeling and hit it left into a bad spot, which was a big lesson for me," Lehman said. "I have a great caddy, Andy Martinez, probably the best caddy on tour.

He's gone along the last four years, he and I as a team, and suddenly I'm not paying as much attention to him as I normally do. It was kind of a rookie mistake. You and your caddy are a team. You need to trust him."

The rain was at its heaviest. Behind them, Couples and Haas continued to struggle. At one point they lost six out of eight holes without making a par and were five down after ten holes. Wadkins was dumbfounded to see one of his favorite teams getting dusted. "It's kind of surprising, but that's golf," Wadkins said. "Sometimes things don't go right."

And sometimes it does. Love and Maggert were on their way to closing out Clark and James. They started out birdie-par-birdie and were four under at the turn. That made the last point of the morning matches crucial. Johansson was hitting it all over the lot, but Langer was saving the team with his short game. At the sixth, he chipped close to save par, and at the ninth, he made a thirty-five-footer from across the green with a hard five-foot break for birdie. Crenshaw and Strange could only shake their heads at that. Soon they would be three down, making bogeys at the tenth and eleventh holes.

Up ahead, the lead group were grinding into the toughest stretch of holes, all square. The U.S. team saved par from the right rough at the sixteenth to stay even and halved the 452-yard seventeenth—which plays to a par five for the members—with bogeys. "By this time it was pouring and it was just survival," Lehman said. "Standing on the seventeenth hole, I was really nervous. I told Corey to give me a pep talk, I was letting it get away from me. He reminded me to stay committed."

The two middle matches were over. Couples and Haas made a mini-rally by winning the twelfth, thirteenth, and fourteenth holes. At the thirteenth, Couples had to hit a shot over the oak trees from the tenth fairway and the Europeans started to wonder if it would slip away. But at the par-three fifteenth, Torrance hit a 6-iron to eighteen feet and Rocca made the putt to go three up again. The match ended on the six-teenth green.

"We played great," Torrance said. "Originally Costantino and I were not foursomes partners. Bernard changed it yes-terday. It was a great change. Costantino played great. He was a rock out there from the start, from the very first hole when he holed a five-footer for par. It got a bit smelly when they got us back to two after we had been five up, but otherwise we were in control. It was a great start for us."

And a disconcerting one for Couples and Haas. "They kept the ball in play and deserved to win," Freddie said. "There's not much to say. It was very difficult out there. When Jay did hit a fairway, I hit a bad iron. We just had a bad run, and when you get five down, you relax a little bit and good things happen."

The consolation was that Love and Maggert closed Clark and James out 4–3, so each team had one point, with the first match all square going to the eighteenth tee and the Euro-peans leading the last match three up with six to go. Puddles had formed on the greens. The grounds crew was out with squeegees, delaying play.

The eighteenth hole at Oak Hill is 440 yards, but in the driv-ing rain the green looked 540 yards from the tee. The Euro-peans had the honor, and Faldo drove into the right rough. Pavin had the driver out, and took his sweater-vest off, care-fully folding it and placing it neatly in his golf bag. This was exactly the spot Pavin wanted to be in, and he was taking his time, making sure everything was right, before addressing the ball. The grip on his club was wet, so he asked Martinez for a dry towel. He called his caddy, Eric Schwarz, over to ask him if he had seen any good movies lately. Then he took his series of practice swings before stepping up to the ball, first putting all the weight on his left foot, then on his right, then on his left, before getting in balance. The ball went 235 yards, but it was in the short grass, 205 yards from the pin.

The Europeans had no chance to hit the green. Montgomerie pitched out, leaving Faldo a wedge to the pin. Lehman had a 5-iron in his hands and Pavin's advice in his mind. Be committed to the shot. Trust it.

"I had a little bit of a downhill lie, 186 yards to the front edge of the green, 205 yards to the pin," Lehman said. "It was a left-to-right wind, and all I wanted to do was get something up in the air, swing hard, and go ahead and rip it. It was raining sideways and 4-iron was the club, but I couldn't get it up out of that lie so I just went with it. I will say it was one of the best shots I ever hit under pressure in my life. That shot will stay with me my whole career."

The ball came down on the green thirty feet below the hole. On a dry green, two-putting from that distance was virtually assurable, especially with Pavin over the first putt. But the green was slow and the ball stopped four feet short of the hole, right in throw-up range.

Again, it was on Lehman's shoulders. The Europeans had a three-footer for bogey after Faldo airmailed the green with a wedge. After coming back from four down after five holes, fighting and clawing their way to all square with three holes to go, they were in the hopeless position of having the match in the hands of their opponents. Azinger called it a defining moment in Tommy Lehman's career, and he responded by rolling it center cut. Standing off the green, Faldo didn't want to see it, but could tell by the applause that Lehman had answered the call.

"In the end it was a disappointment," Faldo said. "We should have won. We clawed our way back, we had great chances at the sixteenth and seventeenth, but we didn't take them. So that was that. We played the last four holes better than they did. We played the better golf, but they got the point. That's the pity."

It was no pity to Wadkins, who ran onto the green and hugged both players around the neck. "I've been watching these guys practice all week and I've hardly seen anybody get it to eighteen," Wadkins said. "To be as strong as Lehman was to get it on the green out of the wet rough from a downhill lie to an uphill green was one hell of shot."

There was one match still out on the course, but the afternoon pairings were announced. Gallacher brought Ballesteros off the bench and set the Spaniard out first with David Gilford, the man in the envelope at Kiawah Island in 1991. They would play Faxon and Jacobsen. Since Torrance and Rocca had played so well, Gallacher kept them together, and they drew Maggert and Roberts. Faldo and Montgomerie also remained together, and would play Couples and Love. Last off, Gallacher kept Langer and Johansson together, but he later admitted that was a mistake. When Gallacher had to submit the pairings, Langer and Johansson were three up. He had never expected that match to go to the eighteenth hole, which it did. They were paired against Pavin and Mickelson, who had rushed out to the golf course when the USA Network had erroneously reported a set of afternoon pairings that did not include his name. Wadkins assured him that he was very much a part of his plans, but it wasn't until the last-minute conversation with Haas that he paired Mickelson with Pavin.

"I needed an honest appraisal from guys who were playing good or bad," Wadkins said. "Jay said he didn't play very well, so I figured I could get Freddie going by pairing him with Davis. I had Haas going with Mickelson in the afternoon, but I stuck Mickelson with Pavin and came back with my gamble team of Roberts, who hadn't played yet, and Maggert, who played well with Love."

With the business of the pairings completed, Wadkins went back out on the course to pull for Strange and Crenshaw, who had won the thirteenth and fourteenth holes to cut the European's lead to one up. This final match of the morning came down to the eighteenth hole. Langer is a slow player anyway, and the rain compounded the crawl of his pace. Johansson followed Langer's lead, and this was driving Strange and Crenshaw crazy. "It was excruciating watching that," Crenshaw said. "On a day like that, you were going to get tight, and as the day went on, I could feel it. It was cold and slow and wet, and the last thing you want to do is stand and wait. God, it took forever. I admire Bernhard for what he is, but God almighty is he slow."

Strange was enraged. "The guy [Langer] just doesn't have any etiquette. They told us before the matches that we'd be responsible for the pace of play and have kind of a gentleman's agreement, but they are going to have to start bringing the clock out here and putting it on some guys. It was ridiculous."

Strange didn't let it affect him. At the twelfth hole, after they had lost three straight, Curtis had to stand over a twelve-footer for par and a halve. He made it. At the fifteenth, after he missed the green left and Crenshaw wedged onto a wet green, he stood over an eight-footer for par and a halve. He made it. The seventeenth hole was playing especially long. Langer left Johansson 243 yards to the green. Strange left Crenshaw 234 yards. Both ended up in the left greenside bunker. Langer had the more difficult of the shots, from forty yards with twenty yards of carry. Crenshaw left Strange with a twenty-yard shot. This is where Langer got a little cute and tried to play a running shot. The ball plugged in the front face. It showed that Langer was human, and that maybe the luck would shift. "He made four or five of the damnedest pars," Crenshaw said. "There was a three- or four-hole stretch where he got them up and down from a hundred yards."

Strange wedged to fifteen feet below the hole, and his bogey ended up winning to halve the match going to the eighteenth. It was just like the first match, except it was the Americans making the comeback.

Crenshaw had the tee. He hit what appeared to be a good drive down the right center. The gallery crowded behind the tee box liked it. Strange did not. "I think it's right," he said to Crenshaw. Crenshaw just shook his head. He knew. Two feet left, and he would have been in Lehman's divot. Instead, he was dead, in a clump of rough.

Johansson was on the tee for Europe. At twenty-eight, the Swede was the youngest member of the European team. That is why Gallacher had put Langer with him. The problem was that Langer couldn't make the swing for him at eighteen. The ball was left right off the clubface, and was heading toward Oak Hill's West Course when it hit an elm tree and came to rest on a patch of trampled grass, 220 yards from the green.

Langer hit a 3-wood, but the combination of water on the clubface and the elevated green resulted in the shot coming up just short, in the bank of deep rough.

Strange had no play but to lay up, leaving Crenshaw a wedge from seventy-five yards to the green. Crenshaw had flashbacks to Muirfield Village, where he had a similar shot in the 1987 Ryder Cup that spun back off the green and into the fairway. Off the downhill lie, Crenshaw chunked it onto the green, but thirty feet below the hole. The advantage was back to the Europeans.

"We agreed the top of the hill was not the best place for Curtis to lay up," Crenshaw said. "Two more feet and I would have had a perfectly flat lie. The ground was wet enough that I didn't make very good contact with the pitch, and I just left him too long a putt. I'm not very proud of that shot. It was at least a pitch you could swing at. I just didn't contact the ball very good."

Johansson was left with a long chip shot from calf-deep rough, and Langer called for the squeegees to come out to clear a patch for his partner. Wadkins rushed out yelling, "Wait a second, boys." Use of the squeegees was not allowed until the player was on the green.

Gallacher concurred. "Bernhard should have known," he said.

Johansson was in a situation where he had to fly the shot all the way to the hole. Gripping the club more firmly than normal, choking down on the shaft, and playing the ball back in his stance, the Swede hit a low driving shot that stopped six feet below the hole.

Again, it was Strange's turn to save the team and silence some of his critics. He hit a good putt, but the ball didn't break and the U.S. team had to settle for a bogey.

Now it was on Langer's shoulders. The putt was similar in length to the one he'd missed at Kiawah Island. This was certainly an easier putt, because it wasn't to determine the Ryder Cup. But it was pivotal, and Langer was the man to stand over it, because in spite of his unorthodox putting grip and his battles with the yips, there is no finer pressure putter on the European Tour. No one was surprised to see Langer make it, not Strange or Crenshaw, and certainly not Gallacher, who was elated to walk off that eighteenth green in the rain that first morning with a 2–2 tie.

"A typically exciting first morning," Gallacher said. "The same score as last time, but better than in 1991 [when the U.S. team took a 3–1 lead], so that's good. I think Nick and Monty did so well to come down the eighteenth. Sam and Costantino played great, as I knew they would. Sam really is playing the best golf of his life, and Costantino is so solid. Howard and Mark were on the end of some very fine American play in very tough conditions. Bernhard and Per-Ulrik came through when it was needed to secure that other point. What a great putt to end the morning session with."

CHAPTER 11

Silent Assassin

David Gilford had that deer-in-the-headlights look on the first tee, the look of a man who was afraid, uncertain, about to be run over, frozen by his own anxieties. The last morning match of the thirty-first Ryder Cup was still being played out on the back nine at Oak Hill, but the Friday-afternoon four-balls were about to begin, and Gilford was scheduled to hit the first shot for Europe. Gary Schaal, the PGA's past president, stood ready to make the introductions. The wall of people down both sides of the tee told him how important this was, that this was nothing like Kiawah Island, and he didn't handle that scene at all.

"You're the best player out here."

Gilford recognized the deep, resonant voice. It was Seve Ballesteros, the great Spaniard, his teammate and partner, telling David Gilford, the shy, quiet Britisher from the Midlands, not to be afraid. To trust it. You're the best player out here. Now go prove that you are.

It was still raining hard enough to hear the big drops splatter on the umbrellas, but Gilford listened. He listened the way Luke Skywalker did to Yoda, the way an attentive son does to his encouraging father. Soon, he *was* the best player on the golf course at Oak Hill. It was Gilford who was carrying Ballesteros, the great Spanish champion. It was Gilford who was almost single-handedly holding off Peter Jacobsen and Brad Faxon. Nobody looked more unassuming than David Gilford, yet it was David Gilford who was playing the role of the lion, it was David Gilford who would save the afternoon, and perhaps the Ryder Cup, for the European team.

The Friday-afternoon four-balls have historically been controlled by the Europeans. Since 1983, they have won eighteen of twenty-four points, sweeping the Americans in 1987 at Muirfield Village and 1989 at the Belfry. But this was a star-spangled afternoon at Oak Hill. The crowd was up and into it, happy that the rain had ended, and the U.S. team was reigning over the Europeans. The United States would win three of the four matches. The only thing that prevented a clean sweep was David Gilford and his chauffeur, Mr. Ballesteros.

The Americans jumped off to a quick start in all the matches. Faxon and Jacobsen were one up after four holes against Ballesteros and Gilford; Jacobsen birdied the second and the fourth. Maggert and Roberts, the two rookies Wadkins had sent out as his "gamble team," were two up through four holes against Torrance and Rocca. Couples and Love were one up through three against Faldo and Montgomerie. Langer and Johansson had a mandatory thirty-minute break to change clothes and grab a quick lunch. Pavin was in no hurry after a tough morning match, but Mickelson was anxious. "The hardest part is waiting," the rookie said.

With Langer setting the pace, the last match was just getting started when Jacobsen, Faxon, Gilford, and Ballesteros reached the seventh tee. Jacobsen drove down the middle of the fairway, but Faxon was right, behind the weeping willows that blocked Pavin after Lehman's errant drive in the morning foursomes. Faxon took a drop and hit a low burning shot under the tree branches that stopped twenty yards short of the green. "Great shot," said Jacobsen, tending to his own business in the fairway.

Ballesteros and Gilford were having their problems as well. Ballesteros was right off the tee and had to chip out. Gilford had already hit his second shot into the greenside bunker. Faxon joined Jacobsen in the fairway to help him with club selection. They were in between 7- and 8-iron on the long par four. Jacobsen decided on the 8-iron, and came up short. "At no time did Brad ever say he was laying three," Jacobsen said. "And we walked all the way to the green." Jacobsen played a pitch shot that was inside Faxon's line. Ballesteros was out of the hole. Gilford wedged from the bunker, ten feet above the cup. "Do you want me to knock the putt in and show you the line?" Faxon said. "I'd love you to," said Jacobsen.

And with that, Faxon made the putt for bogey. The problem was that the crowd and Jacobsen still didn't realize that Faxon had had to take a drop under the weeping willows. "The crowd went crazy, and I felt a great uplift," Jacobsen said. "My caddy even said, 'Wow, what a great four!'" Faxon walked off the green, figuring that Jacobsen knew it was for bogey. The only person who knew was Ballesteros, who was in the trees himself and had seen Faxon take a drop. Of course, he was not going to tell Jacobsen.

Looking down the fairway behind him, Jacobsen noticed that the Couples-Love, Torrance-Rocca match had closed in on them. Normally, Jacobsen likes to putt out on every green, just to keep his touch and rhythm, but in this case, because it had been an Easter egg hunt for Ballesteros on every hole, and figuring his team already had the par, he picked up his marker and followed Faxon over to the side of the green.

"Great four, partner."

"Ah, that was a five."

"Oh."

Ballesteros tried to console Jacobsen.

"We don't like to win holes like that," he said.

This surprised Faxon.

"Seve will win a hole any way he can."

That lack of communication by the Americans changed the momentum of the match, at least in Jacobsen's mind. He just couldn't let it go. "It hit me like I had taken a Muhammad Ali punch to my solar plexus. It was a bonehead move."

Faxon put it behind him, and tried to get Jacobsen to do the same. In retrospect, the Rhode Islander thought the turning point came at the ninth and tenth holes, when Ballesteros miraculously saved par and made birdie on two of Oak Hill's toughest holes. This was typical Seve, and had come to be expected by the American team.

At the long uphill ninth, the Spaniard clipped a tree branch coming off the tee. Walking to his ball, Seve couldn't help but hear an American fan yell to him as if he were a Miami Dolphin playing in Buffalo's Rich Stadium. "Hey, Seve, you almost killed me with that one!" Under his breath, Ballesteros muttered. "That would be a shame, wouldn't it?" All the players heard it. They laughed. Just to reach the green, Seve needed to hit a 3-wood and then a 7-iron, but he made the putt for par and came off the green punching his fist in the air.

At the tenth, Ballesteros hit a long iron into the green, ten feet from the hole, and made that putt for birdie. Suddenly the Europeans were two up and Faxon was trying to hold them off by himself.

At the eighth, Jacobsen blocked his tee shot right, bladed a greenside bunker shot into the gallery, and took an X. With the U.S. team up in the other three matches, Wadkins thought he could snap Jacobsen out of it with a joke. "Will you need a mathematician the rest of the way?" he asked Peter. But Jacobsen, the team's practical joker, didn't find any humor in it and didn't make a birdie the rest of the round.

This is when Gilford started to take over. With zero victories on the European Tour in 1995, he was coming off a missed cut in the British Masters when the team arrived in Rochester on Monday. His form was suspect and his Ryder Cup record was 0-2-1. If this was the best player Europe had to offer, then Europe appeared to be in dire straits indeed.

In 1991, Gallacher had paired Gilford with Montgomerie in the Friday-morning foursomes. They lost to Wadkins and Hale Irwin 4 and 2. Gallacher came back with him Friday afternoon in a pairing with Faldo. That couldn't have been a worse pairing for Gilford, who needed encouragement. Faldo left him out on an island, hardly spoke to him, and they were trounced by Azinger and Mark O'Meara 7 and 6. On Saturday night, Gallacher put Gilford's name in the envelope, but the pairings were made and he had drawn Wayne Levi. The American had won four times in 1990 and was the PGA Tour's Player of the Year, but he was nothing in 1991 and even Gilford could have handled him. But Sunday morning, U.S. captain Dave Stockton claimed that Steve Pate, who had been injured in a minor prematch automobile crash and who had played on Saturday, was not ready to go. That meant Gilford had to sit out, and the news was crushing to him. He dropped out of the top ten in the Order of Merit in the 1992 and 1993 seasons, returning again in 1994 and 1995.

Even before arriving at Oak Hill, Gallacher knew he wanted to pair Ballesteros with Gilford. When Olazábal withdrew with his foot injury, it broke up the famed Spanish Armada and allowed Gallacher the liberty of using Ballesteros the way Jacklin had used him in 1983 at PGA National with the young Brit Paul Way. With Ballesteros as his guide, the apprentice played inspired golf, and it forced Ballesteros to elevate his game. They won one match and halved two others, then Way provided a 2-and-1 upset of Strange in the singles.

The Ballesteros of 1983 was in his freewheeling prime. His cut 3-wood over the lip and out of the bunker on the eighteenth hole at PGA National in his singles match against Fuzzy Zoeller is one of the best shots struck in Ryder Cup history. Ballesteros can no longer pull off those shots. His game is a sad representation of what it once was. But as a leader, Ballesteros still has his fastball. He took Gilford around Oak Hill by the hand and produced one very valuable point, a point that would mean so much on Sunday afternoon.

At the par-five thirteenth, the Americans were two down, but Faxon, one of the best putters in the game, had a very makable downhill left-to-right putt. Ballesteros was once again out of the hole, but Gilford had his third shot pin-high, just beyond the fringe, about two inches in the rough. The line was the shape of a crescent moon, and Ballesteros helped him size it up, pointing to an imaginary spot on the green where the ball should go for it to drop in the hole.

"It's a hundred-to-one putt," Faxon was thinking, but the ball came out of the muff with the right speed and the right line, taking its hard left-hand turn and dripping, dripping into the hole on its last rotation. Ballesteros was so happy he squeezed Gilford around the neck. Gilford's hat fell off, exposing one of golf's barest heads. It looked beautiful to Ballesteros. The Americans were as good as dead. Faxon missed his putt, and they were eliminated two holes later, when Gilford made birdie two at the tough fifteenth. It turned out to be Europe's only point that afternoon, but in the final result, it was a crucial one.

"He did all the work. I just caddied for him," Ballesteros said. "As I told him on the first tee, 'You're the best player out here,' and he proved it. All David needs is a good driver. I was there to lead him. I don't know what David gives to his caddy, but I can ask for a lot of money."

Gilford would gladly pay it. It was Ballesteros's record twentieth victory in four-balls competition, and perhaps his greatest in terms of what it did for the morale of the European team. "All I wanted to do was play, but to play and have Seve as a partner was very special," Gilford said. "He is great to play with. He wants to win so much, it's infectious. I didn't know who I would play with when I came here; I know Howard Clark and Mark James fairly well, and I've played with Philip Walton. But I was obviously delighted to get the chance to go out there with Seve. I didn't think about 1991—my one thought was to play well having got the chance.

"Seve? He's older than me, he's more experienced, he's a great player—so when you're playing with Seve or someone like that you've got to take his advice. We spoke a lot, but only about golf. I listened, but I played my own game. I'm obviously delighted we won."

Wadkins blew it off. Maggert and Roberts had already closed out Torrance and Rocca 6 and 5, with Roberts making four birdies, including a chip-in at the ninth where he was standing with his right foot in the bunker and his left knee tucked up under his chest. That put the Americans four up against a team that had easily dispatched Couples and Haas in the morning. At the eleventh, Roberts hit a 2-iron to eighteen inches for a five-up lead. "I had a great partner this afternoon," Maggert said. "Loren played unbelievable."

Having Maggert as his partner, hitting fairways and greens in regulation, allowed Roberts to become more aggressive. It also put him in Wadkins's lineup for the Saturday-morning foursomes. "A friend of mine from Preston Trail plays with Loren every year at Pebble Beach," Wadkins said. "He said you can count on Loren, and he was right."

What looked like the best match of the afternoon was also handled quite easily by the Americans. Couples and Love had Faldo and Montgomerie four down after six holes, but there was no comeback by Europe's strongest team this time. On the eleventh tee, Wadkins was riding in his cart and asked

Faldo if he wanted something to drink out of his cooler. Wearing a turtleneck sweater under his shirt and vest, Faldo politely declined, then reconsidered. "On second thought," he said, "do you have a bowl of soup?"

This was supposed to be Europe's kind of weather, the type Faldo and Montgomerie played in growing up in England and Scotland. But they just couldn't get warmed up, and didn't make a birdie until Montgomerie rolled in an eighteen-footer at the twelfth hole. At the next hole, Faldo had a chance to cut into the American lead, but missed from six feet and that was the match.

Coming to Oak Hill, Montgomerie and Faldo were 23-15-6 in Ryder Cup play, but their 0–2 start appeared to be devastating to the European side. Would Gallacher split them up Saturday morning? That wouldn't be known until later in the day, when the pairings were announced, and Gallacher was reluctant to share that information.

"In golf I'm ready for anything," Gallacher said. "But I would think—I know that Colin and Nick are disappointed. I would say it's one of those things that happen in golf. The Americans are tough players, and the Americans feel they're up against our best players. And you know, they don't feel they've got much to lose and they're going out there and producing good golf."

The last match of the day was a blowout, with the Americans winning the first four holes. "We're standing on the fifth tee," Pavin said, "and Bernhard turned to me and said, 'Are you in a hurry to get this match over?' He had this big old grin on his face, and I said, 'I am always in a hurry to get a match over.' That's a comment Bernhard and I could share. Not many guys out there have that kind of relationship. It's a lot of fun to play against Bernhard. It was not as adversarial as some of the matches could be. He knew I wanted to beat him, and I knew he wanted to beat me, but that's a given and that's not a problem. We've had a lot of competition over the years."

So have Johansson and Mickelson. They were college teammates at Arizona State from 1988 to 1990, and had talked about facing each other one day in the Ryder Cup. Mickelson responded to it better than Johansson did. After a bogey at the first hole, he played the next thirteen holes in three under. Johansson, meanwhile, was having what he described as a nightmare by playing the front side in 39.

Langer was not much help, either, with three straight X's on his scorecard. That was when Gallacher admitted to himself that he made a mistake in not sending Walton and Woosnam out in the last match of the first day. They were both sitting in the locker room, waiting to get the call, when Gallacher told them he was going with Langer and Johansson.

That was crushing news to Woosnam and Walton. They thought Gallacher was making a mistake, but they wanted to be team players, so they didn't make a fuss. At least Gallacher was being straight up with them. They had to respect that. "I was a bit disappointed in Bernard," Walton said. "Ian and I were rarin' to go."

In practice rounds on Thursday afternoon, Gallacher had made some late switches, replacing Walton with Torrance as Rocca's partner and putting Johansson with Langer. Walton and Woosnam had not been driving the ball well, and Johansson had. At Oak Hill, putting the ball in the fairway was a necessity. Walton and Woosnam both knew that, but in a better ball, they figured to make enough birdies to offset their wildness.

Gallacher took all this with him to the press tent for the customary Friday-afternoon captain's news conference. It had been a long day, and his nerves were frayed. The Bernard Gallacher who sat behind the microphones on the platform next to Julius Mason of the PGA was the defensive, combative Scotsman that John Hopkins had written about in the London *Times*.

It started when Gallacher was asked again about Woosnam, and whether if he was paired with Walton, that would have meant Langer sitting out. It was a legitimate question, one that needed to be asked, but Gallacher had enough of the second-guessing by the media, so he lost his cool and lashed out.

Q: "Bernard, not to hammer this point, but if Woosie would have played the afternoon, would he have played with Walton so Langer would have sat out?"

A: "Well, I mean I can't really answer that question, I mean."

Q: "Well, you said Walton and Woosnam . . ."

A: "What I've said is if I had known that Per-Ulrik Johansson and Bernhard Langer were going to have such tough finishing holes against Ben and Curtis and be soaked, I would have put Woosnam and Phil out. That's what I've said. When I put the pairings in, it wasn't chucking down [raining] as badly, and it looked like the match wasn't going to go much further. So I mean that's it. And I've told them that. There's no reason. I mean, it was just one of those things."

Q: "So you can't say that Langer was going to sit?"

A: "What's he asking? What do you want?"

Mason: "You're asking if Langer was going to sit?"

Q: "You had three pairings set and you were waiting for that last pairing to materialize. And you said Woosnam and Walton would have played had you had the option."

A: "No, I'm not saying that. I'm like—I'm sure Lanny's the same. You see how the matches and the combinations are going in the morning. If players play well in the foursomes in the morning and they look comfortable together, it's only fair that they get a chance to play together in the afternoon. And so obviously that was my thinking at five [minutes] to twelve. Ian Woosnam wanted to come in. He's happy to come in, but at the same time he was leaving it up to me. I was sitting with him watching this on television, and I said to him, 'I'm sorry, Ian. I think they'll both want to play. They're playing well. It looks like I'm going to have to put them back out together. You're going to have to sit out.' He said, 'You just do it. They look good out there.'"

Q: "Bernard, how important does Woosie become for you tomorrow? And indeed Walton, especially dried out and unplayed?"

A: "Sorry?"

Q: "How important do Woosie and Walton become tomorrow as they're unplayed and indeed dry? Woosie can be a very inspirational part of the . . ."

A: "They're all big matches for both sides. You'll see the pairings later. They're all big matches."

Q: "Well, given that we're four minutes away from the pairings . . ."

A: "Well, you go and speak to the press office. Don't ask that question to me."

Q: "I'm not saying—it's not your fault."

A: "Dammit! I take enough responsibilities around here without taking that from you, as well!"

Q: "I'm not suggesting it's your fault about it. I'm just saying . . ."

A: "Jeez, I've already put in the pairings. I don't decide on the timings. The pairings went in twenty minutes ago, with me."

Q: "Nobody suggested it was your fault."

A: "Well, it looks like you said it."

Q: "Well, that wasn't the point."

A: "I can't really tell you any more."

Q: "Well, I'll ask you the question four minutes from now, then."

A: "What do you want to know?"

Q: "How important Ian Woosnam will be tomorrow."

A: "I've said everyone's important, not just one member of the team!"

Later, Gallacher was asked if he preferred to be a captain or a player in Ryder Cup competition. His response broke the tension and resulted in some well-deserved laughter for the tortured European captain.

"Well, I enjoyed my time playing," he said, "and I enjoyed *some* of my time as captain."

Wadkins was much more relaxed and confident when he sauntered in after Gallacher. Mason announced that the pairings were on their way from the tournament office and would be disseminated during the interview. This calmed the European writers fighting deadline. With the five-hour time difference, it was almost midnight in London. With Woosnam having sat out Friday, it was crucial to their stories to see if the Welshman was set out on Saturday morning.

"Obviously I feel like my guys had a pretty good day," Wadkins said. "And like I said yesterday, I've got most of the guys, actually all of them, I think, playing pretty well. I've had a couple of guys that didn't play as well as they had been playing, but, hell, that's golf. And I had some guys play even a little better than they had been playing, so all in all I thought they had a real good performance.

"They had some very convincing wins today. I got some solid golf out of some real good players. So I was very pleased. The only problem I've got is I got a whole bunch of guys that want to go play tomorrow morning and play tomorrow afternoon, and sitting four guys out is real tough right now. Actually I saw a little disappointment on a couple of faces when I said they may not play in the morning. They all want to get in. They all want to play. They all feel like they're playing well. I wish I had a spot for everybody to play every match right now. They're going good.

"What made me feel great was I got to play all twelve guys today. I don't remember that happening in quite a while. That's kind of nice. And we had probably one of the best afternoons in best ball that we've had as an American team in quite a while. I think our guys' games fit this course very well. They're playing solid, hitting some straight shots, a lot of greens, not making a lot of mistakes. And in best ball, it seemed like we had a lot of guys in the hole all the time, and that's kind of the key, having two putts at it. That way you can turn one guy loose.

"Obviously I'm very pleased with today's results. I would have liked for it to have been better. At the same time, I would stress very firmly to my team that this is just Day One, that nobody awards trophies or prize money for being a first-round leader. This is just Day One. And the European team is filled with a lot of very experienced champions and veteran players, and they're not going to lay down and die, by any stretch of the imagination. And I want my guys to stay focused and be ready to go full-bore at eight o'clock tomorrow morning."

At dinner Friday night at the Woodcliff, Wadkins reiterated these words to his team as he went over the pairings—but it was hard for the captain not to feel good about himself and the way it worked out that day at Oak Hill. The 5–3 lead was the first a United States team had enjoyed on Friday since 1981. Everybody had played in at least one match, and eight of his twelve—everybody except Crenshaw, Strange, Faxon, and Jacobsen—had posted wins. His rookies, led by Maggert (2–0), were 5–1 for the day, with only Faxon losing. What's more, the U.S. team had shut out Europe's best in Faldo and Montgomerie.

In the team room, Faxon had volunteered to sit out and let Jacobsen take his place. Fax knew Jake needed to get on the course as soon as possible to purge the mistake of picking up his ball marker on the seventh green. Faxon also wanted to play with Fred Couples in the afternoon four-balls, and figured this was a way to make that pairing. Wadkins was consulting everybody, but he was stuck on Strange and Haas, even though they weren't playing particularly great, and sent them first off. They drew Faldo and Montgomerie. Love and Maggert got the call again, and they would play Torrance and Rocca in the second match. Jacobsen would be paired with Roberts; they drew Woosnam and Walton. Gallacher's other lineup change was to break up Langer and Johansson, sitting down the young Swede and pairing the German with Gilford.

They would face the two bulldogs, Pavin and Lehman, in the last match of the morning.

The hanging face Wadkins alluded to in the press conference belonged to Mickelson. The rookie felt that he had played well enough to warrant a spot in the Saturday-morning foursomes. Wadkins's thinking was that Mickelson had told him before the matches that he felt uncomfortable in alternate-shot competition, and that he was fifteen pounds under his playing weight of two hundred because of a pre–Ryder Cup virus. Mickelson had never sat out in Walker Cup or Presidents Cup competition, and both his ego and his competitive drive made him feel Wadkins was making a mistake.

It also bothered Mickelson when Wadkins singled him out in front of the team. When the captain read off the Saturday morning pairings and saw the disappointed look on Mickelson's face, he confronted the rookie, saying, "You got a problem with this?" Mickelson had been promised that he would play every match from Friday afternoon on, and he had a big problem with it, but he backed off. "I wanted to tell Lanny, 'Play me until I lose,'" Mickelson said. "But I never had the chance."

The rookie had every right to feel spurned. He had played his way onto the team and had played brilliantly with Pavin. He went back to the Woodcliff feeling Wadkins had made a tactical mistake in his pairings, wanting the first opportunity to prove Wadkins wrong. Wadkins brushed it off, admitting that he wasn't at all unlike Mickelson at age twenty-five. Besides, it was too late. The pairings were in. Mickelson would sit until Saturday afternoon.

The bad feelings seemed to be forgotten that night at dinner. Jacobsen took his share of good-natured abuse, and knowing he was going out in the morning, started cracking jokes and doing imitations. The night ended on an emotional note as Wadkins asked everyone around the table to stand up and explain what it meant to be on this Ryder Cup team.

"Ben Crenshaw started it off, and he's got the respect of

everyone in the golfing world," Faxon said. "He started saying, 'I want you to know how proud I am of all you guys.' Freddie was almost in tears. He said he was so happy that Lanny chose Curtis and me. 'I just can't believe I'm here.' It was all he could do to say it. I was the last one." When it came to Mickelson's turn, he started out by describing what it felt like to hit a 3-wood off the first tee, and then his iron shot into the green. When he got to the putt, everybody in the room started buzzing, figuring the rookie was going to take them on a shot-by-shot description of the round. They teased him until he started blushing and sat down.

Jay Haas took the opportunity to talk about Jacobsen. "We need your spirit. We need your humor," he said. "We need you to keep us up."

That meant a lot to Jacobsen, who thanked Haas when it was his turn to stand up and address the team.

"I kind of teared up when Jay said that, because I was still feeling kind of down," Jacobsen said. "Until you play on a team like this, you don't know how your emotions can really swing. Normally in a situation like that, I would have forgotten about it and gone on and birdied the next hole. But I let it get to me. It was like all the air went out of me. I should have said, 'Okay, these guys need a hole.'"

Faxon was last, which was appropriate because he was the last player to qualify for the team at Riviera. Although he had lost that day with Jacobsen, Fax was thinking about the team, and the two-point lead it held, and some of the players in that room. He thought about being in there with Lanny and Curtis and Ben, guys in their forties who will some day be members of the Hall of Fame, guys who could be taking part in their last Ryder Cup. He was so charged up when it came his turn to talk that he made a prediction.

"Starting the week, I had no idea who was going to win," Faxon said. "But after this dinner, my whole attitude has changed. I *know* we are going to win."

Over in their room at the Woodcliff, Gallacher confessed

that it was his fault they were behind, that he had miscalcu-
lated on the Langer-Johansson pairing and Woosnam, who led
Europe in four-balls wins, and Walton should have gone out
that afternoon. David Gilford was already thinking about the
first tee. He was in the last match of the morning, against
Pavin and Lehman, at 8:48 A.M. He would not have Seve by his
side, but he did have Langer. The German might not be as
emotional, but there was no player more respected on the European side than the two-time Masters champion.

CHAPTER 12

Comeback

Autumn arrived Saturday morning at Oak Hill with a cold blast from the north, but Peter Jacobsen was up all night anyway. He could feel the chill coming, because it was already gnawing on his bones. He sounded like Faxon the night before the final round of the PGA. "I didn't sleep well at all," he would say. "I was up, I can tell you, about seven times." Then he counted off four of them. "I was up at two thirty-five. I was up at four. I was up at four twenty-one. I was up at four fifty-two. I kept walking to the john and I was dry. I'd pull down my pants and I'd just sit there."

Jacobsen had won two tournaments early in the 1995 season, going back-to-back at Pebble Beach and San Diego to snap a winless streak that went back to the 1990 Bob Hope. He did this at age forty-one, thanks to dedication to a fitness program and a trip to the Dave Pelz Short Game School. All of a sudden golf's lounge act had a reborn credibility.

Jacobsen's skid was also personal. He lost his father to cancer and his brother to AIDS. The '90s were sad times for Peter Jacobsen, and Peter Jacobsen always was known to have a smile on his face. It was good to see him back and playing well again, having put the tragedies behind him.

Sally Jenkins wrote in *Sports Illustrated* that Peter Jacobsen could do his George Bush for you, with a smooth necktie of a voice, or he could do his Greg Norman, with lips pursed in a baby-man expression, or he could do his flight attendant, explaining with a pair of bugged-out drill-sergeant eyes how to use a seat cushion as a flotation device. But these days the person Jacobsen does best is himself.

Part of the change in Jacobsen occurred one day when he was doing his imitations instead of practicing. His caddy, Mike (Fluff) Cowan, walked in off the range and told Jacobsen to either get serious or he was quitting; he was through wasting his time. They have been together for seventeen years, one of the longest player-caddy relationships on the PGA Tour. As Cowan told Jenkins, "If I didn't think he was as good as he is, I would have gone to another bag a long time ago."

It was basically a case of Jacobsen finding himself, of growing up and realizing his best years were behind him, that it was time to produce or be left behind. The only reason he was playing backup for Hootie and the Blowfish or Huey Lewis was that he was a professional golfer. That's why he was a celebrity, Jack Lemmon's pro-am partner at the AT&T, not because he was a standup comic and mimic. "I was almost there, but not quite," he has said. "Maybe inside I didn't really think I could play at that level. Maybe I was the classic underachiever."

In 1992, Peter Jacobsen finished 127th on the money list and lost his playing card. In 1993, he went to work for ABC, but he soon realized it was a waste of talent and returned to tournament golf full-time. Two years later, he started out the season as one of the hottest golfers in the world.

After the West Coast, he came to Florida and bogeyed the last hole at Doral to finish a stroke behind Faldo. At Bay Hill, he shot thirteen under to finish third behind Loren Roberts. When he came to the Greater Greensboro Open, he was on top of the money list and feeling so confident that at the seventy-second hole of that tournament, he went at a sucker pin, made bogey, and wound up second behind Jim Gallagher, Jr.

That, however, seemed to break Jacobsen's bubble. He did not record another top-ten finish going into the Ryder Cup, five months with nothing better than a tie for thirteenth at the Memorial and three poor finishes in the majors. It frustrated him, and it legitimized the *Golf World* comment about his inability to concentrate in pressure situations. Picking up his ball on the seventh green Friday only compounded the angst, as Jacobsen sat there on his toilet bowl, elbows on his knees, head in his hands, wondering how the morning of September 23, 1995, would turn out.

Temperatures had dropped into the low forties when Jay Haas and Curtis Strange stood on the first tee at 8:00 A.M. to face Nick Faldo and Colin Montgomerie. Jacobsen was on the range, hitting balls and looking at the Jumbotron screen, loosening up for the third match of the morning. Lanny Wadkins was sipping coffee from a Styrofoam cup, trying to stay warm. "We haven't played much in cold weather," the captain thought to himself. Faldo was thinking just the opposite: "We're used to it." It didn't seem to bother Peter Jacobsen. He grew up in the Pacific Northwest, in Portland. When it was cold and raining on Sunday in Greensboro, he played in shirtsleeves. He said it was the old Nordic blood.

Staring into the bright morning sun on the first tee, wearing a bottle green V-neck sweater, Montgomerie drove to the middle of the fairway, right down the sprinkler line. A big roar went up as balata touched grass and hopped into perfect position for Faldo to advance it onto the green. Earlier in the week, Jim Flick and Jim McLean critiqued the big Scotsman's swing, marveling at its consistency in spite of some dramatic technical flaws. But nobody in the world is a better driver or iron player than Montgomerie, and he would prove it by winning his third straight Order of Merit, the money title on the European circuit. Once cast as a spoiled child, Monty has come to be respected if not loved, and when he split the fairway at the first, the Europeans in the gallery roared their approval. "Way to go, Mon-teeeee!" and "All right, Monty!" could be heard from behind the gallery ropes.

Gary Schaal waited for the crowd to die down before introducing Strange, who pinched the bill of his baseball cap and then shielded his eyes from the sun. It had been six years since Strange stood on this tee for the final round of the U.S. Open. That day was Strange's finest moment, but it also began a slump that had gone unabated. After his loss on Friday, the pressure on Strange—and Wadkins—had mounted. The second-guessing had already begun, and Strange was well aware of it. "I didn't ask for this situation. I didn't put in a vote for this," Strange told Rick Reilly in a report for NBC. "Lanny felt like I was the right guy for the job, so I'm here and hopefully I'm going to do the best job I can. There are some players who certainly feel like they should have been picked, and I feel for a couple of players who are playing awfully well, but that's the nature of the captain's picks."

With all of this on his shoulders, Strange pulled his drive into the left rough, deep into the stuff Wadkins had grown purposely to give his team a home-course advantage. That drive, the first of the day for the Americans, was an omen of things to come, not only for Strange and Haas, but for three of the four pairings Wadkins sent out on this Saturday morning in upstate New York.

This was a completely different American team from the

one that went 3–1 on Friday afternoon, that took the 5–3 lead, the biggest for a U.S. team on a Friday since 1979, the first year the Europeans joined the fray, the year the American team won 17–11 at the Greenbrier. This was to be the morning that turned the Ryder Cup around, the swing in the matches that would at least give Europe a chance on Sunday. It would be forgotten by most on Saturday night, but in the big picture, this Saturday morning would be pivotal. It was America's chance to put the Europeans away early, and they would come up empty. It went totally against what Wadkins had told them. If you're one up, go two up. If you're two up, go three up. If you're three up, go four up. And if you're four up, close them out. "These matches aren't over," Wadkins kept warning Friday night. How right he was.

From deep in the grass, Haas hacked it across the fairway into the right rough. Strange chopped it into the greenside bunker. The Europeans, with Faldo's crisp second shot, were on in regulation. The hole was conceded. Europe jumped to a quick one-up lead.

Behind Strange and Haas, Jeff Maggert drove into the trees down the left side of the fairway. Torrance had been puffing one of his hand-rolled cigarettes, the smoke billowing around him like the steam around a locomotive. The Scotsman, with three victories on the European Tour in 1995, drove into the short grass. Once again, the Europeans were one up heading off the green. They birdied the second to go two up and were three up after the third hole, when Love and Maggert made bogey at the par three.

The third match, with Roberts and Jacobsen playing Woosnam and Walton, followed the same form. The Europeans won the first and fourth holes and were two up. Wadkins didn't like what he was hearing on the walkie-talkie. In the final match, Langer rolled in a birdie putt to give Europe a lead in all four of the matches. Then it got really bad for the U.S. team. Rocca stood on the sixth tee contemplating a 6-iron. The pin was cut fourteen paces from the front of the green and four paces in from the left, back on a shelf that was tough to get to. Rocca changed his mind and pulled out a 5-iron, figuring he would grip down on the club and play a knockdown shot. Torrance liked what his partner was thinking. It was hard to judge the wind, but the Italian was being creative, trying to play a golf shot under the most adverse pressure situation.

Rocca's tee shot flew toward the pin as if directed by radar. The ball landed twelve feet short of the cup, took one bounce, and disappeared into the cup for only the third hole in one in Ryder Cup history. Back up at the tee, Rocca had both of his arms in the air, the 5-iron in his left hand, like a knight with his sword. He then jumped on Torrance, straddling the Scotsman in celebration. Gallacher held his breath hoping that the injury-prone Torrance wouldn't hurt himself.

Rocca's immediate feelings were so beautifully simple, yet so brutally true. "It was a great moment for me and for my partner, because with the hole in one, it's very difficult to lose the hole," Rocca would later say. It was the Italian's seventh hole in one, his second in international competition. He also made a one at St. Andrews during a Dunhill Cup, but it didn't mean as much as this one in the Ryder Cup at Oak Hill.

The gallery absolutely loved it. In *Sports Illustrated* that week, Rick Reilly had written a five-page feature chronicling the life of golf's Italian Stallion, and this had brought Rocca to 3.2 million Americans. Rocca had gone from making boxes in a factory to becoming one of the six best golfers on the European Tour, and had reached near-immortality by holing a sixty-five-foot putt from off the green on the seventy-second hole at St. Andrews, nearly stealing the 1995 British Open from John Daly. Rochester also has a large Italian population, who had embraced Rocca from the time he arrived in the city, calling him "paisan." Rocca said they made him feel right at home.

Standing on the tee, even Love had to feel a sense of happiness for Rocca. Their battle at the Belfry had been an epic one and turned out to be the deciding singles match in the '89 Ryder Cup. When Rocca three-putted the seventeenth, then lost the eighteenth, it could have been emotionally crushing. But Rocca was able to deal with it better than anybody, Gallacher included, had expected. When he sent Ballesteros to make sure Rocca was all right, it was Rocca who ultimately had to tell Ballesteros not to worry, that the sun would come up in the morning and there would be other Ryder Cups for the both of them. Rocca had just proved it.

"That was awfully tough to follow," Love said, describing his emotions when Rocca's 5-iron found the hole. "I wanted to crack a joke. But I had to get up and hit it, and I didn't want to pass on my turn. That was probably the best shot I hit all day and I didn't get to putt."

The roar was heard around the course and word was quickly passed about what Rocca had done. It pumped another tank of adrenaline into an already surging European team. Love and Maggert were toast; they would not win a hole and were taken out at the thirteenth hole, 6 and 5. Love could see a change in the Europeans' attitude. "I knew coming out here this morning that Sam was trying to fire Costantino up. He said, 'You can beat him! You can beat him!' But that's what it's all about. I don't know what they did before they got out there, but they were holing shots from the tee and making a lot of putts."

Torrance gave most of the credit to Rocca, but he had played equally well. On Friday afternoon, he had developed a case of the hooks and hadn't been much help as he and Rocca were blown out by Maggert and Roberts, 6 and 5. A call to his father in Scotland straightened the problem out. Bob Torrance always could correct swing faults via fiber optics. "I can tell you one thing, it's a much better feeling winning six and five than losing six and five," he said. "Costantino was just fantastic. You've heard of the Rock of Gibraltar? This is the Rock of Italy. He's so strong. He has so much talent. He's a great partner. We've certainly combined really well."

The first match was another European blowout, with Faldo and Montgomerie breaking their shutout with a 4-and-2 victory over Strange and Haas. The U.S. team won only one hole, when the Europeans bogeyed the fifth, and were five over when the match ended at the sixteenth hole.

Strange accepted blame for the loss. He missed a six-footer for birdie at the fourth that lost the hole. At the sixth, with the Europeans struggling to make bogey, Strange blew a thirty-five-footer eight feet past the hole and Haas lipped out the comebacker for the win. You don't get that many openings against Faldo and Montgomerie, and Strange let two slip away.

"Jay actually played pretty good, but I didn't play well at all," he said. Both he and Haas, former teammates at Wake Forest, were now 0–2. They came into the Ryder Cup with a 3–0 record in foursomes, having won two matches in the 1975 Walker Cup and one in the 1983 Ryder Cup. "During practice rounds we felt like we were a great team," Haas said. "I thought we'd do really good, but that alternate shot, I forgot, that's a hard format."

Faldo and Montgomerie didn't exactly tear Oak Hill up. They were one over and made only two birdies. Faldo was worried until Montgomerie hit a 9-iron to eight feet below the hole at the par-five thirteenth. That put the Europeans back to three up. "I asked Monty to leave me an uphill birdie putt at the thirteenth and he did and I made it, which really did the trick," Faldo said.

Europe added its third point of the morning and took the lead for the first time when Gilford and Langer muzzled the bulldogs, Pavin and Lehman, 4 and 3. There was no quick start by the Americans this time. At the par-three third, Gilford hit an iron to four feet and Langer made the putt to go one up. The Americans again ran into trouble at the seventh and eighth holes; bogeys at the two long par fours put the Europeans three up. The match looked to be swinging toward the United States at the twelfth, when Gilford's approach shot came up short of the green, in eight-inch rough. But Langer chipped in from the deepest greenside rough on the course and Pavin missed from thirty-five feet. Once again, the

Europeans had found the hole from what looked to be an impossible position. Even the usually languid Langer celebrated by leaving the ground.

Three holes later, it was over. Once again Gilford had produced a point for the European team and Gallacher had found the right chemistry. For the first time, Europe led in the matches.

"We are both fairly calm people, always on an even keel," Langer said of his partner. "We have feelings inside, which show on the big occasions like this and help us focus better and play better."

Gilford admitted that Langer had a calming effect on him. This was Langer's eighth straight Ryder Cup, and Gilford was his twelfth different partner. This is a tribute to the German's ability to play with anybody. This was his fifteenth victory in thirty-two matches. "If you hit a bad shot, you always feel he is going to be there," Gilford said. "He's such a great chipper and putter."

So it came down to the third match, the dogfight between Roberts and Jacobsen and Walton and Woosnam. Wadkins sensed the importance of it at the eleventh hole, when he pulled Jacobsen aside and said, "Look, we need this match. We need this match or we're going to get swept."

Woosnam had just birdied the eleventh from forty-five feet to go one up, and seeing Woosie make a putt like that was somewhat shocking, especially to Jan Jacobsen and Kim Roberts. Their mouths dropped wide open as Woosnam's putt took the six feet of break and dove in the cup for a two.

Jan's husband, Peter, was thinking to himself, "This must be me. I played with Seve and Gilford yesterday and they made everything, too. Now it's Woosie and Walton."

Weren't these greens set up to favor the Americans? That was Lanny's plan, but it was the same story at Muirfield Village in 1987, when the European team won for the first time on American soil. What the American captains keep forgetting is that the fastest greens in the world are at Augusta National, and nine of the last sixteen Masters champions have come from Europe.

Woosie owned a green jacket, so it should have been no surprise to see him holing putts on greens rolling at 12 on the Stimpmeter. These greens were actually what he needed to shake a two-year putting slump. When Woosnam came to Oak Hill, he was clearly the more suspect putter on a European team that had three players—Torrance, James, and Walton—using the long, broom-handled putters. At the German Open, in fact, Woosie played with both a broom-handled and a regular-shafted putter in his bag, alternating on long and short putts. That was a determining factor in Gallacher's taking Olazábal over him, and it kind of made him the butt of some good-natured jokes.

"Woosie could use a regular putter," Wadkins said one day at practice, "and it would look like a broom-handed putter."

All teasing aside, Wadkins wasn't surprised that Woosnam found his stroke once the competition began. What caught him off guard a little bit was Walton's coming up so big in his first Ryder Cup, at least early in this match when Woosnam was struggling off the tee. The day off to practice did him well, and with eight Walker Cup matches to draw on, Walton was quite comfortable in a match-play setting

That ended at the twelfth, when the Americans won the first of three straight holes. It was as if Woosie had used up all the magic with that one across-the-carpet rug-burner at the eleventh, and suddenly Jacobsen was back to being the Jacobsen that had dominated earlier in the year. It was his iron shots that set up Roberts for birdies at the twelfth and thirteenth holes. When Roberts made a ten-footer at the thirteenth, it was the first time an American team had led a match all morning.

In a golf cart down in the fourteenth fairway, Wadkins was with Crenshaw, Love, Maggert, and Faxon, going over the afternoon pairings. It was 11:23 A.M. The captain had roughly thirty-five minutes, and he was asking his players, "Okay, what do you want me to do?"—hoping that somebody would step forward the way Haas had Friday, just before the pairings went in. That led to Mickelson being paired with Pavin, one of the afternoon's strongest pairings.

Love made the point that he wanted to play again with Couples, his partner in the World Cup, the Presidents Cup, and Jacobsen's Fred Meyer Challenge, but he was willing to split up and had heard that Faxon wanted to play with Couples; they had won the Shark Shootout. The problem was that Faxon wouldn't just come out and say it, and time was slipping away. Finally, Love took charge. "Let's make it simple," he said. "Put Fred and Brad together and put me and Ben together. I'll be honored to play with Ben Crenshaw. It's something I'll remember the rest of my life." To himself, Love was also thinking it would have created a doubt in his mind if Faxon was paired with Crenshaw—knowing that neither had played together in practice rounds—and he couldn't be stepping on the course that afternoon worrying about what somebody in another match would be doing. Plus, Faxon had unselfishly stepped aside for Jacobsen. The least he would do was the same thing for Faxon, the guy he brought cigars to at Couples's outing in Seattle when he made the team.

Meanwhile, Jacobsen and Maggert had won the fourteenth hole with a bogey and were now two up with four to play. Bob Trumpy of NBC caught Wadkins for a quick interview.

"The guys had a flat morning and the Europeans played wonderfully. They played great golf," the captain said. "I've seen great shot after great shot from the Europeans and a lot of great putts. They're world-class players and great champions and I would expect nothing less. Our guys have not responded too great this morning, but they've got a lot left in them and I expect a great afternoon for us."

At the par-three fifteenth, the Europeans surged back again, with Woosnam making a fifteen-foot putt that cut the lead to one up with three to play. This one was going down to the wire, and thanks to Woosie, it did.

At the sixteenth, the Welshman pulled off a Seve-type miracle shot, wedging from a bad lie right of the green to gain a halve. At the long seventeenth his putter once again came through with an eight-footer to save par. It was his tee shot at the last, and he hit the fairway to put the pressure on Roberts.

Roberts had not missed a fairway in two days, but his ball drifted just enough to catch the worst patch of rough on the golf course. Jacobsen had no chance to reach the green; he could barely see the ball.

"If you can get me to seventy-five yards, I'd appreciate it," Roberts said. Jacobsen took out a 9-iron and hacked the ball a little farther than what Roberts would have liked, but it was back in play and looked even better when Walton's iron shot from two hundred yards came up short, in the bank fronting the green. The shot plays longer than it looks, and Walton caught it a little bit heavy.

Now it was on Roberts, who was on a flat lie, forty-three yards from the front of the green, fifty-six yards from the cup. It was a hard shot to get a feel for, the type where he couldn't take a full swing. Under that kind of pressure, it would require all the nerves Roberts had to pull it off. "The softness of the green really helped," Roberts said. "It allowed me to play more aggressive."

Although 150 yards shorter than Lehman's 5-iron through the rain on Friday morning, Roberts's wedge was just as crucial to the American side. It came down on that soft green and checked up three feet short of the hole. In the NBC booth, Johnny Miller called it a "huge, absolutely huge golf shot."

Woosnam had an uphill chip for birdie that he virtually had to make for a chance at the halve. During practice rounds, he had given Walton a lesson on how to chip the ball from the deep rough, and when he applied it to his own hands and own wedge, the shot came off frighteningly close to finding the cup. Woosnam could not believe it when it didn't go in. He grabbed his face in disbelief. "Just a little bit softer," he thought, "and it would have gone in."

Jacobsen had it right where he wanted it, the match riding on the face of his putter. In the NBC booth, Paul Azinger said, "Peter Jacobsen is facing one of the biggest putts in his career right here." Beside the green, the players and wives from both teams were crouched next to the photographers in front of the bleachers.

Jake thought back to the 1985 Ryder Cup at the Belfry. So did Wadkins. Craig Stadler had a similar putt at the end of play on Saturday morning. It was Stadler and Strange vs. Langer and Sandy Lyle, and the Americans were two up with two to play. At the par-five seventeenth, Lyle hit two monstrous shots and made a twenty-two-footer for eagle to win the hole. Still one up with one to play, it came down to a putting contest on the eighteenth green. Stadler had a fifty-five-footer for birdie that he left eighteen inches away from the hole. Under normal circumstances, that putt would have been conceded for the halve, but these weren't normal circumstances. Langer and Lyle missed birdie putts, then stood silent while Stadler replaced his marker with a ball, and hovered over a putt that would have given the United States a 6½–5½ lead going into the afternoon four-balls. Again, under normal conditions, Stadler would have tapped the ball in. But he stabbed it left of the hole, stood over it in disbelief, then walked away grabbing the back of his neck, the ball unmercifully resting at the back edge of the cup. Europe went on to win the afternoon four-balls 3–1 and then the singles 7½–4½ for its first Ryder Cup victory in twenty-eight years. Jacobsen wished he could do a Vulcan mind meld to every member of the media who criticized him for being unable to handle the pressure, just so they would know what this felt like, to be fighting off all those negative thoughts.

"I remember—I think it was Bobby Jones said one time, a long time ago, he said, 'It's an amazing thing what goes through your mind when you stand over a two-footer to win,'" Jacobsen said. "You're thinking that you're going to miss the hole, you're going to drop the putter, you're going to whiff the ball, anything. All the negative thoughts that go through your mind. The thing you do is you try to shove them all aside and grab onto that positive thought and knock it in."

And that is exactly what Jacobsen did. With what felt like the entire United States on his back, he rolled that putt center cut for the biggest par save of his life. From off the green, Wadkins and Strange came pumping their fists. Lehman had hustled over from the fifteenth green. "Peter, Peter, Peter, Peter," he said. "Give me a hug." Roberts had now been involved in two Ryder Cup matches, and he was 2–0, having won a 6-and-5 blowout with Maggert and now having survived this one with Jacobsen. This, he learned, was the essence of the Ryder Cup, a match where one team was two up, then two down, then fighting and scratching for its life while he was just trying to hold on.

"They just wouldn't let their teeth out of it," Roberts said. "I tell you, it was a tough fight."

Woosnam and Walton could hardly feel too disappointed. They were two down with four holes to go and took the match to the eighteenth green. If there were moral victories, this was one. "I don't like losing, but there's no disgrace in losing a match like that," Walton said. "It was terrific, a great match and a lot of fun."

Woosnam was thinking back to that chip he'd hit from off the eighteenth green. "If I'd hit it just a tad softer it would have gone in," he said. "What a finish that would have been. But it was a great match with a lot of magic moments."

Reporters from all over the world surrounded Jacobsen on the eighteenth green. He went over again what happened at the seventh Friday afternoon, and how it was Faxon who had lobbied with Wadkins to let him take his place in the Saturday-morning matches. He talked about dinner the night before, about how the team had teased him into finally laughing about it, about Faxon saying stuff like "Peter, I have one fork," and "Peter, I have one glass."

Jacobsen could smile about it now, because he had come

through, because he had become a big part of Ryder Cup history. Yeah, he had messed up. But he'd had the guts to come back and make a putt when the match was on the line. When Wadkins told him they needed the match, Jacobsen and Roberts had gone out and gotten it.

"We're six–six after three rounds, playing a tough team," Jacobsen said. "It's kind of like we thought it would be, all tied."

Up in the TV tower behind the thirteenth green, Johnny Miller and Paul Azinger were wrapping up the morning telecast. The afternoon matches were getting ready to go off. Both captains had juggled their lineups.

"That's a huge point for the American team right there," Miller said.

"That was big for Peter after what happened yesterday," said Azinger.

The afternoon pairings were Faxon and Couples against Torrance and Montgomerie; Woosnam and Rocca against Love and Crenshaw; Haas and Mickelson against Ballesteros and Gilford; and Pavin and Roberts against Faldo and Langer. It was four completely different teams for the Americans and three new teams for the Europeans. Azinger commented afterward that he thought it was good strategy on Gallacher's part, not making the same mistake as he had made Friday afternoon, because teams that play well in alternate shot don't always mesh in best ball.

But what happened on this Friday morning had clearly caught Azinger off guard, and he was the first to admit it. He thought that this was the morning the American team would put the matches away, that the depth of the European team would lead to at least a three-point lead going into the afternoon. Instead, it was all square, and that made him realize that nothing had really changed, that these matches were going to come down to Sunday no matter how strong the U.S. team looked on paper, no matter what kind of home-course advantage it supposedly held.

"I'm a little bit in shock," Zinger said. "I thought the Americans would go out there and make a statement this morning, but it seems like in the tradition of the Ryder Cup, at least the years I've been involved, a team gets a lead, the other team comes out inspired. That's what happened today. The Europeans played spectacular golf. It's not that the Americans played bad. It's just that the Europeans played better. The pressure was squarely on the European team today, and they've done well. In my opinion there was big-time danger of a blowout. Fortunately for TV, it hasn't happened. Unfortunately for Lanny, it has."

Wadkins was just happy that Jacobsen had come through.

"That was just a mistake," he said. "Good God. I mean, I've backhanded putts before and missed them. Mistakes happen, accidents happen. I told Peter the best thing is to get fired up from your mistake. I even used one of my deals that I did when I was talking to him about it. I said, 'Listen. The time I missed a backhander at the ninth hole at Augusta when I was near the lead. I went back and shot thirty-two the next nine and got myself back in the tournament.' You know, that backhand really kind of fired me up, because I was having a very lackluster day to begin with. And all of a sudden, it woke me up, and I had a big back nine and got back in where I had a chance to win the golf tournament the rest of the weekend.

"So I said, 'Just use it to your advantage. I mean, if you make a mistake, you know, let it piss you off, and use it to your advantage and go out there and do good. Don't worry about it.' There's no question it bothered Peter, but Peter came back real big—that was a huge win for us. That could have been disastrous if they had gotten ahead at that point in time. I think that would have been a real downer for the team, no question."

CHAPTER 13

The Go-to Guy

During lunch break on Saturday, Lanny Wadkins needed somebody, one of his veterans, to take over this Ryder Cup and put his signature on it. The way Joe Montana did in Super Bowls. The way Michael Jordan did in NBA Playoffs. What he needed was for Corey Pavin, the littlest American, to come up big.

Pavin's Ryder Cup career began at Kiawah Island, where he was best remembered for a wedge shot played from a pot bunker on the seventeenth hole at the Ocean Course. It was in the Sunday singles, and Pavin was so pumped up he beat the ball to the flagstick, chasing it across the green as it rolled nearly inside leather from what looked like an impossible lie in one of Pete Dye's obstacles. That put away big Steve Richardson of Great Britain and gave Pavin his only point of the week. He had lost two four-balls matches, with Mark Calcavecchia and Steve Pate as his partners.

The Europeans, quite frankly, didn't know how to take to Pavin. He wore the Desert Storm camouflage baseball hat, and that charge across the seventeenth green, they felt, had crossed the line of sportsmanship.

But in the last two years, Pavin had emerged as America's best player, and even the Europeans had grown to respect and admire him for his tenacity, shotmaking, and ability to close. Nobody played harder than Pavin did at the Belfry in 1993, and he was 3–1 before Peter Baker made every putt he looked at in the Sunday singles and knocked him off. He had won two matches as Wadkins's partner, then when Faldo and Montgomerie beat them in the Saturday-morning foursomes, Tom Watson sent Pavin out with Jim Gallagher, Jr. With Pavin holing a 9-iron for eagle, they produced a convincing win on the afternoon of America's big rally. Putting points up early is important in the emotional swing of a Ryder Cup, and Pavin showed an ability at the Belfry to do just that.

Match play is Pavin's arena. He was 5–2 on the PGA Tour in playoffs and won the Toyota World Match Play in 1993, defeating Faldo in the thirty-six-hole finals at Wentworth. He backs down from nobody.

"I think it's all what you have in your heart," Pavin has said. Heart is winning tournaments with a swing that looks like a woodchopper's and length that wouldn't pass the longest hitters on the LPGA Tour. Pavin has survived and excelled—winning thirteen tournaments, including a U.S. Open—by having an innate ability of being able to manufacture shots and get the ball in the hole.

He is a throwback to the Hogan-Nelson-Snead era, when players could work the ball left to right and right to left. He excels by being able to outcompete anybody, and there is no statistical category for that. Coming down the back nine at Shinnecock it was Greg Norman, the number-one-ranked player in the world. Pavin didn't care who it was. Norman just happened to be standing in the way of destiny.

"I just love those situations," Pavin has said. "I thrive on the pressure."

Johnny Miller has long said that the PGA Tour needs more wolves stalking its fairways like Corey Pavin, that there are too many American-born lambs playing golf for this country, and it showed through in 1985, 1987, and 1989, when the United States team went 0-2-1 in Ryder Cup play. At twenty-four, Pavin stepped into a playoff at the 1983 German Open in Cologne and took down Seve Ballesteros. He hasn't backed off a day in his life since.

"He's like a little dog that gets ahold of your pants leg and won't let go," says Mark O'Meara.

Pavin grew up small and stayed that way, developing a chip on his shoulder the first time he stepped on a golf course near his home in Oxnard, California, over thirty years ago. He's had plenty of practice getting the most out of his game. Pound for pound, and Pavin has only 147 of them, there's no better player in the world.

Faldo looked across from him at Wentworth and felt as if he were playing a pocket-sized version of himself. The intensity and the sneer on his face go back to Pavin's junior golf days in Southern California, where at seventeen he was the youngest to win the Los Angeles City Men's Tournament and where at UCLA he played for Eddie Merrins and won eleven tournaments, including the 1982 PAC-10 title.

His swing hasn't changed much over the years. While it has its idiosyncrasies, it repeats and is textbook through the hitting area, where it matters most. That warmup move he does, where it looks like he's starting a lawn mower with his right hand, is designed to keep him from coming over the top.

"Everybody has their own individual body movements," Pavin says. "Some guys pick the club up and swing it picture-perfect from the start. But there is no picture-perfect swing in golf. As long as you get back to the proper position at impact to hit the ball, it doesn't matter."

In match play, Pavin just wears down opponents. As O'Meara said, he gets ahold of your pants leg and won't let go. That's why it was surprising for Wadkins to see Pavin and Lehman go down so easily against Langer and Gilford on Saturday morning. He already had two wins, but he needed more out of Corey. He needed some sort of slam dunk that would excite the crowd and his team, that would send them into Sunday on a high.

"Corey Pavin is one of the toughest competitors out here," Wadkins said. "He's probably the littlest guy with the biggest heart I've seen. I mean, he is as tough as just about anybody in the game." Wadkins needed Pavin because he just wasn't getting it out of Fred Couples, who was 1–1 and had just sat out the foursomes because of his sore back. Jay Haas was 0–2 and coming off a loss. Curtis Strange and Ben Crenshaw, his two oldest players, guys he had counted on, were 0–3 combined. Behind the scenes, they were still important to the team's chemistry, but on the course neither one had been productive. He needed points, and he needed points immediately, otherwise this Ryder Cup was going to turn around, and turn around in a hurry. That grandiose prediction Wadkins made to friends Wednesday night at the Gala Dinner had gone by the boards. The Americans had been in position to put the matches out of reach on Saturday morning. It was all set up as Wadkins had envisioned. A two-point lead. Playing at home. Riding momentum. But Gallacher's side came out smoking and his team had been flat. Of the first forty-four holes played that morning, his team had produced only one birdie. The momentum had shifted. Wadkins no longer controlled the dice.

"Listen," he told the guys. "We had a bad morning and we're still tied. So that's the good part. We had a bad morning and we're still just tied. We've got a real strong group of guys this afternoon. Let's go out and take advantage of that and put some wins on the board."

Gallacher could see the change in his team. For the first time, they were starting to believe that they could win this Ryder Cup without Olazábal, with Ballesteros way off his form, and on American soil, on a golf course that supposedly wasn't suited for their games.

"We did what was required," he said. "It could have been better, but we got all square. I've been optimistic from the start—and I remain that way."

The European captain was getting big efforts out of Sam Torrance and David Gilford, but it was Rocca who had emerged as the star of the European team. With his hole in one and his two wins, the Italian had lit a fire for Gallacher. The Europeans were not surprised by this. They had watched his game improve and his confidence grow in the days that had passed since the 1993 Ryder Cup at the Belfry. Gallacher had waited until Saturday afternoon to give Rocca his first match two years ago, and with Mark James as his partner, he had lost to Pavin and Jim Gallagher, Jr., 5 and 4. "What carries Rocca through is his technique," Torrance had said. "Rocca's got a great swing. He's a great technician, and on a big course like this and a tough course like Oak Hill, the best strikers of the ball and the best methods come through. And Rocca is just churning it out."

If there was a surprise star like Rocca for the United States, it was Loren Roberts, the Ryder Cup rookie, who had posted wins in both of his matches. Wadkins's thinking was to put Roberts off last and pair him with Corey Pavin, who had gone 2–1. They were last off against Nick Faldo and Bernhard Langer, who between them had won seven major championships. It had the potential to be the match of the day. This was the first time Faldo and Langer had been paired in Ryder Cup competition. Back in the '80s, Tony Jacklin would put Faldo with Ian Woosnam, dubbing them David and Goliath. They produced a 5-2-2 record until the magic rubbed off at

Kiawah Island and they were split up by Gallacher. Although Langer did play with a number of partners, he was strongest in 1987 at Muirfield Village, when he and Sandy Lyle were 3–0. Two of those victories were against Wadkins and Larry Nelson. Their Saturday match, which ended in the gloaming with Nelson conceding Langer the winning putt on the eighteenth green, is one of the classics in Ryder Cup history.

Roberts was considered a late bloomer who had shown his mettle in the 1994 U.S. Open at Oakmont, where he was one putt away from the title. In the Monday playoff, he went to the twentieth hole before losing to Ernie Els. At Preston Trail, Wadkins had met a mutual friend in Bob Gibson. Gibson played the AT&T Pro-Am every year with Roberts and knew Roberts a lot better than Wadkins did. He told Wadkins, "When you need somebody to count on, Loren's your man."

The day almost couldn't have gone better for Wadkins—or worse for Gallacher. Couples and Faxon, who had won the Shark Shootout, ham-and-egged the death out of Montgomerie and Rocca. Faxon answered Torrance's birdie at the third, then Montgomerie's at the tenth. At the eleventh, he ran in a fifteen-footer for a two to put the U.S. team one up.

Couples took over at the twelfth with a wedge to fifteen inches to go two up. At the thirteenth, Torrance went on the counterattack, nearly holing out his third shot from the fairway for a gimme birdie. Faxon had a birdie putt for the Americans, and Couples was off the green, chipping his fourth shot uphill. He couldn't have picked a better place, or a better time, to hole out.

The ball traveled out of the first cut of rough and traveled roughly ten yards in the air before it started tracking toward the hole. The crowd noise started to swell as it approached the cup, and when Couples's Maxfli dove in, it set off an explosion that shook the NBC booth behind the green.

For the U.S. team, it was the clarion's call.

Even the normally placid Couples reacted to it, high-fiving Faxon, and the caddies, John (Cubby) Burke and Joe LaCava.

You could see Couples mouthing "Yeah!" and "Whooooooo!" but you couldn't hear him because he couldn't hear himself.

"That's the loudest roar I've ever heard in championship golf right there," Miller said when it quieted down.

And Miller was standing on the seventeenth tee at Augusta in 1978 when Jack Nicklaus rolled in a snake across the sixteenth green to take the Masters. There is no place louder in golf than down in that amphitheater at Augusta National, where the patrons are packed in cheek to jowl. But the thirteenth at Oak Hill, the club's Hill of Fame, can pack in more spectators, and it seemed like most of the 25,000 ticket holders who had jammed through the gates were there to see Couples chip in.

Couples just figured, "It was a thrill I'll never forget, and I figured I might as well just let the people realize it. It was pretty exciting."

Pretty exciting? That's just Couples.

"It was deafening," Faxon said.

The Europeans were through three holes later, losing on the sixteenth green to Faxon's fourth birdie, 4 and 3. For Montgomerie, it was especially demoralizing. He had come into the matches as arguably the best player in the world and was 1–3. He had also said, "The strength of our team is theirs."

While Couples hit the most exciting shot, it was Faxon who played the best golf and made the most crucial putts. Like Jacobsen, he had made amends for the seventh hole Friday afternoon. This was the Brad Faxon who had shot 63 on Sunday at Riviera to make the team. "Fax put on a putting show," Couples said. "He was phenomenal. I'm sure Sam and Colin are shaking their heads."

The second match was the only one that Europe controlled. Once again it was Rocca who was going to get a point. Paired with Woosnam, he birdied the second, eleventh, and twelfth holes, while the Welshman, who had played so well in a losing effort with Walton that morning, chipped in with a two at the par-three third. That improved Woosnam's four-balls record to 9-3-1 all-time, but it wasn't so much a case of the Europeans playing well as it was of the American team of Crenshaw and Love just not jelling.

They had just one birdie between them, Love's three at the 429-yard tenth. Even on a hard golf course such as Oak Hill, players of that caliber should make more than just one birdie, especially when one of the players is Crenshaw, recognized as one of the best putters in the world. "You go out there in best ball and make one birdie. That's a joke," Love said. "I go out there and play that course in a U.S. Open, and I make two or three birdies a round, at the least. We just never got it going. It just didn't happen."

Love had played the most solid golf for the U.S. team on Friday, and was 2–0. But he was shut out on Saturday, losing both matches without ever seeing the seventeenth tee. Crenshaw was even more bummed, going 0–2 in these matches to run his four-balls record in Ryder Cup competition to 0-4-1. "Making all those pars was just like a dial tone," Crenshaw said. "I kept it in play, had opportunities, and nothing, just nothing."

Gilford felt the same way in his match, except he was going at it alone. Ballesteros spent most of the afternoon in the woods, searching for both his ball and his game. It was sad to see such a great player struggle so badly, but it was quite predictable. He had started the year working with Mac O'Grady, the eccentric guru, and obviously had too many technical swing thoughts in his head. Ballesteros had since split with O'Grady, but the damage was done. His shots had a weak sound to them, causing David Leadbetter to say, "Seve's game is simply awful. I'm amazed he's even playing."

Paul Azinger had the theory that Ballesteros was victimized by analysis paralysis. The obvious indication: There was no pattern to his misses. They were either right, or left. "Seve is an instinctive player who has lost his instinct," said Azinger, who was Ballesteros's adversary in the 1989 and 1991 Ryder Cups. "He should pretend he's hitting every shot from out of the trees, because that's the only time he forgets technique and just concentrates on target and trajectory and shaping the shot. He should just try to curve every shot instead of trying to hit it straight and seeing it spray off in one direction or another. If he can do that in the singles and get it around the course, he is still very hard to beat."

With José María Olazábal as his partner, Ballesteros had forged an 11-2-2 record in foursomes and four-balls play from 1987 to 1993. With Gilford, he would go 1–1, which was acceptable considering the way he was playing.

Haas and Mickelson had the good fortune of drawing Seve when he was down. They came out in high gear and overran Gilford before he could get started. It wasn't like the Jacobsen-Faxon match, where Gilford could get some confidence going and feed off Ballesteros's leadership. John Schroeder, the former tour pro working as an on-course reporter for NBC, compared Gilford's situation to being on the wrong end of a two-on-one fast break.

"I had talked about playing with Phil for months," Haas said. "But I just kind of told him, 'Hey Phil, I don't want to go oh and three, take care of me.' He was great. He kind of gave me the pep talk I was supposed to give him. We went out and had a great time."

Before he teed off, Haas saw Byron Nelson standing beside the first tee. He asked reverently, "Can I have some of that magic, Mr. Nelson?" and Byron just smiled and passed some on.

Haas was a different player from the one who had lost matches paired with Couples and Strange. He birdied the second and fourth holes and didn't make a bogey all day. Mickelson kept pouring in pars until the eleventh. At the 192-yard par three, Haas had come up short of the green while Mickelson had sailed his iron shot thirty feet from the hole. It looked like Mickelson's hole, but Haas found himself in a position to help his partner by innocently blading his chip shot past the pin and in a direct line with Mickelson's putt. "It looked like I did it on purpose," Haas said.

He was about ready to pick up his marker when Mickelson made him realize how he could help.

"Putt this down there. Let me have a look at it."

Haas did, showing Mickelson the line and the speed. After that, it was like stealing.

"It was a fooler-type putt," Haas said. "It was quick and there was not as much break as there looked and Phil just poured it in like Vermont maple syrup."

Mickelson looked at Haas and winked.

"You did great, partner," he said.

When the match ended on the sixteenth green, Gilford and Ballesteros had not made a single birdie. Haas and Mickelson were a modest three under, but it was good enough for a 3-and-2 win. That put the United States back up in the competition 8–7, with the final match lagging over two holes behind because of the deliberate play of Langer and Faldo. When Mickelson and Haas closed out their match, Pavin and Roberts were hitting their second shots into the fourteenth green. "I just can't believe they haven't penalized Langer," Wadkins said. "He's been warned in every match."

Wadkins could only blame himself for that. He had signed a captains' agreement before the matches whereby pace of play would be loosely enforced by the players. It didn't seem to bother Pavin, but the tenseness of the final match, and the way it was dragging on, started to hit Roberts at the fourteenth hole. He pulled Jacobsen over for some help.

"I'm dying," he said.

Jacobsen understood.

"Breathe in all this fresh air, it's what your brain needs," he told Roberts. "Just think, with four holes to go, it's like having eight more practice balls to hit on the range."

The United States had gone one up with Pavin's ten-footer for birdie. It was his fourth birdie for the afternoon, but the

Europeans came back to even the match at the par-five thirteenth when Faldo broke his streak of twenty-eight straight holes without a birdie by running in an uphill eight-footer.

The match stayed locked there for four more holes. Pavin had a chance to put the U.S. one up at the par-three fifteenth, but missed a five-footer for birdie. Faldo got the halve by making a three-footer. Just as he putted, Faldo heard a lout behind the green yell, "Miss it!" Faldo stared the jerk down, gave him the thumbs-up with a twisting right hand. It was as if he was saying, "Up yours, buddy."

"Hey Nick, not everybody's like that!" yelled another American fan. "Good putt."

The players and an entourage of writers and cameramen walked through the oak trees up the hill to the sixteenth green. Europe had a chance to go one up at the sixteenth, but Pavin made par from out of the woods, and Faldo, who hit a perfect drive, missed a six-footer for birdie.

That surprised just about everyone watching in the fairway, and it seemed as if everybody from both teams, players, wives, caddies, and officials—including Great Britain's Prince Andrew—was there.

"You had to figure he was going to make it," said Couples's caddy, Joe LaCava.

"Would you ever expect that after those two drives?" said *Golf World*'s Chris Millard.

At the long seventeenth, Seve was stalking the right rough, his visor pulled down low. Gallacher was out in the fairway, watching Faldo and Langer go over their club selections. The standard-bearers were carrying signs that said ALL SQUARE. In the gallery, a European fan waved a Union Jack and yelled, "C'mon, Nick." John Hopkins of the London *Times* compared the match to the Azinger-Couples/Faldo-Montgomerie duel at the Belfry in 1993 that was completed Saturday morning. Jaime Diaz of *Sports Illustrated* called it one of the best Ryder Cup matches in ten years. Certainly it was huge from a momentum standpoint. If the United States won, the Americans would go into the singles with a 9–7 lead. If Europe won, it would 8-all. Pars were scraped in at the seventeenth green, and the foursome headed through an opening in the ropes to the eighteenth tee.

"C'mon, Corey," Wadkins said to Pavin. "Hurry up and make a putt so we can go to dinner."

Over on the driving range, Faxon was hitting balls with Jacobsen and Haas. Dottie Mochrie was there, along with Mick Potter, his golf coach at Furman. Watching the match between shots, he was thinking to himself, "Corey is our go-to guy. He's like Michael Jordan. He wants the ball."

Back on the tee, the caddies were having a hard time getting the crowd to settle down. Up in the bleachers behind the eighteenth green and down behind the practice range, American fans were chanting, "USA! USA!"

Fanny Sunesson, Faldo's caddy, was trying to get control of the situation. Faldo was ready to hit. "Stand still, please!" she yelled with a thick Scandinavian accent. "Stand still!"

Langer's longtime caddy Peter Coleman got a kick out of Sunesson's determination. "Get 'em, Fanny," he said.

It was 6:35 P.M. There was barely enough light to get the hole in before dark. Faldo took two practice swings, and it was so quiet you could hear the whoosh of the clubhead going through the cold late-September air. His line was down the left rough, with a cut back into the fairway. Faldo didn't like the shot. He pointed to the neck of his driver. It wasn't the cleanest hit, but under the circumstances, it was in play.

Langer was up next, but he peeled one off near the corporate tents in the right rough. "That's trouble," said someone in the gallery.

Now it was Roberts's turn. Sitting on the bench by the tee were Curtis and Sarah Strange. He remembered what Jacobsen had said, and took a deep breath through his nose, blowing it out of his mouth. This was the next-to-last shot on the practice range. Two more swings and he would be done for the day. This time, unlike in his alternate-shot match with Jacobsen that morning, Roberts hit the fairway. The crowd er-rupted. "Big-time," one man yelled. "That's big-time."

Finally, it was Pavin. He had come through all day, and there was no reason to expect anything less now. But the pres-sure was too much even for Pavin. His drive sliced into the right rough. It looked as if it would come down to Faldo and Roberts.

With his short drive off the neck of his driver, Faldo was away. He hit a high 3-iron, the type he used to hit from 1987 to 1992, when he won five major championships. The ball came down seventeen feet from the hole, and a large roar went up from the European fans. Watching inside the gallery ropes was Gill Faldo. She had walked every hole of every match her husband had played since Friday. "Nick has really clicked in, he's totally focused," said Leadbetter. "This is what he lives for."

But Pavin wasn't out of the hole. His ball landed on a tuft of grass, not far from where Jacobsen had been forced to lay up from that morning. It was an unbelievable break, and Pavin intended to make the most of it.

He was 189 yards from the front of the green, uphill, into a left-to-right quartering breeze. Club selection might have called for a 3-iron, but Pavin doesn't carry a 3-iron. It was ei-ther a choked-down cut 4-wood or a hard 4-iron. The 2-iron he couldn't get up high enough.

On the seventy-second hole at the U.S. Open, Eric Schwarz persuaded Pavin to hit the 4-wood. Here he told Pavin to whack the 4-iron, knowing it was plenty of club considering how much adrenaline was flowing through his player.

"It was a pretty big 4-iron, but I was juiced up," Pavin said. "I just swung as hard as I could and tried to get the ball up in the air." The shot flew over the flag and stopped in the back fringe. Wadkins was watching from the fairway. "I got a chill after that shot. Damn!" he said to Strange's caddy, Frank Williams.

Pavin walked up to a group of American players and got a

thumbs-up from Maggert. Pavin blew enough air into his cheeks to look like a squirrel with a mouthful of acorns. "Just a walk in the park on a Saturday afternoon," he said.

Over on the practice ground, Faxon was thinking, "Corey's so good at nonchalanting it."

This opened it up for Roberts to go after the pin with a 5-iron, but he pulled it to the center of the green. Ultimately, this worked in favor of the Americans. It allowed Roberts to putt first, lagging a sixty-footer that seemed to take ten seconds to get to the hole. It was close enough to give Pavin a run at the hole.

It was now 6:50 P.M. Pavin told Roberts's caddy, Dan Stojak, to keep the flag out. The lie wasn't great, but it didn't matter. Pavin was locked in on making it. With Faldo seventeen feet away, par wasn't going to do a bit of good. Faldo was off to the side of the green, practicing his stroke, preparing himself mentally should Pavin chip it in. So was Langer.

In the 1987 Bob Hope Chrysler Classic, Pavin chipped in on the ninetieth hole at PGA West to nip Langer by a stroke and win his fifth tournament. Nothing Pavin does surprises the German.

It was one of those sweet moments in time when everything goes in slow motion. The ball came off Pavin's pitching wedge, and the crowd started to rise in anticipation, except to Pavin the sound was muffled, because he was in such a trance, so locked into the shot, that it all seemed surreal.

He was six paces from the hole, roughly eighteen feet. He saw it breaking right to left, about three feet. The contour of the green would feed the ball into the hole. It was a picture he drew in his mind, visualizing the ball going in the hole, just flipping it on the green and watching it track down the hill as if it were part of a telestrator. What do they say about golf? The game is 90 percent mental. Actually, it's 90 percent mental and . . . 10 percent mental.

The ball circled the cup and went in. Pavin showed no emotion. He had enough composure to realize that Faldo still had a putt to tie, that a celebration like the one across the seventeenth green at Kiawah, or like the uppercut he had thrown on the fourteenth green Friday, would have been unsportsmanlike.

"When I chipped in, and I looked up, it was right at my team," Pavin remembers. "They were all jumping up and down, hugging each other, so I kind of felt I was doing it through them."

Before Faldo even putted, Langer came up to Pavin and Pavin looked like he wanted to apologize. Langer stuck out his right hand. "Nice chip," he said with a grin that was saying, "That was a great shot."

Pavin appreciated that moment almost more than making the shot itself. "He's such a good friend and a good buddy . . . that grin meant everything to me," Pavin said.

Two years earlier, Faldo made the seventeen-footer on eighteen to halve the hole and the match against Couples and Azinger. But in 1995, Faldo was not the Faldo who once dominated golf. He had his worst record in the majors since 1986, and only a victory at the Doral-Ryder Open had salvaged his first year of playing golf full-time on the PGA Tour. The birdie putt was pulled coming off the putter and never had a chance. With Pavin now joining the celebration, he tried the putt again and went straight to the putting green to practice until dark.

"Trying to force them on these greens is very tough," he said.

It was at that moment that you could not have taken a bet on Europe's winning the Ryder Cup. Only twice in the last forty years had the Americans lost the singles. Down on the range, Faxon, Jacobsen, and Haas were high-fiving and hugging and dancing. They sprinted up the hill to join their teammates and wives on the eighteenth green. Out in the fairway, Maggert started sprinting toward the green like a halfback. Crenshaw was waving a seat cushion over his head. The crowd was chanting, "Cor-ey, Cor-ey, Cor-ey." Pavin was up there somewhere, in the middle of it all.

"A birdie from that spot? From a shank lie? Unbelievable," Crenshaw said, more impressed with the 4-iron from the rough than the chip from the fringe.

"Unbelievable," said Couples. "The ball's below his feet— just to get it on the green—and he took it right over the flag. Wow!"

"That's why he's the U.S. Open champion," said Strange.

"I was not really surprised," said Wadkins. "I was sitting up there with Curtis and I said, 'You know, he's got the flag out. He can make it.'"

Faldo was still putting when Pavin walked through the gauntlet of fans behind the barriers and along the clubhouse with Shannon. He never looked up, as Leadbetter worked with him on his stroke, using both hands to make sure his shoulders were on line with the hole. Afterward, Diaz stopped him going to the locker room. Not many people could get Faldo to do an interview at that point, but Diaz is perhaps the most respected of the writers among the players, somebody who always asks the inquisitive questions.

"Corey is simply magic with the putter," Faldo said. "He holed a fifty-footer on the first hole. I watched him when he went out on the practice green. He threw down three balls and made two of them every time. I knew he had his eye in it."

What did he think when Pavin made the chip?

"Expletive deleted, expletive deleted, bleep, expletive deleted, bleep."

Faldo admitted that the greens and the course setup had been the deciding factor, but he wasn't ready to concede the defeat. "We've got to play great tomorrow. Everyone has to go for it," he said. "But it's not so cut and dried. I think we look good."

CHAPTER 14

Mind Games

There was no time for Lanny Wadkins to celebrate or Bernard Gallacher to hang his head. The pairings for Sunday's singles had to be in Kerry Haigh's office one hour after the final match finished, which was 7:10 P.M. In the parking lot, spectators were queuing up on bus lines to take them back downtown, or to the malls in suburban Rochester that were being used to handle the 25,000 people that poured into Oak Hill every day. It was quite an operation, but it was not as complicated as the mind games that Wadkins and Gallacher were dealing with.

Wadkins sat at a table in the U.S. team room surrounded by Davis

Love, Curtis Strange, Brad Faxon, Fred Couples, and his brother, Bobby. Lanny had on his reading glasses and was looking at a piece of paper numbered 1 to 12. He was trying to figure out how to stack the lineup.

"There was a huge buzz," remembers Faxon. "A lot of people had stayed around and were still watching when Corey chipped in. We were up nine–seven and I was thinking, 'Hey, perfect.' Lanny was not going to save the big guns for last. He wanted to send them out early and in the middle. Lehman's was the first name I saw down. He had Jacobsen second, Maggert third, and then he started loading. He had Pavin tenth, and originally he had Mickelson down in the middle. Lanny said, 'Hey, Phil, I hope you're ready for one of the prime spots.' I know Lanny's feelings were that somebody in the middle would clinch it, somebody like Davis or Freddie."

Across the hall in the Oak Hill clubhouse, Gallacher was doing the same thing as Wadkins, but Gallacher went at it alone. The big criticism of him in 1993 was that he relied too much on his players to make decisions, that ultimately the inmates ran the asylum. That wasn't going to be the case this time. He had consulted only with Ken Schofield, executive director of the European Tour and a member of the Ryder Cup committee. The only member of the team who knew when he was playing was Ballesteros, who would go off first. Faldo and Langer were still out putting. The rest of the team, except for Per-Ulrik Johansson, were headed back to the team hotel. It was 7:25 P.M.

"Per-Ulrik had some slight misgivings about playing twelfth," Gallacher said. "I persuaded him that it was actually the best spot to be in. The way I read it, I was taking a bit of a gamble, but as I told him, say you play Corey Pavin, what have you got to lose? In your position, nobody will think anything if you get beaten. What an opportunity this is for you—this is a chance you'll want."

As the captains finalized their lineups, Pavin and Roberts were in the media center, being asked to replay the events on the eighteenth green and assess their team's position.

Q: "Corey, if you could step outside of Corey Pavin right now and look at yourself, why do you think you're so good under pressure? If you could just kind of do a little self-examination."
A: "I don't know how to step outside myself."
The tent broke up in laughter.
Q: "Why are you so good under pressure?"
A: "I don't know. I just—I don't know if I can really answer it, but you know, I just concentrate really hard and focus very well under situations like that. I really see what I need to do very sharply, very keenly, and just try to execute. I just try to be as relaxed as I possibly can and as—and just let my game flow as much as I possibly can and picture everything I want to do."
Q: "What do you think that the victory in your match did to the European team?"

Roberts: "I'll tell you, I don't really think it did anything to them other than made the score nine to seven. They came out really good this morning. I mean, they putted great. They all played good this morning, and all we did basically this afternoon was get the two points back that we lost in the morning. You know, we've got a long way to go in this thing. That's about all I can really say about that."

Pavin: "I mean, there's still twelve points out there to be had, and we only have a two-point lead. And I think all of us—everybody on the team is very aware of what could happen tomorrow. And we want to make sure that we're ready. Obviously we're very pleased with the afternoon, the way it went, about as displeased as the way the morning went. So it was good to end the day that way because we needed a boost after the morning. I was just as proud of everybody on the team for playing tough this afternoon because it was like we lost the first hole this morning, it seemed like, and we came back and won the second hole this afternoon. So tomorrow is where everything happens. You have twelve points out there. A lot of stuff's going to happen tomorrow, and we'll see what happens."

Outside the clubhouse, Mark Love saw it differently. Davis's brother and caddy saw this as most people saw it, as a big psychological swing for the Americans. "I think everybody on the European team is in a state of shock," he said. "Now we've just got to win five of the twelve matches. Everybody can go out there more relaxed."

Wadkins was trying to think like Gallacher and Gallacher was trying to think like Wadkins. It was a chess match, and when Haigh got the lineup sheets in the tournament office, he could see a lot of changes had been made by both captains. Gallacher went with Ballesteros, Clark, James, Woosnam, Rocca, Gilford, Montgomerie, Faldo, Torrance, Langer, Walton and Johansson. He had the two Ryder Cup rookies going off last, figuring the matches might be over by then anyway, so it didn't matter. His thinking on Ballesteros was that out of respect, he didn't want the Spaniard involved in a pivotal match. Maybe he would get a good matchup and steal a point. If not, he would be around to walk the other matches and serve as a presence on the course.

Wadkins went with his strength in the middle, because he felt that was what Gallacher would do, but he also wanted someone leading off who would get a point early, which is why he put Lehman there. Also it would be cold in the morning, and cold weather doesn't bother Lehman. He then put in Jacobsen, another cold-weather player, and Maggert, the rookie who had played so well the first day in victories with Love and Roberts. The heart of Wadkins's order was in positions four through ten, with Couples, Love, Faxon, Crenshaw, Strange, Roberts, and Pavin. For anchors, he went with Haas and Mickelson. Mickelson had lobbied to go last; he wanted the pressure on him if it came to that. Wadkins relented.

"The guys are really involved, and I think there's some

great pairings there tomorrow," Wadkins said. "That's been the interesting part, working with the pairings and working with the guys. I think that not only did I work guys' games that complemented each other pretty well, but I worked the personalities that were comfortable playing with each other out there pretty well. And that was a big part of it.

"I think that sometimes you have to listen to your players a little bit, and I think I listened well this week and communicated with them pretty good. I don't think anybody was out there with a player this week that they were uncomfortable with, whether they won or lost."

The pairings almost looked as if Wadkins and Gallacher had consulted each other before making them. It seemed impossible that this was a blind draw. There were rematches from 1993, Love playing Rocca and Couples playing Woosnam. In a rematch of their 1988 U.S. Open playoff, Strange had drawn Faldo. Pavin would be playing his good friend Langer for the fourth time. And finally, Mickelson would be playing Johansson, his old college teammate. "I think it turned out to be great strategy," said Faxon, who would be playing Gilford. "We got the matchups we would have liked. I was sure psyched."

So was Gallacher. He threw the piece of paper containing the pairings across the table at Schofield with a rueful look on his face. In the press tent, Gallacher told the golf media, "This is a good draw for us," but the British golf writers didn't agree. That night at the lobby bar at the Holiday Inn, they would go over the pairings again and again and not a one of them saw any way that Europe could win—not seven and a half out of twelve points.

"As far as I'm concerned, we had a great day," Gallacher said. "We came out this morning. We showed our temperament. We showed how strong we are and how determined we are. This afternoon didn't exactly go our way, didn't exactly go the way we meant, but this competition is by no means over. They're disappointed they're behind. They feel they're better than the American players, and they want to prove it tomorrow."

It was pointed out to Gallacher that this was the first time since 1981 that the U.S. team had led on Saturday night, and that the Europeans were 1–6 in the singles since then. He cut off the question before it was completely asked. It was time to head back to the Woodcliff and go over the pairings with the players, time for this news conference to end.

"We live in a very changeable time, a very fluent time," he said. "Things have changed. Our players are stronger going out there. These players don't—amateurs think of history; professionals think about the future. They're going out to win tomorrow."

CHAPTER 15

Morning Glory

Tom Lehman and Seve Ballesteros shook
hands on the first tee at Oak Hill
Sunday morning, sizing each other
up, squarely looking each other in
the eyes. Neither man dared to blink,
the Spanish bullfighter or the bull from
Minnesota.

Lehman tried to remember what
Azinger had told him on Wednesday night,
that no matter how nervous you may feel,
the other guy feels just as nervous. He
took off his pullover. It wasn't as cold as
it had been Saturday morning; it was
the start of a brisk day that would
surely heat up before it was over. His

blood was already boiling. It was just after 9:00 A.M. His arms were bare.

Saturday night, when they did the pairings, Wadkins had pulled Lehman aside.

"Tom," he said, "they're going to send a stud out first. You need to go out and handle him."

There was no hesitation in Lehman's voice.

"I'm there," he said.

And now he was there, on the first tee against Europe's stud of studs, trying to handle all the mind games that Ballesteros had been known to pull. Physically, he could stand up to Ballesteros. Mentally, he would have to deal with Seve's nervous cough and who knows what tricks of gamesmanship. He would have to be ready for it, because it was sure to come.

Ballesteros had on a sweater, a baseball cap, and the worried look of a man who had lost his golf game. He had started the year with a victory at the Spanish Open, but he had missed the cut in five of nine U.S. events and had not played much better in Europe, where he was twenty-five over par in seven tournaments since that victory in May at Club de Campo. His victory on Friday with Gilford was Ballesteros's twentieth in Ryder Cup competition. That put him just two behind Arnold Palmer for career Ryder Cup victories. He still had that aura working for him, but not much else.

The Lehman-Ballesteros pairing was the first of twelve singles matches on this Sunday at the thirty-first Ryder Cup. For Lehman, it was the first time he had gone one on one with anyone in Ryder Cup competition. He hadn't played since a Saturday-morning loss, so he was well rested and somewhat upset that Wadkins had given him only two matches. If he could take out the Spaniard hard and early, it would send a message across the course, perhaps demoralize the Europeans and certainly psych up his teammates. Ballesteros had been through seven of these singles matches, and had not fared particularly well, recording a 2-3-2 lifetime record. In his last match, he failed to break 40 on the front side at the Belfry and lost to Jim Gallagher, Jr., 3 and 2. Maybe he could lean on his short game and perhaps steal a point or a half point against Lehman. Maybe he could summon some of that old Ballesteros magic once again.

Ballesteros had the honor. In his two four-balls matches, he had had a partner to lean on. Now his game would be exposed. His drive went into the left trees, not drawing any reaction from the gallery crowded around the tee. Lehman, who had hit the first ball for America on Friday, that towering 290-yard 3-wood, stepped up and busted it down the middle.

Advantage Lehman.

Ballesteros had to take a drop for an unplayable lie and made bogey. Lehman won the hole with a par and went one up. The rout was seemingly on.

At the second, the 401-yard uphill par four, Ballesteros drove into the right rough and couldn't get his second shot on the green. Lehman was on in two, pin-high and twenty feet away, looking at going two up, when Ballesteros holed a wedge from off the green. It didn't shock Lehman, because he knew that Seve still had his short game.

At the third hole, Ballesteros established what kind of match it was going to be. Lehman had it inside two feet for par to halve the hole. Ballesteros made him putt it. Lehman tapped in and moved on.

It went like this until the twelfth hole. Ballesteros would miss a fairway, miss a green, but get a halve. Lehman was hitting fairways in regulation, but walking away with pars. At the fifth, Ballesteros sliced his drive across Allen's Creek. He moved the crowd and hit a shot over the trees, over the creek, and onto the green. From sixty-five feet he two-putted, making a ten-footer coming back. At the eighth, Ballesteros was out the hole but hesitated before conceding. All Lehman had to do was two-putt from ten feet, but the Spaniard was up to his old tricks, trying to unnerve Lehman, trying to get under his skin. It wouldn't work.

At the tenth, Ballesteros pushed his drive into a fairway

bunker but made a twelve-footer for par. Lehman knocked a six-footer for birdie eighteen inches past the hole. Ballesteros made him putt it.

"I just wasn't going to get sucked into it," Lehman said. "A lot of times with a guy like him, you think you've got it in the bag, he's fifty yards right of the green, and makes par. I kind of expected him to do that. I just felt if I could play steady golf, it would eventually get him."

They came to the twelfth with Lehman two up. Any other golfer might have been closed out, but Ballesteros kept finding the hole, staying close enough to make it interesting. Lehman had a fifteen-footer for birdie, leaving it six inches from the hole. Ballesteros indicated that he wanted Lehman to mark his ball. The crowd started buzzing. Lehman looked at Ballesteros funny, forgetting that in match play there is no continuous putting rule. What he wanted was Lehman to leave his mark so he would have something to aim at. Lehman didn't understand. Neither did the gallery. The referee, former PGA president J. R. Carpenter, intervened. He tried to explain to the gallery what had happened, that Ballesteros had every right to ask Lehman to leave his marker on the green. Finally, it was settled. Both players made pars, with Lehman picking up after Ballesteros had putted out.

Lehman seemed inspired. He won the thirteenth hole with a par and birdied the fourteenth to go four up. With four to play, Lehman closed Ballesteros out by hitting the fifteenth green and two-putting for par. That made him fifteen for fifteen in greens hit in regulation. When the match ended, Ballesteros shook Lehman's hand and said he had meant nothing on the twelfth green. Lehman nodded that he understood, then took a step back as the Spaniard walked off the green. With the first point of the day on the board, Lehman let loose and punched the sky in three different directions. Wadkins came out for a hug. So did Lehman's wife, Melissa.

"As long as I've been a golfer, he's been one of my idols," Lehman said of Ballesteros. "You know he's just never going to give up. He'll keep fighting you even if he's spraying shots all over the place. Lanny and Zinger told me before the match to expect him to chip in from everywhere, that he'd never be out of a hole. I knew that if I kept it on the fairway and on the greens I'd put pressure on him to save par."

Lehman tried to downplay the incident at the twelfth green, but reporters grilled him on it. He claimed that Ballesteros was a gentleman, that he was just trying to win, that it wasn't gamesmanship.

"He told me, 'I'm not trying to play games with you. I just want you to handle it correctly,'" Lehman said. "It was the kind of thing where he had every reason to ask me to put my mark back. I had tapped in and putted out of turn, so that was all the confusion. We weren't really sure if it was a loss of hole. It was my fault. I had putted out of turn."

Ballesteros was encircled behind the green. Questions came at him from everywhere. General comments first. "He played very well, and I just could not hit the fairway or the greens. That has been my problem all year and this week. I cleared all the rough and all the branches on the golf course. And I'm sure all the members at Oak Hill, they're not going to lose any more balls."

What happened on the twelfth hole?

"Nothing happened. I didn't want him to hole the putt. I was just looking for the coin. No problem, it was just a misunderstanding. I wanted to use his ball for a mark to line up my putt. It was within my rights to do."

Comment on your play.

"I was trying everything to hit the ball straight, and nothing worked. That's why Bernard didn't play me in the foursomes. I couldn't hit the ball straight. It was a very frustrating week. I tried to do well for the team but nothing happened."

Are you still working with Mac O'Grady?

"No. Mac is very busy in Palm Springs."

What was it like playing against Lehman?

"It seems to me that he didn't miss a shot all day. He's a nice guy, a gentleman. He just didn't give me any chances."

Would you consider being a playing captain in 1997?

"That's not possible in these days. Now it's too big and there are too many things to do. It's impossible. I think the role of the captain is too important."

The crowd got hostile.

"They thought we were going to have a fight. But I wouldn't fight him. He is a heavyweight. I am a light heavyweight."

Would he be Europe's captain at Valderrama in 1997?

Ballesteros looked at the scoreboard to the right of the fifteenth green. He saw a lot of blue. Blue on a Ryder Cup scoreboard is for Europe.

"We might still win. Bernard might have to defend the title over there."

Nobody believed him, because at that point, the United States was only four points from retaining the Cup, four and a half points from an outright victory. With eleven matches out on the course, a European victory seemed impossible.

CHAPTER 16

Clark & James

In the United States, Howard Clark and Mark James were probably two of the least respected members of the European team, two nondescript career grinders who had won their share of tournaments on the European circuit but who never had the games to do much in major championships or the Ryder Cup. Paired on Friday, they were defeated convincingly by Davis Love and Jeff Maggert. In singles, they figured to be two sure points for the Americans on Sunday at Oak Hill. Clark lost his last singles match by an 8 and 7 score to Tom Kite at the Belfry in 1989. James was 1–4–1 in Ryder Cup singles. While the European team fought to stay alive on Saturday, they were on the practice tee, trying to find a game.

It didn't bother James that Gallacher had him out Friday afternoon and all day Saturday. Clark was more edgy. He thought Gallacher might send him out Saturday afternoon, but the European team went 3–1 that morning and Gallacher kept Clark and James on the bench. Clark worked with David Leadbetter, James with his coach, Gavin Levin.

"I practiced and then I played the first six holes and then practiced again," James said. "Then I went out and heard I wasn't playing so I had some lunch and practiced again. Then I played another six holes, and practiced some more. After I went out to watch some of the fellows finish, I had a spare half hour, so I practiced again. I practiced five times that one day. I like to practice little and more often at times, because golf is a game about finding your game each day. It's not about blasting balls for six hours."

The American players knew not to take Clark and James lightly. They weren't paying attention to the Sony Rankings, which had James listed as the fifty-eighth best player in the world and Clark at sixty-third.

Peter Jacobsen and Jeff Maggert knew they would have their hands full, and they did. Although Clark hadn't won in seven years, he and James had twenty-nine career victories between them. They knew how to win—not that Jacobsen and Maggert didn't, but between them the Americans only had seven career victories.

The first sign came at the second hole. Jacobsen had a par putt of three feet. Clark had missed the green, then tried a flop shot that cleared the bunker but not a deep patch of rough short of the green. It looked like Jacobsen's hole.

Clark holed out the chip for the halve.

It went that way all day. Jacobsen went one up four times. Every time, Clark would come back at the next hole to draw even. Jacobsen hit driver, 9-iron at the 429-yard tenth and made an eleven-footer for birdie to go one up again. At the par-three eleventh, he hit 6-iron in the hole from 186 yards. When the ball came off his club, Clark didn't like it and dropped his head. He thought he'd pulled it, but the wind was left-to-right and it redirected the shot over the bunker and onto the green. It pitched three feet short, kicked right, hit the stick, and disappeared. Clark patted his heart.

At the uphill twelfth, Jacobsen hit 9-iron twelve feet above the hole. Clark was in the front bunker and blasted out to six feet, just inside Jacobsen's line. Jacobsen missed, but Clark got a good read on the break and made his putt for the halve.

"Those were two big momentum shifters or boosters to Howard," said Jacobsen.

James was giving Maggert fits. At the par-five fourth hole, with Maggert looking at a ten-foot putt for birdie, James holed out from a greenside bunker. Maggert missed to go two down. At the next hole, he dumped his second shot in the water, made double bogey, and was three down in a hurry.

Maggert could never make it up and was the first American knocked out of the singles. James had birdied the second, fourth, sixth, eighth, and twelfth holes. It was only his second victory in seven Ryder Cup singles matches, but it got Europe on the scoreboard and made the score 10–8. "The thing about match play," Maggert said, "is that things can turn against you or for you quickly. Every time it looked like I was going to win a hole with par, he would make a ten- or a fifteen-footer to halve. In match play, it helps when you get a gift, and after that hole-out from the bunker, Mark just never messed up. I was three down early, and I never had a chance to close the gap."

Clark kept grinding. Jacobsen gave him a hole by three-putting the fourteenth, and then the lead by three-putting the sixteenth from the back of the green. Clark got up and down from a greenside bunker to go one up for the first time all day. Was this the same guy who had missed the cut in four of his last seven European Tour events? Outside he looked calm. Inside, Howard's nerves were doing a dance.

"When everything is moving except for the ball," he said, "it's dangerous."

At the seventeenth, Clark and Jacobsen both hit big drives over the crest of the hill on the 458-yard par four, leaving them 167 and 173 yards respectively. Clark left himself three feet for the halve, but made the putt to take a one-up lead to the eighteenth tee.

Jacobsen just couldn't shake the guy. At eighteen, Clark had 199 yards to the flag, 187 yards to carry his shot onto the green. He changed clubs, went with the 5-iron, and hit it fifty feet below and right of the hole.

Jacobsen had just a 7-iron in his hands, but he should have hit 6-iron. His shot just cleared the bunker, leaving him an up-hill thirty-footer that he probably would have to make, depending on what Clark did.

Clark was definitely in three-putt range, but he didn't short-arm it, rolling his ball four feet past the hole. Jake still had to think birdie, and he hit one of those putts that did everything but go in. As it burned the left edge, Jacobsen backed away in agony.

Without taking too much time to line it up or think about it, Clark made the putt to win the match and make the score 11–9. Europe had just stolen two points, and had swung the momentum away from the Americans. "James and Clark had played great in practice," Gallacher said. "But they didn't play as well as they could have on Friday, and most people took it that they were playing badly because they weren't sent out on Saturday. People forget that in a Ryder Cup, four people can't play every day. Some of the British press were coming out and saying they weren't on the course supporting the team or watching, but I told them to keep going out and play the course, it's going to be crucial, and it was. Their victories canceled out Seve's lost point."

Behind the green, Jacobsen was disheartened. All week, players had been holing out shots and making putts on him. It had happened with Gilford on Friday. It had happened with

Woosnam on Saturday, but he'd managed to escape with a win. On Sunday, it happened again when a guy he should have beat chipped in from the deep rough, made a hole in one, and drained two throw-up putts on the seventeenth and eighteenth holes for a one-up victory. Sometimes it's just not meant to be.

The first person to shake Howard Clark's hand when he walked off the eighteenth green was Mark James. Clark had the ball he'd made the ace with. With a Sharpie pen, he wrote on it, "Hole In One, 1995 Ryder Cup," and stuck it in his pocket.

"Shows what you have to do to win out here," he said.

CHAPTER 17

Rematch

The photographers wanted them to pose, so Fred Couples shrank six inches to stand head to head with Ian Woosnam. They mugged for the cameras. It was a light moment, one of the last they would share this day.

Out ahead of them, Davis Love had already driven into the trees and Costantino Rocca had split another fairway. Love had teed off thinking that it was probably again going to be his match that decided it, that he hated to do it to Rocca again but he had no choice. Couples and Woosnam just wanted to get this thing over. No matter how it turned out, it was going to be hell.

At the Belfry in 1993, Woosnam drew Couples in the first match of the Sunday singles. It didn't end until the eighteenth green, when Woosie slithered in a four-footer for par to halve the hole and halve the match. When they shook hands, Woosnam told Couples, "You know, they really should be paying us for this." It was the first time in six Ryder Cup singles matches that Ian Woosnam, the Masters champion and then winner of twenty-eight events on the European Tour, had not gone down in defeat. He was simply relieved to walk off the course that day in the British Midlands with a half point.

When the pairings came out Saturday night, Woosnam and Couples almost couldn't believe it. Neither could Love and Rocca, for that matter. Brad Faxon had come by Love's room with the news. Love thought he was putting him on, the same way Love put Faxon on by calling the locker room at Riviera wanting to know how he'd played in the final round of the PGA.

"You drew Rocca again," said Faxon.

"Yeah, real funny," said Love.

"No," said Faxon, "you drew Rocca again."

Love had been disappointed at himself for losing two matches on Saturday, especially making only that one birdie in the four-balls match with Crenshaw as his partner. He was 2–2 at the Belfry in 1993, and had it in his mind that he was going to win all his matches, that he and Pavin were going to play all ten matches and win eight or nine points for the Americans. It may have been overconfidence, but 1995 was the year when Love's game really matured, when he won at New Orleans knowing it was his only way to get a spot in the field at the Masters, then played so well at Augusta, shooting 66 in the final round to finish one stroke back of Crenshaw. It was Jaime Diaz's observation that Davis was "starting to look like a full-grown man instead of a youthful beanpole full of potential," that he had "gained stature among his peers, which should help him believe he is ready for bigger things."

The Rocca pairing made Love uncomfortable only in that

they had grown so close since the Belfry, when the Italian three-putted the seventeenth and bogeyed the eighteenth to lose a lead and lose the pivotal match. The first person Love looked for that day was Wadkins, because it was Wadkins who had volunteered for the envelope when it became apparent that Sam Torrance might withdraw with his "septic toe." He wanted to tell Lanny, "This one's for you," and since that day, Love and Wadkins had grown closer the way Love and Rocca had grown closer. When it was earlier in the 1995 season, and Love hadn't been doing much, Wadkins had implored him, saying things like "C'mon, you've got to get off your butt, because I need you on this team. I don't want to have to pick you."

Although it was only his second Ryder Cup, Love had evolved into one of the team's leaders, helping Wadkins with strategy decisions, then stepping up on Friday with two wins. Rocca had also come up big for Europe, and there was no American happier than Love when Rocca holed that putt on the seventy-second hole of the British Open to tie John Daly. It was nothing against Daly. Love wanted the American to win. But he had grown much closer to Rocca than he had to Daly.

"Robin and I were watching from our rooms at the Old Course Hotel," Love said. "We could see Costantino outside our window playing eighteen, and we had it on the TV. They showed a picture of Daly watching it on a TV by the scorer's trailer, and you could hear him say, 'It's over.' I said, 'Hey, it ain't over yet.'

"When he made that putt I jumped up off the foot of the bed and hit my hands on the ceiling. Brad Faxon was in the room, and he looked at us like we were crazy. He said, 'You're not pulling for John Daly? You're pulling for Costantino?' I said, 'No, you don't understand, and you won't until you're in a Ryder Cup.'"

The night before his singles match with Rocca at Oak Hill, Love tried to explain to Robin how nervous he was feeling.

Robin tried to help by saying maybe Davis should get Jack Lumpkin to watch him hit balls before he teed off on Sunday. Davis sort of snapped at her. "That ain't gonna help," he said. "I'm hitting it perfect on the range. The pressure just got to me today. I didn't play well today."

Robin said, "Well, you played well under pressure before, at New Orleans and the Masters."

Davis came back by explaining, "It's different," then made the mistake of saying, "You don't know what it's like."

That was the wrong thing to say. Robin was just trying to be supportive. Davis hadn't meant to insult her, but he wasn't thinking, he was just talking, and it came out wrong. He was thinking, "I shouldn't have started this with her, I just should have agreed with her."

"It's just so hard to explain how much pressure there is," said Love. "The next day, I was never more nervous. Because I told her how much pressure there would be, I was tight in my chest, I could hardly breathe. It was the most nervous I had ever been for the longest period of time."

Love started out shaky, pitching out into the first fairway, but hitting a full wedge to ten feet and making the putt for par to halve the hole. He bogeyed the second to fall one down, but got it back with a par at the fifth and then started to play really well, entering that zone golfers talk about when the game is so easy, the hole looks so big, and the ball does the things the mind tells it to do. With birdies at the seventh, eighth, tenth, and eleventh holes, Love moved to four up. It was the best stretch of golf anybody had played in the Ryder Cup, and Love went on to close Rocca out with a birdie at the sixteenth, 3 and 2.

He counted them up: six birdies. Where had they all been on Saturday? He couldn't worry about that now. With that point, the U.S. team led 11–8. They were just three points from retaining the Cup, but Love could see trouble on the board. He could see a lot of blue. In the match ahead of him, Clark had just gone one up on Jacobsen. Behind him, Couples was having trouble with Woosnam. His point was a welcome relief. He doubled back to root Couples home.

Woosnam had gone to the first tee thinking, "I've got to improve my record. I've got only one half with Fred. It means such a lot to me to win a singles for the team. Maybe I put too much pressure on myself. I'm an older member of the team. I need to win a singles. Maybe I should go out there and play my own game."

Couples had been in a good mood since the engagement. Tawnya noticed, "Fred always gets a little uptight at the Masters and the Ryder Cup. But I've never seen him so relaxed." The Woosnam pairing was good for him. He liked Woosie, was comfortable around him both on and off the golf course. But this was Sunday at the Ryder Cup. It's a little different.

What Couples wasn't comfortable with was his putter. He was one up with a par at the first, but reeled off three straight three-putt greens to lose the third, fourth, and fifth holes. He was two down through ten, realizing he'd better get it in gear, when Woosnam gave him a break and made bogey. He had a chance to level the match at the twelfth, but missed a six-footer for birdie, then stayed locked with Woosnam until the seventeenth, the 458-yard monster that had given everyone fits all week.

Woosnam still had honors and hit a good drive over the crest of the hill. Couples felt a surge of adrenaline and blew it forty yards past Woosnam. With just an 8-iron in his hands, Couples hit it to eighteen feet and made the putt for the first birdie of the week on the seventeenth. They were all square going to the eighteenth tee.

Now Couples was really pumped up. Down in the fairway, Love was thinking, "Hit the 3-wood," but Couples wasn't linked up to the telepathic communications channel. He took out his driver and busted it. His caddy, Joe LaCava, could tell it was too long. "Bite, bite," he said, the way golfers usually yell at iron shots hit into greens. The ball didn't listen. It flew through the dogleg and into some matted-down rough and took off running into the trees. When it finally came to rest, forty yards past the longest drive of the week, Couples's ball was behind two giant fir trees, apparently dead, or in jail, as the pros say when they have no shot to the green.

Woosnam's normal flight is a right-to-left draw, but with the pressure he slap-cut a drive into the right rough, 185 yards from the front of the green, but in a good lie. While Couples was trying to figure out what to do, Woosie hit a 5-iron pin-high, twenty feet left of the hole. With Couples in so much trouble, it looked like a sure point for the Europeans.

But Couples manufactured something, spotting some air up in the tree branches and carving a cut 9-iron from 140 yards that came down in the front bunker.

Watching from the fairway, Wadkins was relieved to see it bounce off the sand into a good lie. "It didn't plug," he said into his walkie-talkie.

From the bunker, Couples had to get his shot up quick. That was no problem. Stopping it was. The ball released four feet past the hole, leaving Couples a slick comebacker with a little right-to-left break. It wasn't a putt he liked.

Woosnam then put the purest stroke on a putt he had all week. As the ball approached the hole, the Welshman went down on his right knee and looked as if he were throwing the dice up against a sidewalk curb. He did this when he sank the winning putt at the '91 Masters. But this time, the putt did not fall. When it didn't take the break and cruised the left lip, Woosnam covered his face with his hands. Just a little easier and he would have made it.

"I couldn't've hit a better putt," Woosnam said. "I thought I got it. I was just concentrating on the pace because I knew Freddie had a tricky putt."

Couples looked as if he wasn't sure whether he was relieved Woosnam had missed or apprehensive knowing it was now on his shoulders. But there was no turning away from it. It was right there on the green in front of him. His ball. The hole. Four feet of grass. The grandstands packed. The television cameras on him. All around the world, Fred Couples was being watched, and his career would be judged by how he handled the next ten seconds of his life.

The scoreboard showed that Europe was leading in seven of the remaining eight matches. This half point was vital. Behind him, Brad Faxon had just fanned a 6-iron at the seventeenth and missed the green, Bernhard Langer had just left it in the bunker at twelve to go two down to Pavin, and Colin Montgomerie was in the middle of four straight threes, a run that would close out Ben Crenshaw. Couples didn't know the details, just that his team was suddenly in trouble. The putt was just like the one Woosnam had had to make at the Belfry to halve him in 1993.

When it went in, America had eleven and a half points, Europe had nine and a half points, and Fred Couples had the relief of knowing he could still make the big four-footer when he had to. Plus, he was one of Lanny's captain's picks. That gave him a 2-1-1 record for the week. It justified Wadkins's decision to take him, bad back and all.

"I didn't hit a whole lot of good putts," Couples said. "I was nervous all day, and obviously it showed. I just feel fortunate. I'm glad I had a downhiller. All I had to do was get it started. I was just atrocious on these greens."

Atrocious until it counted, and then Fred Couples ran in two putts on the seventeenth and eighteenth holes that made the scoreboard look a little bit better, but not much. Couples looked back down the eighteenth fairway and saw Faxon one down to Gilford, Crenshaw two down to Montgomerie, Torrance one up on Roberts, Walton two up on Haas, and Johansson one up on Mickelson. Freddie added it up. "We're in trouble," he said.

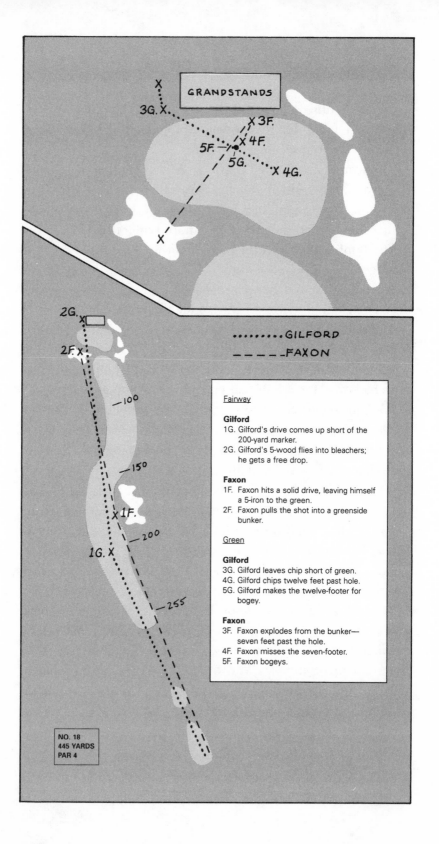

GRANDSTANDS

3G. X

X 3F.
X 4F.
5F.
5G.
X 4G.

2G. X

2F. X

·········· GILFORD

– – – – – FAXON

—100

—150

X 1F.

—200

1G. X

—255

Fairway

Gilford

1G. Gilford's drive comes up short of the 200-yard marker.

2G. Gilford's 5-wood flies into bleachers; he gets a free drop.

Faxon

1F. Faxon hits a solid drive, leaving himself a 5-iron to the green.

2F. Faxon pulls the shot into a greenside bunker.

Green

Gilford

3G. Gilford leaves chip short of green.

4G. Gilford chips twelve feet past hole.

5G. Gilford makes the twelve-footer for bogey.

Faxon

3F. Faxon explodes from the bunker—seven feet past the hole.

4F. Faxon misses the seven-footer.

5F. Faxon bogeys.

NO. 18
445 YARDS
PAR 4

CHAPTER 18

Gilford Again

What's Loren doing at thirteen?"

From the eighteenth fairway, Lanny Wadkins was working his walkie-talkie, trying to stay current, trying to put it all together. It was starting to happen fast now, and he could sense it slipping away. That two-point lead the American team had had Friday and Saturday nights meant absolutely zip on Sunday afternoon. So did that chip-in by Corey Pavin on this same eighteenth green not twenty hours ago. Maybe that shot by Pavin had brought the house down, but it certainly hadn't brought the Europeans down. As he suspected, they'd come out fired up, and were holing shots from everywhere. It looked bad. Real bad.

Wadkins had a white earplug coming out of his right ear. He was biting the antenna of his walkie-talkie. These matches had gotten out of his control. He had fixed the golf course to suit his team. He had done the pairings the first two days. Everybody had played at least two matches, and it was the first time a U.S. Ryder Cup team had led going into the Sunday singles since 1981. He had made out the lineup for Sunday. He had told his team to be prepared for an onslaught. But he couldn't go out and hit the shots for them. All he could do was watch, cheerlead a little bit, and keep track of it on his walkie-talkie.

Up on the eighteenth green, Fred Couples was sizing up a four-foot putt for par, and a halve. A lot was riding on it. Wadkins had already seen Peter Jacobsen and Jeff Maggert lose, and Ben Crenshaw was going down fast to Colin Montgomerie. Roberts, who had gone 3–0 as a Ryder Cup rookie, was two down to Torrance. Only Pavin had things under control, but that figured. Pavin you could count on. No matter who you put him up against, no matter what the situation, Pavin would get the job done.

"This is big-time right here," the captain said.

Bobby Wadkins was out by the fourteenth green, giving reports on the pivotal Curtis Strange–Nick Faldo match. Tom Lehman was there. So was Davis Love. Bernard Gallacher was watching up by the green.

"Curtis has a four-footer to stay one up through fourteen."

Couples figured it out and stroked the putt. When the ball went down in the ground, Wadkins went up in the air about the same distance, but for a forty-five-year-old Texan, five inches felt like five feet.

"Yes, Freddie! Oh, my God! What a big putt! Yes!"

Wadkins could now turn his attention to the Faxon-Gilford match. Back out at seventeen, Gilford had it four feet for par.

Faxon was one down. Gilford had made everything. He made another one. He was now one up going to the eighteenth tee. If Faxon could scratch out a halve the way Couples had, it might mean the difference.

"That match," said Wadkins, "is an absolute must."

Faxon had made only one birdie, but that was matched by Gilford at the par-three sixth. At the eighteenth, they both hit the fairway, but Faxon had the advantage. Gilford was back where he needed a five-wood. Faxon was up at comfortable yardage. He had 175 yards to the front, 187 yards to the hole. Perfect distances for his 5-iron. He looked back and saw Gilford taking the head cover off his wood. Even from 210 yards, Faxon thought his opponent had too much club, and he was right. Gilford put a smooth pass on the ball, but instead of cutting it flew straight—straight over everything. There was a big commotion behind the grandstands. Faxon waited for the gallery to settle and talked it over one more time with Cubby Burke, his caddy. He pulled the 5-iron and thought he hit it perfect. He was posing on it when it came down in the front bunker. The weight of disappointment buckled his knees. He couldn't believe it.

"My ball definitely got caught up in the wind," he said. "I thought the wind would help the shot, not hurt it. Even though it was a little left, I'm thinking it's on the green. Two feet right and it's perfect. It was really close to a good shot."

Walking up to the green, Faxon was approached by Wadkins and Love.

"Fax, we need this point, *We need this point!*" said Wadkins.

Love was especially charged up, and nervous.

"Fax," he said, "think about holing it."

Faxon didn't want to look back at the scoreboard and start computing things, but he could tell the situation was not great, that his point was huge, that in fact it could be the deciding point. He thought back to Riviera, and what a stud he had been there at the eighteenth hole. He could do it again.

And it looked like he was getting a lot of help from Gilford, who for the first time in the Ryder Cup seemed to be coming unglued.

As the situation was getting sorted out behind the green, bad news had arrived. Pat Rielly, the past PGA president, was the referee of the Crenshaw-Montgomerie match. Crenshaw had been closed out 2 and 1 when Montgomerie went 3–3–3–3 starting with a sixty-footer for birdie at the fourteenth and ending with only the second birdie of the matches at the seventeenth. For the second day in a row, Crenshaw hadn't made a single birdie.

"Ben came up to me coming down the eleventh hole and said he was so nervous, he was going to throw up," said Julie Crenshaw.

"I haven't read a putt for him in four years, and on Sunday he had me reading everything," said Crenshaw's caddy, Linn Strickler. "Julie saw us on the thirteenth hole and said, 'I don't know what you guys are talking about, but tell him to get it to the hole.'"

At the fourteenth, Crenshaw had ten feet for birdie, but Montgomerie knocked in what Crenshaw called a diabolical putt, and that set the Scotsman off on a run. Crenshaw missed the putt at fourteen, then ran another birdie try across the hole at fifteen. He could never get the speed of the greens, could never see the lines. All week, he was beating himself up over the putter, and it never got any better.

"I have never been wrung out like that," Crenshaw said.

Montgomerie's victory over the Masters champion moved the Europeans within one point, 11½–10½. Behind the eighteenth green, Gilford had a chipping club out. He had received relief from the grandstands and was trying to run his ball through the rough onto the green. The lob shot simply was not in his bag, and he dared not try it in this situation. Behind the green, this drove Ballesteros crazy. He knew what the outcome would be. It was inevitable.

"I knew he was going to have to hit a great chip to make four," Faxon said. "Running it through that stuff was impossible. I was nervous anyway, and I remembered that whenever you're nervous, try to stay busy. So I went up to the flag and actually paced off who was away. I said, 'David, you're two steps further away.' Seve or Gallacher said, 'Bullshit!' So the referee paced it off and he told David, 'You're two yards away.' It was just like I told him."

Gilford's ball skimmed across the rough behind the green and stuck like burlap to Velcro. He was now lying three. Advantage Faxon.

"I was actually thinking I had an easy shot, that I could hit a good shot and still make four, but I was still thinking about making it."

So was Love, who down in the fairway, at the crest of the big dip, stood up and yelled out, *"Hole it, Fax!"*

The bunker shot looked as though it had a chance. It looked like Jacobsen's putt as it cruised the left lip. Faxon though it might go, but it was hit just a little too hard. *"Check, check, check!"* said Maggert from the fairway. The shot left Faxon seven feet back down the hill, with what looked like a right-to-left break. It was almost the same putt Couples had had, except just a little shorter.

Gilford had yet to reach the green. He had a delicate little chip shot down the hill, and he played it about as well as could be expected. Gravity took over, and the ball just released and picked up speed as it rolled past the hole. "Roll, roll, roll," Wadkins said, quietly, because you're never supposed to root against your opponents. The ball stopped twelve feet from the cup.

The captain pushed the button on his walkie-talkie. "Talk to me. What's Jay doing?"

Bad news. Haas was two down with five holes to play. He needed Gilford to miss the putt. He needed to catch a break. He didn't want to see Faxon have to attempt that putt, not that he doubted Faxon. It was just that luck wasn't running his way.

Faxon had no time to think about the big picture. It was just him and Gilford. Gilford had twelve feet. He had seven feet.

"The thought was going through my mind, 'Always assume your opponent will make the putt,' but sometimes you get feelings and I really did not think that he was going to make it," Faxon said. "That was my gut. For some reason, I didn't think it was going to go in."

Gilford short-circuited everything. In a calm, almost Langer-like manner, he stepped up and hit the putt of his life, a putt every bit as good as the one Faxon had made at Riviera, maybe better considering an entire continent was riveted on it and not just an individual trying to make his first Ryder Cup team.

Maybe it surprised Faxon, but not Gallacher. "He is a good putter, with great temperament, and it turned out, it happened," he said.

So it was Faxon's turn to face the firing squad. If Couples had only gone out there and told him. "It doesn't break as much as you think." But Couples was in no position to do that. He figured Fax could handle it. Fax is one of the best putters in the world. Fax would drain it, just as he'd drained it at Riviera.

The putt never broke.

Faxon hit it right where he wanted to hit it, but it stayed on line and never touched the hole. Faxon was stunned. Back down the fairway, you could read Wadkins's lips.

"That's too bad," he said.

Faxon walked off the green in shock. He shook Gilford's hand, and Gilford's caddy's hand, but it was impossible to say a word to anyone.

"Davis was the first guy who came up. He said, 'Great try, Fax.' Then he took off running down the fairway like Edwin Moses. Freddie came up and slapped me on the back and said, 'Just sit down and try to relax,' because he'd been there in '89. I sat down and looked at the board and my stomach was tied in knots. I couldn't go out and root anybody on. At that time, it was hard to feel that way."

Love reached Wadkins.

"Where you going, Lanny?"

"I guess I better go bring Curtis in."

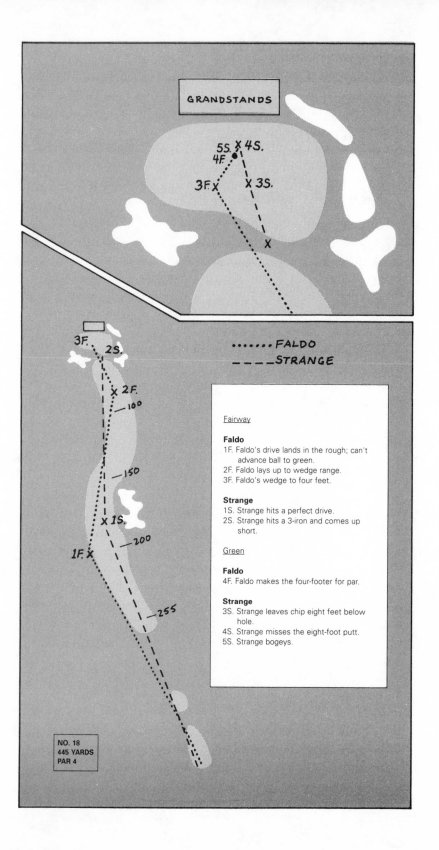

GRANDSTANDS

5S. X 4S.
4F.
3F. X   X 3S.

X

········FALDO
_____STRANGE

3F.
2S.

X 2F.
—100

—150

X 1S.
—200

1F. X
—255

Fairway

Faldo
1F. Faldo's drive lands in the rough; can't
     advance ball to green.
2F. Faldo lays up to wedge range.
3F. Faldo's wedge to four feet.

Strange
1S. Strange hits a perfect drive.
2S. Strange hits a 3-iron and comes up
     short.

Green

Faldo
4F. Faldo makes the four-footer for par.

Strange
3S. Strange leaves chip eight feet below
     hole.
4S. Strange misses the eight-foot putt.
5S. Strange bogeys.

NO. 18
445 YARDS
PAR 4

CHAPTER 19

Very Strange

They say the worst part for an athlete is watching, but Curtis Strange and Nick Faldo probably would have debated that coming down the stretch on Sunday at Oak Hill. They were trapped inside a pressure chamber, and there was no way out.

In the NBC tower behind the thirteenth green, Johnny Miller admitted he was a nervous wreck. Standing behind the gallery ropes near the crosswalk at the eighteenth hole, Dottie Mochrie said the same thing. They had both won major championships. Miller had competed in Ryder Cups. Mochrie had competed in Solheim Cups, the women's equivalent of this international torture.

"Getting kind of tight, isn't it?"

"Too tight," she said. "My hands are clammy."

There were five matches still out on the course. The U.S. led in three, but Europe apparently had one locked up and momentum in another. Torrance was one up on Roberts with a near hole in one at eleven. Walton had just birdied the fifteenth and Haas was dormie.

Only Pavin looked like a lock for the United States. At the thirteenth, he made a downhill fifteen-footer that curved the last two feet into the hole. That put him three up. No way he was going to lose that lead, not even to Langer. That would give the U.S. twelve and a half points. Still not enough.

At the seventeenth green, Lanny Wadkins was back on his walkie-talkie. He had sent Peter Jacobsen back to threaten Phil Mickelson with his life.

"What's Mickelson?" he said to his brother.

Lanny was told that his rookie anchorman was one up after a birdie at the eleventh. It might not matter.

The European team was starting to gather, sensing the upset if Faldo, their best player, could pull out this match. Montgomerie was there with Woosnam, James, their wives, and Gill Faldo, who again walked every hole.

This was a death match. Strange was the only American golfer to get the better of Faldo in a major championship, winning the eighteen-hole U.S. Open playoff by four strokes (71–75) in 1988. Before that, Faldo had taken advantage of Paul Azinger's bogey-bogey finish in the 1987 British Open at Muirfield. After that, Scott Hoch missed a two-foot putt in a 1990 Masters playoff, the following year Raymond Floyd dumped a 7-iron in the pond at the eleventh in a playoff against Faldo, and in 1982, again at Muirfield, John Cook three-putted the par-five seventeenth for par, and then bogeyed the eighteenth to hand over another major to Faldo.

Strange hadn't slept well at all Saturday night, knowing he was 0–2, knowing that it was Faldo who would be on the tee at 10:39 A.M. "I respect Nick and enjoy the way he goes about his business," Strange was thinking. "But nothing would please me more than to beat him head to head, because he's one of the world's best players."

Strange went one up with a birdie at the sixth, but Faldo won the seventh and then matched Curtis's birdie at the eighth. It was about that time that they both realized that theirs would be the swing match. Words were not spoken. It was just understood.

Strange went one up again with a birdie at the eleventh, and had a chance to go two up with a fifteen-footer at the fifteenth, but came up short. You don't want to give Faldo an opening like that. Strange knew it going up the hill to the sixteenth tee.

His swing hadn't felt good all day. It seemed as if he were surviving on Band-Aids. It was as if he had to manipulate the club just to put the ball in the fairway. He hit a good drive at sixteen, and Faldo was in the woods. He had a 6-iron from the left side of the fairway to a pin cut right middle. All he had to do was hit the green. Faldo was still in trouble, right of the green in two. If he hit the green and two-putted, chances were he would win the hole and Faldo would be dormie. The U.S. would get its half point and retain the cup.

But the Band-Aids came off. Curtis got the club trapped behind him and missed the green short and right. Later, he would say, "I honest to God couldn't have imagined hitting a worse shot, and it shocked me that it was going where it was going. You can't imagine what went through my mind."

Strange was so shaken he blew a par putt four feet past the hole and had to make that coming back just for the halve. One up with two holes to go, he went to the seventeenth tee.

This was not Curtis's favorite hole. He'd parred it on the Sunday when he won the U.S. Open. But that was six years

ago. A lot had gone on since then, most of it bad as it related
to his golf game. He was happy just to hit the fairway. So was
Faldo, for that matter.

Azinger made the observation, "I've never seen Faldo take
deep breaths before, but he's noticeably takin' some air."

This is where Wadkins picked them up. Curtis had 200
yards to the hole and 190 yards to the front. It was a 4-iron
shot. Faldo was just inside him, with 188 yards to the front
bunker.

Down on the sixteenth green, Torrance went two up with a
birdie putt about the length of his broom-handled putter. Roberts would have to win the seventeenth hole, or that was another point for Europe.

Bob Trumpy of NBC stuck a microphone at Wadkins.

"You don't look comfortable, sir."

"I'm not. I'd be a lot more comfortable if we were way
ahead. But it's looking like a typical Ryder Cup Sunday. It's
nail-biting time. I need some guys to finish things off. I've got
some good guys out there. I hope they can handle it."

Strange couldn't. His once-galvanized swing, a swing that
had won two U.S. Opens and sixteen tournaments in the '80s,
let him down, deserted him, at the worst possible time. He
didn't even come close to hitting the green, blocking the shot
right, into the spectators, short of the bunker. Faldo didn't do
much better, landing in the front left bunker. The scoreboard
said "USA 11½" in red and "Europe 11½" in blue. Lanny went
up to check out what kind of shot Curtis had. "It's a good lie,"
he reported. Then he went back to the walkie-talkie. "What's
Jay, two or three down?"

Strange came out of the tall grass with a wedge, the ball
trickling twelve feet below the hole. Not a bad shot. Not great.
But not bad.

Faldo exploded out to ten feet, just inside Strange's mark.
Paul Azinger said into his microphone, "Johnny, this is a classic match-play situation here. I'm sure Curtis loves it. These
guys are grinding."

But Curtis didn't necessarily love it—not when he missed his putt. This was the third straight opening he had given Faldo, and now there was nothing to do but watch as Fanny Sunesson lined up Nick's putter, took her six steps to the right before stopping on cue, and froze. Faldo stroked it in, and Gill Faldo was the first on her feet, clapping as a devoted wife who was out there supporting her husband. That leveled the match and sent it to the eighteenth tee.

Wadkins was waiting for Strange to walk off the green. There was a stampede to the walkway. He slapped Curtis on the back. "C'mon, Curtis, you can do it," he said. Strange had a strained look on his face. He kicked the wood chips that had been put down after Friday morning's rain. If Stephen King wrote a novel about a golfer trapped in his own worst dreams, this is what it would be like.

Faldo had honors. He missed this fairway in the foursomes Friday morning, and this one was in the same spot, down the left side into an area where it would be impossible to get home in two.

"You can do it, Curtis!" somebody yelled.

Again Strange hit the fairway. Again he missed the green, this time with a 3-iron, catching it thin and coming up short in the tangle of grass below the green. This after Faldo had to lay up. Three straight fairways. Three straight bad iron shots. Strange. Very Strange.

Behind them, Pavin had closed out Langer 3 and 2, but Torrance had matched that point with a 2-and-1 win over Roberts. That made it 12½–12½, with three matches still out. Walton had Haas dormie. Mickelson ran in another long putt on Johansson, and was one up. Strange and Faldo were all square. It was Strange and Faldo, just as they'd thought on the front side.

Faldo did what was expected. He hit a pitching wedge that stopped four feet from the hole. As Fanny went to retrieve the divot, he threw the club at the bag, a defiant gesture. Later, Faldo would say he was lucky to lay up in the first cut of rough rather than the fairway. The wedge shot had less spin on it that way, and didn't suck back.

Back at sixteen, Haas holed out from a bunker for birdie. The cheers could be faintly heard at eighteen, where Strange was walking up the bank to his ball. On each of his practice swings, the club grabbed in the deep rough. He did well to hack it out eight feet below the hole.

Out in the fairway, the Oak Hill members marshaling the hole were already second-guessing Wadkins's decision.

"Curtis is choking all over himself."

"I never liked him as a wild-card pick."

Strange lined up the putt, but he had bad vibes working. Faldo couldn't look. Azinger read it breaking a little left, but Curtis shoved it through the break. It was now out of his hands. He took a seat beside the green.

Faldo stood over the putt, and like Clark, had trouble with his equilibrium. Everything was shaking but the putter, but this was a classic Faldo situation; he was there to feed off someone else's mistakes. The putt poured in the hole. Strange's head went up on his mantel next to Azinger's, Hoch's, Floyd's, and Cook's.

"Just a hair outside and left and once I saw it ticking along nicely, I thought, 'Well, that's good,'" Faldo said. "It's a four to remember, that one."

Ballesteros was the first to hug Faldo. His eyes were red from crying. Gill Faldo gave her husband a hug. She got a half-hearted response. That gave Europe the lead for the first time, 13½–12½.

Strange was man enough to talk with reporters behind the green. "No matter how hard the press beats me up, I deserve it," he said. "They won't be any harder on me than I am on myself."

CHAPTER 20

Toast

Curtis Strange headed to the locker room, head down, walking through the gauntlet of hushed fans, not believing what had just happened. He was numb.

Corey Pavin was chasing after him, making sure he was all right, wanting to let Strange know that it was not just him, it was a team. Strange heard him, and he appreciated it, but sometimes those words have no meaning.

Cubby Burke came into the team room. He was broken up over Faxon's loss to Gilford. Then it was Strange who became the voice of reason. "C'mon," he said. "We've got to get back out and support the last two matches."

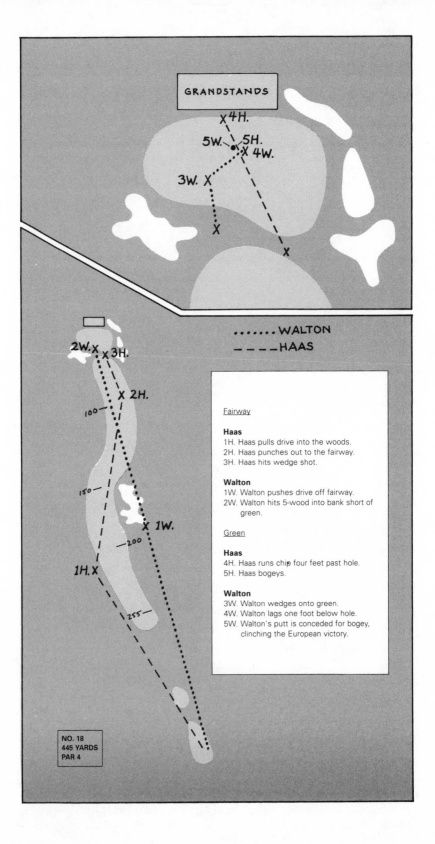

GRANDSTANDS

X 4H.

5W. 5H.
X 4W.

3W. X

X

········WALTON
— — — —HAAS

2W. X
X 3H.

X 2H.

100

150

X 1W.

200

1H. X

255

Fairway

Haas
1H. Haas pulls drive into the woods.
2H. Haas punches out to the fairway.
3H. Haas hits wedge shot.

Walton
1W. Walton pushes drive off fairway.
2W. Walton hits 5-wood into bank short of
green.

Green

Haas
4H. Haas runs chip four feet past hole.
5H. Haas bogeys.

Walton
3W. Walton wedges onto green.
4W. Walton lags one foot below hole.
5W. Walton's putt is conceded for bogey,
clinching the European victory.

NO. 18
445 YARDS
PAR 4

The United States team had one last desperate chance.

Jay Haas. Maybe Strange's old Wake Forest teammate could bail the U.S. team out and get Strange off the hook. He had already holed out from a bunker at sixteen. Maybe there would be a happy ending to this after all.

If Haas could just get his match against Philip Walton, maybe he could sneak out a halve and the Americans would escape with a 14–14 tie and retain the Cup the way Europe had in 1989.

The twelfth and final match suddenly did not mean anything except to the friends and families of Phil Mickelson and Per-Ulrik Johansson. It was inconsequential.

Haas had to get a half point, otherwise it was over.

Walking back out to the seventeenth green, Wadkins was followed by Sam Torrance and the European contingent. It was 2:47 P.M. From behind the ropes, a European fan called out, "Sam, have we won it?"

The Scotsman pointed to the green. "We're two up with two to play."

When Torrance walked through the gallery ropes, Mark James was there to reassure him. "All we need are two halves."

Haas had already hit one of the best iron shots of his career, from two hundred yards out, under tree branches, to fifteen feet below the hole. Walton hit a bump-and-run shot he learned as a boy who grew up playing the hardpan links courses around Dublin.

"That looks short," said a hopeful American fan.

"No, that's a great shot," said Derek Lawrenson, a British journalist.

The ball stopped four feet short. Very makable, even for Walton, who was nervously toting the long putter.

A lady broke out the European flag and started to wave it.

An American fan in the crowd said, "He makes that putt and we're toast."

Haas plumb-bobbed the putt and checked it out from every

conceivable angle. It was so quiet you could hear the blimp's motors whirring overhead.

"Funny how it's always the Irish, isn't it?" said Peter Higgs, a London columnist. He made a good point—it was Eamonn Darcy who clinched it for Europe at Muirfield Village in 1987, and Christy O'Connor, Jr., who did the same at the Belfry in 1989.

It was 2:54 P.M. on a perfect afternoon in Rochester, New York. The sun was shining. The sweaters were off. On any day, men shouldn't be subjected to such crazed torture, but this is what they spend two years fighting for, the right to decide it. It had come down to a fifteen-foot putt for Haas and a four-foot putt for Walton. Who was going to blink?

They both did.

First Haas, then Walton.

Neither one as much as touched the hole.

New life for the Americans.

Heartache for the Europeans. They tore handfuls of grass getting up off the ground.

"I realized when I missed that putt how important our match was," Walton said. "The crowd in the stands went totally wild. I couldn't see the end match on the scoreboard, because there were people standing there and there were heads blocking it. Sam Torrance came up as I walked through the crowd and said, 'C'mon, you're still one up!' Then I realized this is it."

Haas had won the sixteenth and seventeenth holes with a birdie and a par. He had one more hole to go and needed one more miracle. His kids were out there in the crowd somewhere. So was Billy Harmon, and his wife, Janice. It was a madhouse. An utter madhouse. How were you supposed to play golf in the middle of something like this?

"*C'mon, Jay!*" someone yelled. "*Work hard!*"

Haas hadn't played the eighteenth hole since the practice rounds. He hadn't liked it then and he didn't like it now under these conditions, 440 yards needing a par from himself and a disaster out of Walton.

Azinger: "Your arms are hot, they feel heavy. Your fingertips are throbbing. You can feel your pulse in your eyeballs. It's unbelievable."

Haas has a little hitch at the top of his backswing. It helps him to set the club. But with this type of pressure, the type of pressure Calcavecchia felt at Kiawah Island and Rocca at the Belfry, Jay Haas hit one of the worst drives of his life. Just by the sound, Miller could tell in the broadcast booth that he had popped it up. Torrance went sprinting down the fairway to tell Gallacher where Haas's ball had landed. He didn't get there before Walton hit a weak slice into the right rough. By the time he reached the ball, Gallacher had already scouted it out. He gave Walton the thumbs-up. That meant a good lie.

"It was just a nerve-wracking experience," said Walton. "I went back to the tee, and people are right behind you, close enough to touch you. I could feel the hair standing on the back of my head, and then my right leg started shaking. It wasn't my favorite tee shot all week anyway. I was trying to squeeze the thing down the left side, and it just moved on me."

It was 3:02 P.M., and Haas had hit it in a spot only Seve Ballesteros and the club's 15-handicappers had seen. It was deep in the trees. He had not gotten the type of bounce Johansson got Friday morning, when his drive came down in an opening, on a trampled lie. This was Jail City, branches and tree trunks and a green that looked four miles away. It was hard for Haas to even figure an avenue of escape. The marshals tried to move the gallery. Ben Crenshaw took a drag on his cigarette. It went on like this for a while, Haas trying to figure out whether to play a draw or a cut, just to lay up. Walton was in the right rough, pacing, already knowing his yardage and what club he would hit to the green. He had a metal wood in his hands.

"When I was playing that last hole," Walton would say one

month after the Ryder Cup, "it felt like I was never going to get to that green."

Haas finally elected to go with the hook, drawing a shot into the fairway, near where Faldo had to lay up. The ball had barely stopped rolling when Walton hit his shot into the bank short of the green. From there, the worst he could make was bogey. Haas had to get it up-and-down, or it was over.

From ninety-seven yards, Haas would save par maybe eight times out of ten. But in this situation, one of the best wedge players on the PGA Tour couldn't even put the ball on the green. His shot carried ten feet on the putting surface, but spun back into the fringe. Haas would have to pull a Pavin and chip it in.

"All I wanted to do was get it to ten feet," Haas said. "I wish I could have that shot over."

Walton was already down by the bank, looking for his ball in the deep grass. "I nearly walked on it," he said. "I was halfway up the bank and I thought to myself, 'Hold on,' and as I stopped I looked down and there it was between my two feet. One of the spectators said, 'Hey, did you walk on it?' I had a feeling I was pretty close."

Shots such as the one Walton faced are not common in Europe. But during the practice rounds, Woosnam gave Walton a lesson on how to pitch from deep U.S. Open–style rough. This was a hell of a situation to try that shot, but Walton went with it, dropping the club on the ball and watching as it came out of the rough.

Out in the fairway, PGA CEO Jim Awtrey was watching with PGA Tour commissioner Tim Finchem. Their knees buckled in unison.

"It looked like the ball wasn't going to clear," said Awtrey.

"It looked like he chunked it into the bank," said Finchem.

"That ball was within an inch of hanging up," said NBC's John Schroeder.

"I just didn't want to get it above the hole," said Walton.

"From the back to the front of that green is treacherous. You can have an eight-foot putt and run it fifteen feet past."

Haas didn't have a Pavin in him. He didn't want to leave it short again, so he ran the chip shot six feet past the hole. It was a shot of desperation and frustration. The sentence had been pronounced. It was now just a formality of the executioner pulling the rope on the guillotine, sending the blade down for its final act of death. All Walton had to do now was two-putt from twenty feet, straight up the hill.

It wasn't until after, flying home on the Concorde, in a quiet moment of reflection, that the Irishman realized what a mess he could have made of that situation. "Over the putt itself, my concentration could not have been better. On the plane, on the other hand, I suddenly started thinking: "What if I do something crazy over this putt? . . . What if I whack it miles past the hole and mess things up for everyone?"

It didn't happen. Philip Walton, who practiced his putting on the beaches of Malahide, just across from Portmarnock, lagged up to two inches and was conceded the tap-in and the match. His name would go down in Irish lore next to Darcy's and O'Connor's as the man who won the Ryder Cup. The nineteen-inch gold trophy Sam Ryder bought for £250 sixty-eight years earlier would be flying back on the Concorde. It would be going home.

CHAPTER 21

Blue Sunday

Back out on the seventeenth green, it was Davis Love's job to tell Phil Mickelson that the matches were over, that Jay Haas had lost to Philip Walton, essentially that it didn't matter what happened in his match with Per-Ulrik Johansson. They were just playing for pride. They had talked about doing this someday when they were at Arizona State, playing each other in the last singles match to decide the Ryder Cup. They thought that's what they were doing, bringing up the rear on Sunday at Oak Hill.

By the time they teed off, it was 11:07 A.M. and the day had taken shape. Warming up on the range, they could watch the Jumbotron and see Clark chip in at two and James hole from the bunker at three. They could see a lot of blue on the board, which meant a shift in the tide.

It was important for Mickelson to prove to Wadkins that he was not some selfish wet-behind-the-ears kid who thought he could take on the world. He felt Wadkins had had a chip on his shoulder ever since he and Azinger had beaten Lanny and Tom Watson in a practice round the Tuesday before the Masters. It was supposedly the first time Wadkins and Watson had ever lost on a Tuesday, and the veterans didn't take kindly to it. The joke on the U.S. team had become that Mickelson wanted to play in six of the five matches, and his confrontation with Wadkins on Friday night had really become the only uncomfortable scene of the week for the U.S. team.

And it was equally important for Johansson to prove something to Mickelson, because it was Mickelson getting all the publicity at Arizona State by winning three NCAA titles and the U.S. Amateur and the 1991 Northern Telecom Open as an amateur. Per had a game, too. And he was out to show it.

The Swede came out smoking with birdies on the second, third, fourth, and sixth holes to go three up. He had seven putts walking off the sixth green, and had won four straight holes. The turning point came at the seventh. Johansson was in the greenside bunker in two. Mickelson was to the left of the green, on a tight lie, hitting to a pin cut tight to the left edge. He had no green to work with and a skull lie off a crosswalk, and was looking at going four down in a hurry.

But Mickelson hit a soft lob shot that not too many people can pull off. He got the club under the ball, and the ball plopped on the green as if it were made of cookie dough. "I've seen him do that before," Johansson said. Mickelson holed his putt and Johansson lipped out, the ball doing a 180 and coming back at him. Instead of four up, he was only two up. That's a big psychological difference in match play, especially with eleven holes to go.

"At the turn I looked at the board and saw the Europeans

were beating us in almost every match," Mickelson said. "We needed to do something to turn around, which I thought I could do by making some birdies. I thought it would be a lift for the entire team, if they heard the roars."

Mickelson went on a tear starting at the tenth. With three straight birdies, he went one up. "At twelve he was putting downhill, forty feet away, and he makes it dead center," said Mickelson's caddy, Jim McKay. "He made that putt like you and I make a two-footer. The roar was scary. It was one of those things I'll never forget. We go one up, and get to the next tee, and he hits 3-wood two hundred and seventy yards down the middle. He handed the club to me, pointed to his own arm, and it had goose bumps on it. I did, too. We were both in the middle of something really exciting."

It was getting crazy. Coming off the twelfth green, Mickelson heard a guy in the gallery tell his fiancée, Amy McBride, "Excuse me. Are you going to marry him? Well, you better hurry up, because if you don't, I will." The man was smitten.

Johansson won the fourteenth with a par, but lost the fifteenth with a three-putt bogey. They were both watching the scoreboard, trying to see what was going on with Faldo and Strange, and Haas and Walton.

"Don't worry about anything else, just win your match, you're playing great, just close this guy out," Love said to Mickelson coming down sixteen.

They came to the seventeenth with Mickelson one up. Mickelson was so pumped up he reached the green on the 458-yard par four with a 3-wood and a 6-iron. That's when Love gave Mickelson the bad news. Mickelson waited until Johansson had played his fourth shot.

"Per," he said, "it's over. You won. You won the Ryder Cup."

Johansson didn't know how to feel. He wanted to beat Mickelson so badly, but there was something more important than that. He embraced Mickelson and looked for somebody to celebrate with, but they were all down by the eighteenth green, dancing and crying and hugging.

CHAPTER 22

Celebration

The shock was felt on both sides. Up on the eighteenth green one team was celebrating, the other was in denial. Two points down going into Sunday, the Europeans had pulled off the biggest upset in Ryder Cup history. "It doesn't seem possible," a stunned Azinger said in the NBC booth. But it was possible. Europe had stolen the Ryder Cup, and now Gallacher was leaving the celebration to pick up Johansson at the seventeenth green. He saw Wadkins and stopped his golf cart. The two captains embraced.

"Bernard," Wadkins said. "Enjoy it."

Prince Andrew, the Duke of York, was walking in from the final match.

He stopped to offer condolences to Wadkins and his wife, Penny.

"We'll do it again in two years' time," the prince said.

"We'll be there in full force," promised Wadkins.

Love was walking in from seventeen, and Rocca was walking out to find Johansson. Away from the cameras, they embraced like brothers. Love was glad nobody caught that on film. It was too private a moment. "People wouldn't understand the emotion between the two of us," he said. "That's the one thing I'll take away from this Ryder Cup."

It was 3:23 P.M. Mickelson was riding in with Amy McBride.

"I thought it would be enough looking at the scoreboard," he said. "What happened? Did Curtis bogey the last hole?"

It was 3:24 P.M. Johansson appeared in the passenger seat of a golf cart, both arms extended, the wind blowing through his hair. Rocca spotted him, ran to the cart, pulled Johansson into his arms, spun him around, and carried his teammate forty yards down the fairway, heading toward the green, where magnum bottles of champagne were popping.

"He's so strong, and I'm not so heavy, he almost squeezed me to death there," Johansson said of Rocca. "He's like a big bear."

The European players were being interviewed by NBC, Sky Sports, BBC Radio, and the writers covering the event. It was already after 8:00 P.M. on Fleet Street in London. There was still time to get quotes for the morning papers.

"We've gone into the singles ahead the last four times, and it's very difficult to lead from the front in this competition," said Woosnam. "Everybody got psyched up, pumped up, thinking we're going to do it, we've got nothing to lose. And we came up trumps this time."

An interviewer said in a coddling British accent that there were cheers of despair at Kiawah, but cheers of joy at Oak Hill. Woosie beamed.

"I said it was going to be a close match, and it was," he said. "It's going to be close every time. We had a fantastic week. It just shows that European golf is getting bigger and stronger. For any sponsors out there, get on the bandwagon. What a day for us. This will go down in history. The one in '87 was the best, because it was the first time we won on their soil. This was close to it. The new young guys on the team have done terrific. It's a great feeling for them. And these old guys can do it, too."

Gallacher was holding a glass of champagne.

"I feel so much for this team," he says. "The last two Ryder Cups have been so hard going out there to the prize-giving when the Americans had won the trophy. I want to walk out there to get the trophy tonight. I want to say, 'Bad luck, Lanny.' And I want to take that trophy back to Dublin first and then take it back to Wentworth."

Any chance of you being Ryder Cup captain, again? he was asked.

"No chance. No chance."

Bernhard Langer was more analytical.

"It's difficult to put into words right now," he said. "We've lost the last two Ryder Cup matches by the very smallest of margins possible. It's been extremely close, which is good for the game of golf. But all that nonsense that the Americans would run away with the thing was just that—nonsense. They won very closely the last two times and we won closely this time. That doesn't mean we're dominating, but this time we were just that little bit better. We're looking forward to the next one, which will hopefully be just as close again."

Bob Trumpy asked the tough question to Curtis Strange on network TV.

"Do you beat yourself up for this?"

Curtis could barely get the words out.

"Oh . . . sure . . . yeah . . . for a long time."

CHAPTER 23

Handling Defeat

The door closed in the team room, but it couldn't muffle the sounds coming in from outside. The European fans were raucous, singing, "We won the Cup. We won the Cup. Heigho, the derry oh, we won the Cup." Over and over they sang it, louder and louder. Then they started a new ditty, led by the European wives, which was a takeoff on *West Side Story*. "We won the Cup in *A-mer-e-ka!* We won the Cup in *A-mer-e-ka!*" There were loud roars of laughter. Ian Woosnam had opened his mouth wide while a glass of champagne was poured down his throat. Not a drop was spilled.

Most of the U.S. team were

stunned. Ben Crenshaw sat there, birdieless and winless, unable to say a word. Players were crying. The players' wives were crying. About the only player who had it under control, who had already put it in perspective, who accepted this for what it was, was Pavin.

"I thought the whole thing was a great experience," he would say. "It was the first time I was on a losing team. In some ways, it didn't matter that much. Certainly I wanted to win, and that was very important, but I was happy for them, for the Europeans, too. Those guys worked just as hard as we did. We all worked hard, all competed hard. The whole idea of the Ryder Cup is to have friendly matches between the Europeans and the U.S. players. That is what they're all about, for goodwill and the game of golf. Sure, we want to win, and sure, they want to win, and sometimes we tie, but that's the way it is. I didn't know how I was going to take it, actually, being on a losing team, but it didn't bother me, really. The only time I had tears in my eyes, almost, was when Sam walked up to me, and I congratulated him, and he was kind of crying, and he almost made me cry, watching him. That was about the only time I almost lost it a little bit. I was happy for him, and sad for our guys. Those guys are very experienced players, and they know how to handle it and keep it in perspective. We go through times that are tough, and times that are good, and we learn how to deal with both of them."

Azinger didn't realize how devastating a loss this was until his wife, Toni, came to the NBC booth. She was in tears. It made Azinger realize that he owed it to the team to speak to them, to share with them a little bit of what he had gone through.

When Azinger came into the room, Curtis and Sarah Strange were sitting at the same table with Ben and Julie Crenshaw. They were the two oldest members of the team; between them they had four major championships and over thirty-six PGA Tour victories. Yet this week, they were shut out, a combined 0-for-6. Crenshaw was in a stupor. Strange was in the deepest of funks.

"I just want to put this in perspective for you," Azinger said. "I'm sorry this happened, but you know, eighteen months ago, I was dying of cancer. The reality here is that this is just golf. You lost as a team. There is not one individual in this room who has the burden to bear for this loss."

Peter Jacobsen heard that speech and felt guilty for feeling so bad. Yeah, he was down after losing to Clark, about not being able to close the deal, but what Azinger said really hit home. He thought about his father dying of cancer at seventy-five and his brother dying of AIDS at thirty-two and he looked up and saw Azinger crying as he gave his talk and then he, too, started crying. He was proud of Azinger for having the courage to come into that room and say that. He was crying tears of shame, because he felt so bad about losing a stinking golf match.

"That was the defining moment for me of the Ryder Cup," Jacobsen said. "At that point, I put the loss behind me. I was just glad to be there with eleven other players and all the wives and Lanny and Penny. Lanny did everything that was humanly possible. He was just an unbelievable captain."

The players had to get dressed for the closing ceremonies, putting on their gray blazers for the forty-five-minute public send-off. And they dreaded it. Wadkins told them, "Go out there and hold your heads up and act like the champions you are. In golf, it doesn't always work out, you don't always win, regardless of how hard you work or how good you play. If you've got to lose, let's show some dignity and class. Nobody likes to work on being a good loser, but we are the hosts this week, and we should go out there and hold our heads up."

The teams marched out in alphabetical order, the same way they had marched out for the opening ceremonies. Wadkins was next to Gallacher. They were followed by Ballesteros and Crenshaw, and it went all the way down to Woosnam and Strange. Curtis looked fine. Azinger had made him realize there are people in this world facing life-and-death struggles.

Then he got up on the stage and looked down at Sarah. She was crying. He started crying, too.

"I was crying because I couldn't be up there for him," she said. "I feel like having been Lanny's choice, and pick, we felt more pressure. To have felt honored that Lanny did that, respected his golf game that much to pick him, and to not come through for Lanny, that was the hardest part for us."

This team had become so close, so much like a family, that they had shared a communal togetherness that was not normally part of life on the PGA Tour. To have it end like this just didn't seem right. It was a total shock, and it would take some of them months to get over it. The shame was, they would be remembered as a losing team, but people on the outside would never comprehend just how tight they really were, or how much heart they put into this Ryder Cup.

"It was all so special, a very, very meaningful time," Sarah Strange said. "It was just a heartwarming feeling to be a part of that. Plus, it's such a patriotic thing, and I'm emotional anyway. We have Halloween parties and I cry at that."

Wadkins walked by Sarah as he was about to walk up to the stage. He saw she had been crying. He said, "It's all right," and that set her off again. At the podium, Tom Addis, the PGA's president, announced that Europe would be keeping the Cup for the first time since 1989. Up on the Jumbotron screen, there was a 38 x 20-foot image of Curtis Strange with his hand covering his face.

The business of presenting the trophy to the Europeans was the hardest part of the ceremony. Handing over that nineteen-inch gold cup with little Abe Mitchell on top was like handing over the Holy Grail. Wadkins commended the Europeans for being great sportsmen and great gentlemen. He had his U.S. team stand up and applaud them. He singled out Gallacher for a job well done. "I know what Bernard's been through," he said. "I'm very, very happy for Bernard."

When he started talking about his own team, about what it

meant to captain them, Wadkins started to lose it. His voice breaking up, Wadkins was saved by Gallacher, who stepped to the podium and said, "Let me help you out, Lanny."

Wadkins response: "Been there, done that."

He concluded by telling Gallacher and the Europeans to savor their victory, because 1997 would come quickly, and he might be there in Valderrama as a player trying to wrestle the Cup back. "Enjoy your time with this pretty little thing," he said. "'Cause two years from now, we're comin' to get it."

It was 4:28 in the afternoon when Bernard Gallacher thanked Lanny Wadkins for being the greatest American captain of all time, when Bernard Gallacher, after eight Ryder Cups as a player, and three as a captain, could finally take the Ryder Cup home with him. But he didn't gloat. He was as much a gentleman in victory as he had been in defeat.

"I've been saying for six years there's nothing between these two teams," he said. "It's the team of the day. Today was our day. No doubt in Valderrama, it will go down to the last green again. And we'll begin practice on Tuesday."

At 4:49, after all the national anthems were played and the flags taken down, the teams filed back to the clubhouse. Ballesteros and Crenshaw had their arms around each other. They were talking not only about Sunday, but the whole week, and what an emotional week it had been. A big part of Crenshaw was happy for Seve, and happy for the Europeans even. It was a clean fight. Even Seve was on his best behavior.

"I've watched him play, all of us have, and although he was certainly not at his best, I had to admire him for doing what he did," Crenshaw said. "He fought for whatever he had."

He also admired the European team, for doing what they had done, for coming back from two points down on Sunday, for coming to Oak Hill and winning on a course they were not supposed to win on, winning with a team that certainly wasn't Europe's strongest Ryder Cup team.

"They scrapped with everything they had," Crenshaw said.

"Forget about the hole in ones. They holed out more than we did, they got up and down more than we did, they made more crucial ten-foot putts to keep their matches alive and keep their confidence going into the next hole. I didn't feel we did enough of that. I think we did well hitting the ball. All of us play good golf tee to green. But we didn't see enough of our own putts go in. We didn't do the things necessary to keep you in an eighteen-hole match. I remember, Bobby Jones detested an eighteen-hole match. He didn't feel like you have enough time. But that's beside the point. The Europeans got the ball in the hole quicker than we did."

The American press was waiting outside the clubhouse. There were a few one-on-one interviews.

Faxon's lip was quivering.

"I feel terrible," he said. "For the guys. For Lanny. I let them down."

"I didn't think they could beat us today," said Strange. "I thought we were too good."

The team went to the press tent as a unit. Strange hung around outside afterward. Maybe he thought it would soften the blows he would take the next day.

"I was in a position where I was supposed to come through, and I didn't," he said. "My team needed me and I let them down. I feel for them."

The dinner that night went on forever. There was harp music and too much time between courses and Prince Andrew was there, so the European team didn't really party like they wanted to. Faxon was still being hard on himself, thinking about his shot into eighteen. "Okay, was I there mentally? Was I over the ball thinking good thoughts?" He had to answer yes. In fact, he had this vision of making that putt against Gilford, and raising his arms the way Love had after beating Rocca at the Belfry, then looking back down the fairway to Lanny.

But then he thought: "I had a seven-footer to win the Ryder

Cup and I missed it." He went back and forth, back and forth with it, until Pavin told him to forget it, put it behind him, don't beat up yourself.

"Hey, listen," he said. "I know that's the easy way to think, and we all think that way, but everybody could have made a difference."

The Loves were sitting with the Wadkinses, and it wasn't very exciting dinner conversation. "It was the saddest thing I've ever been through," said Love. "Lanny with his head down, staring at his plate, not wanting to eat, having to make a speech. It was awful. Robin kept saying, 'Let's talk about something.' And I'd say, 'What do you want to talk about?' It was hard. Everybody wants to deal with it their own way, but there's nothing you can say."

Maybe sadder than Wadkins was Gill Faldo. The picture of her late that afternoon, sitting in a clubhouse window, toasting the European fans with a glass of champagne, was truly a telling one. Nick was nowhere in sight, and she was there alone, framed in that window, probably knowing it was over but not quite ready to admit it.

That night, after a few more glasses of champagne, she was asking Fred Couples, of all people, to convince Nick that leaving her was the wrong thing to do. "To me, the saddest thing wasn't losing the Ryder Cup," said Julie Crenshaw. "It was Gill Faldo on the American side of the room saying goodbye and asking us to put in a good word for her. I told her, 'You don't need it. You're a great gal.'"

Love found himself in an awkward situation. When the dinner was breaking up, he was giving Gill Faldo a big hug, and she was talking to Robin, crying on her shoulder. Davis didn't really know Gill Faldo that well, but he was trying to be nice, trying to say the right thing, something like " We'll all be thinking of you," when Nick came up and said, "All right, dear," as if nothing were wrong.

"I'm sure he was mad at all of us for that," Love said. "Everybody kind of knew it was over. She had been tough all week. I told her she should be proud of herself for hanging with him. 'You deserve a lot better.' That was unbelievable that she did all that. I guess it was disbelief for her, maybe, hoping that it wasn't true."

In his bed that night at the Woodcliff, Wadkins was just getting to sleep when the phone rang. It startled him, and when he looked at the clock, it was midnight. Who in the world? Wadkins picked up the receiver. It was Tom Watson calling from his home in Kansas City. Wadkins was physically and emotionally gone. Watson just wanted to tell him, one captain to another, that he'd done a hell of a job.

CHAPTER 24

Monday

They woke up at the Woodcliff, turned on *SportsCenter*, and started getting ripped almost immediately. Keith Olbermann had changed the name from Oak Hill to Choke Hill. Later in the show, the ESPN anchor read from a report filed by Jim Litke, the Associated Press columnist. Litke had called it a clinic in how to throw up.

The Concorde was fueled and waiting at Rochester International Airport. On the TV, Colin Montgomerie was being interviewed on the eighteenth green. "To get seven and a half out of twelve points is a daunting task," he said, his jaw set. "But it just shows how good our tour is and silences our critics."

It would be the U.S. team that would have to deal with the critics. Strange would take most of the shots, but Wadkins would be second-guessed for taking him as a wild-card pick instead of Janzen. It would go on for weeks. There would be charges of cronyism. The U.S. points system would be examined. *Golf World* and Jim Herre at *SI* would look back at their charts and see they hadn't been far off. The PGA Tour would be called soft once again, because four players, Jacobsen, Faxon, Strange, and Haas, hadn't been able to win the eighteenth hole on Sunday. It had been the same in 1987, when the United States didn't win one match at eighteen. It had been the same in 1989, when Stewart, Calcavecchia, Couples, and Ken Green lost the eighteenth hole in succession. People would forget that of the four matches that went to the eighteenth hole on Friday and Saturday, the U.S. team had won three of them. Lehman hit the big 5-iron in the rain and made the putt Friday morning. Roberts hit the wedge shot and Jacobsen made the three-footer Saturday afternoon. Pavin chipped in Saturday evening.

On the streets of Europe, the newspapers had done a 360. Giant pictures ran of Ballesteros, tears running down his face, hugging Walton. The *Sun*'s headline was: "Hankie Doodle Dandy! Tears As We Spank Yanks in Ryder Cup." One paper called it the "Cryder Cup." The Spanish sports daily *Marca* said that "Seve, although he lost his [singles] match, was once again the glue that held Europe together." The paper quoted Gallacher as saying. "The whole team felt it was about time we did something for Seve, because he's been the inspiration behind this team on many occasions."

At the Rochester airport, Ken Schofield, the executive director of the European Tour, was talking about the difference between this team and the one Tony Jacklin coached at Muirfield Village, how Jacklin had three teams that were six of the best players in the world—Ballesteros-Olazábal, Faldo-

Woosnam, Langer-Lyle—while Gallacher had to keep shuffling his lineup trying to find the right combinations just to
keep it close. This vindicated Schofield and the European
team selection process. They didn't need three or four wild-
card picks after all. They won without Olazábal, with Ballesteros playing at substandard form, and with Faldo in the
midst of what the players on both teams knew was a separa-
tion from his wife.

"This was perhaps our greatest victory," Schofield said.
"This was not our best team, but it came over here and won
on their soil. The credit goes to Bernard Gallacher and the
twelve players."

The European team was in the international departure
lounge. A bite from Lanny Wadkins, taped Sunday night outside the clubhouse, was being shown on ESPN.

"Bernard's been through a lot of criticism, particularly
from Tony Jacklin, who's been a real jerk," says Wadkins.

The U.S. captain was asked about the criticism he will certainly face over the selection of Strange.

"I could care less," he says. "Tell me something that's going
to worry me."

David Gilford, who had played in four matches for Europe,
winning three of them, was brought out for an interview. He
was asked about what it had been like Saturday night in the
team room after Pavin chipped in, and the way Gilford described it, Faldo and Langer had simply come in, taken their
shoes and socks off, and had a drink. When they acted as if it
were nothing, the rest of the team had, too.

"Bernard Gallacher liked the draw," Gilford said. "But we
were wondering if Lanny had the room bugged."

Most of the questions were about Ballesteros being the captain at Valderrama in 1997. Bernhard Langer predicted that
Seve would have his game in shape by then, and would qualify
for the team. Gallacher once again claimed that he had captained his last Ryder Cup match, but he had said that twice
before.

"It's going to feel great to get home, to get to Wentworth and play Saturday golf," Gallacher said. "I'm going to be there [at Valderrama], but I'll be there behind the ropes."

The team rode an escalator upstairs to the departure concourse, passing under a Kodak picture of the Concorde parked at Rochester Airport the previous Monday morning. Lester Calkins and his wife, Hazel, had been waiting since 6:00 A.M. They made the drive in from the town of Greece, New York. "We're golf fans," Lester explained. "We came up to something we couldn't see in person. We couldn't get tickets. So we watched on TV."

There were not two thousand people at the airport on this Monday morning. There were maybe twenty people there to send the European team off. A Spanish man said, "*Muy bien,* Seve," as Ballesteros walked past. Jimmy Kidd, Tom Younger, and Ian Ferrier were there from Gleneagles Golf Developments in Scotland to catch a commercial flight back to New York and eventually Glasgow. They were all still hoarse from the celebration at the clubhouse, especially after singing the *West Side Story* rendition of "We Won the Cup in America" led by Jane James and the European wives.

"I can't speak for the others," Younger said, "but I was definitely sober."

Schofield, from the town of Auchterarder, Perthshire, spotted the three Scotsmen from Gleneagles and mentioned that it was a great day for their country. St. Johnsone and Hibs both won in football, too, and Younger remembers thinking how the executive director had his priorities in order.

Three hours later, the Concorde came down through the clouds over Ireland, and they could see the roads jammed leading to the airport. "It was amazing when we landed in Dublin," said Johansson. "For ten miles, everybody was flashing their beams." Forty miles from the runway, the team got the news that there were five thousand people at the airport, including Prime Minister John Bruton. It was raining hard when the Concorde taxied to a stop. People were on the roof of the terminal, umbrellas up, trying to get a glimpse of the plane as the door opened.

The first man out was Philip Walton.

He was carrying the Ryder Cup.

EPILOGUE

Is it worth it?

They always seem to come away from the Ryder Cup asking that question. What will happen to Curtis Strange? Will he become like Calcavecchia and take four years to recover, or will this rekindle an old fire?

"It's getting almost too much to bear, this Ryder Cup," Gallacher said on the eighteenth green Sunday.

They started saying that in 1989 when the two teams tied at the Belfry. They said it again after seeing Calcavecchia and Langer go through the wringer at Kiawah Island. They said it after the Rocca Choke-A in 1993. And now they were saying it again at Oak Hill, after seeing Jay Haas fail to hit a green with a wedge from less than a hundred yards away.

"There's too much pressure, too much pressure," said Ballesteros. "People don't realize how much pressure Jay Haas was under."

Yet, they will be back at Valderrama, some of them anyway, subjecting themselves to this form of torture. The Ryder Cup was given a new life by the European victory. Players will want to make the American team even more now, to win the Cup back. The excitement in Europe will be taking the matches to Spain for the first time, where Ballesteros is king.

The letters started arriving in Lanny Wadkins's mailbox as soon as he got home to Dallas. There were piles of them, and most were positive, but some were vicious personal attacks. In August, Wadkins had said he could take the heat, that it was his butt on the line. But when the criticism hit him, Wadkins knew what it was like to be the losing football coach in a Super Bowl or baseball manager in a World Series.

He got a call from Raymond Floyd, supporting him. Those who had been there, who had captained a Ryder Cup, knew that Wadkins had done a hell of a job. "When our team has a lead going into Sunday, it should be a cakewalk," Wadkins said. "The guys were up. On Saturday night, they wanted to see the video I showed them on Monday night of the past captains. It's pretty damn inspirational."

Two weeks later, at the Walt Disney World Classic in Orlando, Wadkins was asked if he had had time to reflect on what had gone wrong that last day. There was nothing he would have done differently.

"Nobody got off to a good start that last day," he said. "I never saw the guys up. The Europeans were ahead in every match, or even. We never had six or seven guys on the board up, which has happened in the past. We never got a foothold. We never had one guy except for Lehman who won semi-big. We've always had a couple of guys, like Kite, take guys out six and five, and get some quick points on the board. I think the amazing thing about the whole thing is that some people thought we were too high after Corey's chip-in, but I didn't think so. Standing on the first tee that last day watching the guys come out to play, they were ready. I mean, it looked like they were almost floating, like they were walking a half stride quicker than normal. They were pumped up. They wanted to go. These guys wanted to win. They wanted to win big and hard. The Europeans, I thought on the first tee, had the attitude of, 'Well, let's go play.' A lot of times when you go out with that attitude, you just let it go. They had three chip-ins or hole-outs in the first three groups, and I said, 'This is not good. This is not a good sign.' You can read signs in golf, and that's one of the things you don't like in golf when you're on the other side."

Curtis Strange went to Bermuda the day after the Ryder Cup and won the Merrill Lynch Shootout. Then he went home to Virginia and started reading the papers. By Thursday, *Golf World* and *Sports Illustrated* had arrived. He was wrong about one thing. The press wasn't as hard on him as he was on himself.

The Tuesday of the Disney World tournament, Strange spent an hour talking to Big Al Coleman's morning sports talk show on WRVH in Richmond. He wanted an open forum to air some of his feelings. He took calls. What hurt him most was Rick Reilly's story and the "Wrong Man, Wrong Time" headline in *SI*. He tried to explain that yes, he was a friend of Lanny's, but that in eighteen years on tour, they had never once been out to dinner.

"He honestly felt I could help the team and bring some things to the team other than my golf game, and hopefully I did," Strange said. "Lanny's a very proud person. He enjoys and loves the Ryder Cup, but more than that he loves his country and he wants to represent his country the best way he can. He wouldn't have jeopardized that by picking me."

Wadkins had waited eight days before calling Strange. He said at Disney World, "I was as concerned about him and it turns out he was concerned about me. But we're both big boys. We've had adversity before. It wasn't the first time and it won't be the last, unfortunately. I just told him not to worry about it. Number one, he didn't ask to be picked. He's probably the only person who didn't ask to be picked, quite honestly."

Two weeks later, at the Texas Open, Tom Kite was asked what he thought Strange's reaction would be. Kite was quite honest. "Certainly what he went through at the Ryder Cup was a tough experience, but he didn't get to where he has been by rolling over and playing dead, and I don't anticipate he will now. It would shock me. Obviously he's got two choices. He can say, 'Well, that was more than I can handle,' and roll over. Or he can say, 'This is gonna make me a better player,' and come back and show people he can handle it."

Until he saw him at the Las Vegas Invitational, Davis Love was uncertain about which direction Strange would go. "I was worried about him at first, right afterwards, thinking he had already done a little bit of TV, he hasn't been playing that much, he kind of makes a comeback, gets on the Ryder Cup team, has it thrown on his shoulders the last hole, and he doesn't come through," Love said from his home at Sea Island, Georgia. "I thought he might be saying, 'I've had enough. I don't want to deal with this anymore.' But when I saw him in Vegas, he was in a pretty good mood. He was grinding and playing some golf. It just looked like Curtis."

In November, *Golf World* came out with a cover that had Strange's picture on it and the caption "I will prove people wrong." *Golf Magazine* came out with a first-person story by its playing editor that had the headline "I'm Not Through." Strange would not be interviewed by *SI*. He told Jaime Diaz at the Shark Shootout it was just on principle.

Strange also told Diaz that he had returned to swing instructor Jimmy Ballard, the man who had helped him win all those titles in the '80s. He said the old feeling came back within thirty minutes.

"I don't think this changes him at all," said Strange's twin brother, Allen. "I think he's been pretty stubborn about it. I don't think it changes his practice habits or his desire or his ambition at all. God forbid all his past accomplishments are forgotten because of one match. Thank goodness he's been awfully successful over the years. The Ryder Cup can't destroy that. Does it change him? Probably. It may motivate him, but I don't think it changes his attitude about his life or his career. He can be a pretty hard and coarse son of a gun when he needs to be."

The week after the Ryder Cup, Loren Roberts went to the Buick Challenge at Callaway Gardens in Pine Mountain, Georgia. He didn't really want to be there, not after Oak Hill, and neither did his caddy, Dan Stojak, who had asked for the week off in advance of the event.

Roberts picked up Russ Steib as a temporary caddy in the

parking lot at Callaway Gardens, but he kept hearing these rumors about Stojak that he didn't like. The other caddies were saying that Stojak had placed a $1,000 bet in Las Vegas on the Ryder Cup. A bet on the Europeans.

It bothered Roberts enough that he called Stojak. Stojak admitted to Roberts that he had placed the bet, then denied it later to *Sports Illustrated*. "It really broke my heart," Roberts said at the Texas Open. "I'm still friends with Dan, but he put me in a position where I couldn't do anything but let him go. It was really an unfortunate thing, because it really hurt my feelings. Not only do I consider him a good caddy, but I really consider him a friend. Obviously I know he was trying just as hard as I was. It was just the fact he did put me in a tough position. It made me look bad."

It looked even worse for Stojak when Roberts finished second in the Buick Challenge and then third at the Texas Open. It was Stojak who nicknamed the smooth-putting Roberts "Boss of the Moss." They had been together since 1988, winning the Nestlé Invitational back-to-back in 1994 and 1995, and losing a U.S. Open playoff in 1994.

Roberts brought Stojak back for the Doral-Ryder Open, explaining that it was never intended to be a permanent firing. "The thing really took on a life of its own last year," Roberts said. "We talked about it in the off-season, and we had planned for him to come back in Florida. He's back and everything's fine. Obviously, he and I have done well together. It was an unfortunate situation and I still don't know exactly what happened. But that's old history. He tried as hard as everybody did at the Ryder Cup. All's forgiven and we'll move on."

Not every gambling story at the Ryder Cup turned out bad. Walton was the only player to be paid for his efforts. Before leaving Dublin, he put down £1,000 on the Europeans in a better-shot at 5–2 odds.

And Malcolm Mason, who works for Sam Torrance, and Eric Schwarz, who works for Corey Pavin, made a $100 bet at the Canon European Masters in Switzerland.

"Right afterwards, when we were in the caddy room, I had the hundred-dollar bill waiting," Schwarz said. "You know, fast pay makes fast friends. Of course, he wanted me to sign it. He started yelling. 'Look at this! Look at this!'"

Bernard Gallacher went back to the professional's shop at Wentworth Club, Virginia Water, Surrey, England, and was vindicated. He had suddenly become a hero, but in the mind of the team, he had always been an able captain. "Bernard has always made good decisions," Sam Torrance said at the Sarazen World Open near Atlanta in late October. "He has the heart of a lion."

Said Mark James, "Bernard has never deserved the stick he was getting. You have wallies like Jacklin sticking their nose in, and we didn't need it. Bernard's a fair guy. If he doesn't like you, he'll probably tell you. In my estimation, Bernard has always been a very good captain. In 1991, it was really his captaincy that gave us a chance. Without him shuffling the pairings around, we wouldn't have been in a position where Langer could have nearly scraped a halve for us."

Bernard Gallacher appreciated the support, but he wasn't going to be talked into another term. He liked playing his Saturday golf with the members.

Lee Janzen went to the Dunhill Cup at St. Andrews with a chance to prove what a strong match-play player he was—and essentially prove Wadkins wrong in his wild-card decision. Standing on the eighteenth tee in his opening-round match against Darren Clark of Ireland, Janzen pumped one out of bounds that bounced off the blacktop on Golf Road and into the parking lot of Rusack's Hotel. In his second-round match against Per-Ulrik Johansson of Sweden, Janzen birdied eighteen to stay alive, but lost to a birdie on the first hole of a playoff. In his final match, Janzen lost to Rick Gibson of Canada. He went 0–3, the same record as Strange. So much for his vindication.

*   *   *

On November 1, the day after Nick Faldo attended a Celine Dion concert at London's Wembley Arena with his wife, Gill, and children, Natalie, nine, and Matthew, six, he packed his bags and bolted from the family's $4.5 million mansion in Windlesham, Surrey. The *Sun* also reported details of Faldo's relationship with Brenna Cepelak, a twenty-year-old golfer on the University of Arizona women's golf team. Cepelak had met Faldo in January at the Northern Telecom Open in Tucson, and they had been seeing each other in the months since. *People* also reported that Faldo had been in Tucson the week before the Ryder Cup matches. The *Sun* said that while in Arizona for that tryst, Faldo had attended a University of Arizona football game wearing a pair of dark glasses.

It made for scandalous tabloid headlines such as "Faldo Seduced Me Like a True English Gent" and "No Sex Till Third Date." When Faldo played in the Tour Championship at Southern Hills Country Club, he was accompanied by a bodyguard. On campus at Arizona, Cepelak was dodging the paparazzi, riding to class in the trunk of her roommate's car. Photographers had to be chased from her garage and classroom.

So it was all true, after all.

Faldo had played the Ryder Cup, had beaten Curtis Strange, knowing his marriage would probably end, knowing Gill would want at least £11 million out of him, knowing that he would be leaving not only his wife but his children.

"Nick's just an amazingly focused person," Gallacher said. "If I had one player on the team who I wanted to make a fourfoot putt for me, I'd want Nick. It was a difficult week for him, and quite a number of people. Gill was terrific on the course. It was a terrific professional performance by both of them."

*   *   *

On November 29, the PGA of America officially named Tom Kite as its 1997 U.S. Ryder Cup captain. Kite will go to Valderrama with all the credentials. He has won a U.S. Open. He has a 15-9-4 Ryder Cup record. And he knows today's players.

It was that last element that separated him from Larry Nelson, the two-time PGA champion who will turn fifty three weeks prior to the thirty-second meeting of the Ryder Cup in Spain. That knocked Nelson out of the running, since he will play the Senior Tour full-time. Kite could sympathize with him. "There are more qualified captains than there are Ryder Cups," he said.

Kite knows that since the 1983 Ryder Cup at PGA National, Europe has won three times and the United States three times, and there has been one tie. He also knows the European team leads in overall points, 100–96. Kite, who has a 5-0-2 singles record and is the second all-time leading money winner in PGA Tour history, knows that Valderrama will be a tough venue, and that bringing the Cup back home from Spain will be one of the greatest challenges in his career.

When he walked into PGA of America headquarters in Palm Beach Gardens, Florida, the day before his news conference, Julius Mason, the PGA's director of public relations and media relations, pointed to an empty trophy case in the lobby. It was the trophy case that had housed the Ryder Cup from 1991 to 1995.

"Your job is to bring it back," Mason said.

Kite just grinned.

"That's what I'm here for," he said.

AFTERWORD
by Brad Faxon

As a youngster growing up at Rhode Island Country Club I often would hit putts on the practice green adjacent to the first tee. Many of these putts would be to win the U.S. Open in a playoff over Jack Nicklaus or to surge ahead of Tom Watson at the Masters. On the cool, windy days with a northerly blowing by Narragansett Bay these putts often would be to secure the British Open Trophy over Seve Ballesteros.

Never once can I remember having a seven-footer to reach the Ryder Cup. Although one can trace the Ryder Cup's history back to New England's Worcester Country Club in 1927 it has only recently become a tournament of tremendous proportion. The United States's early domination of the Cup kept the biannual event from capturing front page news. In 1979 the Europeans were allowed to join Great Britain and Ireland, and they subsequently won the cup in 1985, at the Belfry, and then for the first time on American soil in 1987, ironically, with Jack Nicklaus captaining the American team at his own Muirfield Village in Ohio.

No tournament ever developed with such rapid fervor. This "friendly golfing match" has evolved into a "battle" and the "war." Media attention spans the entire year of the event and all over the golfing globe. Suddenly every U.S. PGA Tour player wants to qualify and participate in what many people call the Olympics of Golf. My own qualification on the '95 Team wasn't solidified until the final day of the final PGA event on the points list: The PGA Championship. My final round sixty-three at the famed Riviera Country Club was not only the best round I have ever played, but it came at the ultimate crunch time.

Attaining a goal is always self-satisfying, but realizing a dream that's shared by so many others is overwhelming. One of the first questions anyone asked was, "Would you like to have a putt to win or lose the Ryder Cup?" Mindlessly, I answered yes, no problem. It was then I started imagining all kinds of scenarios.

It was about this time that Tim Rosaforte congratulated me and added that he was writing a book on the '95 Ryder Cup matches. I was not only impressed that a *Sports Illustrated* writer would be writing such a book, but that it was an individual the players knew could be trusted. Journalism in sports has become a hot issue among many athletes. Stories are reported that stray outside the boundaries of sport, which are often very critical of athletes on and off the playing field.

It's the memories of spending a week with twelve players and their wives, including Captain Lanny Wadkins and his wife, Peni . . . of having Ben Crenshaw and Curtis Strange watch you in a practice round—that couldn't be shared with just any writer. Many writers could have undertaken a book about a week at the Ryder Cup, but I don't think that all the players would have been as open and honest as they were with Tim Rosaforte. Tim's been out on the tour for a while, he's written for several different golf magazines, and he's established a trust among the players. To me, that's important if you want the inside story of what it was really like at Oak Hill. I think that this book does just that.

Barrington, Rhode Island
January 4, 1996

AFTERWORD
by Corey Pavin

The pressure you feel at the Ryder Cup is unlike any pressure I have ever felt, including that of the last shot on the last day of the U.S. Open. At the 1993 Ryder Cup at the Belfry, when I was about to hit the first shot of the competition, I didn't really think much about it until the announcer said, "The United States has the honor." Then I really got nervous. As I teed the ball up, I remember being very worried about placing the ball on the tee because my hands were shaking so much. I got a quarter inch above the tee and nearly dropped the ball. That's how much the Ryder Cup means to me and how much pressure there is in the Ryder Cup. Thank goodness I got up there and hit a really good drive.

The Ryder Cup is such a great competition, but it had gotten away from that. I think the last two years, 1993 and 1995, were back to the way the Ryder Cup should be. The players were out there playing hard, there were no incidents of poor sportsmanship, and the fans were well behaved. It was what Sam Ryder wanted when he invented the Ryder Cup. He wanted guys to go out there and play hard, play for their country—and may the best team win.

There're some vivid memories I'll take away from the three Ryder Cups I played in. I'll always remember the shot I played out of the bunker at Kiawah in 1991, on the seventeenth hole, to win my first Ryder Cup point. I'll always remember watching Hale Irwin and Bernhard Langer play the last couple of holes that year, and how nervous I was and how helpless I felt watching. It gave me great appreciation for all of our wives out there on tour, having to watch us play and not being able to do anything about it. I remember turning to Shannon and saying, "I don't know how you do this all the time. This is so nerve wracking." It's a situation that the players aren't in very often. It was new ground for me.

In 1993 I'll always remember Davis Love's putt on the eighteenth green to keep the cup in our possession and guarantee the tie. This last Ryder Cup had a lot of neat moments in it for everyone. For me, it seemed like every match was pretty exciting, from Tom Lehman hitting the great shot on eighteen Friday morning to help us beat Colin Montgomerie and Nick Faldo. And of course my chip-in on Saturday afternoon was exhilarating, but I also enjoyed watching the matches finish on Sunday. Obviously, some of them didn't turn out the way we wanted them to, but the thing that came out of 1995 was that both teams tried their best, gave it their all, and the competition was fantastic. I think we all walked away from there thinking of it as an experience we would carry around for the rest of our lives.

I remember trying to put it in perspective for Brad Faxon, who was pretty upset. Specifically, I asked him, about the last putt, if he read it correctly, if he was totally decisive on the putt he wanted to hit, and if he hit it where he wanted to hit it. The thing about Brad's putt is, it just didn't go in. He did everything from a routine standpoint and execution standpoint perfectly. He did everything he could do mentally and physically to succeed and it just didn't happen. I told him the execution and the routine were more important in that case than succeeding. That's the perspective I wanted him to have. He just had to swallow hard and accept it.

The 1997 Ryder Cup is going to be even more interesting to all the fans and the players than Oak Hill. Since we did not win this time, we'll be even more motivated to win at Valderrama. I certainly hope to be part of the team. That's my goal, to be on the 1997 Ryder Cup team, because I want to be on the team that brings the cup back to the United States.

Orlando, Florida
January 27, 1996

APPENDIX

Match 1

Corey Pavin and Tom Lehman (U.S.) defeated Nick Faldo and Colin Montgomerie (Europe), one up.

Comment: The first match turned out to be a classic. Pavin and Lehman went four up after five, but were only one up at the turn and had to hang on for a one-up victory. In the rain, Lehman hit a 5-iron into the eighteenth green and made a four-footer to win the match.

Match 2

Sam Torrance and Costantino Rocca (Europe) defeated Fred Couples and Jay Haas (U.S.), 3 and 2.

Comment: Couples and Haas never jelled, losing five holes in a six-hole stretch. Rocca hadn't teamed with Torrance in practice until Thursday afternoon, but Gallacher played a hunch and it panned out.

Match 3

Davis Love III and Jeff Maggert (U.S.) defeated Howard Clark and Mark James (Europe), 4 and 3.

Comment: A surprise pairing by Wadkins paid off. The Americans started out birdie-par-birdie, were four up at the turn, and didn't lose a hole until the thirteenth. By then it was over.

Match 4

Per-Ulrik Johansson and Bernhard Langer (Europe) defeated Ben Crenshaw and Curtis Strange (U.S.), one up.

Comment: Langer made a fifty-footer for birdie at the ninth to gain the momentum. The U.S. pulled even at the seventeenth, but lost at eighteen when Crenshaw's drive drifted into the right rough and Johansson caught a break when his drive hit a tree and came down on a good lie. The Europeans scrambled for a par, with Langer getting retribution for his Kiawah putt by winning the match with a four-footer.

Friday-Morning Results
U.S. 2, Europe 2

Friday-Afternoon Four-Balls

Match 5

Seve Ballesteros and David Gilford (Europe) defeated Brad Faxon and Peter Jacobsen (U.S.), 4 and 3.

Comment: The match swung in Europe's favor on the seventh green, when Jacobsen mistakenly picked up a four-foot putt, not realizing his partner had just made a putt for bogey, not par. The U.S. team did not win another hole as Gilford emerged as an unlikely hero. It turned out to be Europe's only point of the afternoon.

Match 6

Jeff Maggert and Loren Roberts (U.S.) defeated Costantino Rocca and Sam Torrance (Europe), 6 and 5.

Comment: Wadkins gambled by putting two Ryder Cup rookies together, but Maggert and Roberts played like Nicklaus and Palmer. Roberts hit the shot of the afternoon, chipping in at the ninth for birdie with one foot in the bunker and the other foot in the rough. He was four under through thirteen holes.

Match 7

Fred Couples and Davis Love III (U.S.) defeated Nick Faldo and Colin Montgomerie (Europe), 3 and 2.

Comment: Many people were wondering why Wadkins didn't play Couples and Love in the morning, since they were three-time World Cup champions. This was the second loss of the day for Faldo and Montgomerie, Europe's best team. They didn't make a birdie until the twelfth hole.

Match 8

Corey Pavin and Phil Mickelson (U.S.) defeated Bernhard Langer and Per-Ulrik Johansson (Europe), 6 and 4.

Comment: This turned out to be an admitted mistake by Gallacher. He figured Langer and Johansson were going to close out Crenshaw and Strange early. When the match went the distance, it sapped the Europeans. Mickelson was fresh and Pavin proved to be the perfect partner as the U.S. won the first four holes and coasted to an easy win.

FRIDAY-AFTERNOON RESULTS
U.S. 3, EUROPE 1
SUMMARY
U.S. 5, EUROPE 3

SATURDAY-MORNING FOURSOMES

Match 9
Nick Faldo and Colin Montgomerie (Europe) defeated Curtis Strange and Jay Haas, 4 and 2.

Comment: Former Wake Forest teammates Strange and Haas were undefeated in Walker Cup play and won a Ryder Cup match at PGA National in 1983. But they only won one hole and went 0–2 for the matches. Faldo and Montgomerie snapped their shutout, but didn't play particularly well. The Americans were six over when the match ended at the sixteenth.

Match 10
Costantino Rocca and Sam Torrance (Europe) defeated Davis Love III and Jeff Maggert (U.S.), 6 and 5.

Comment: The Europeans won the first three holes and then Rocca made his hole in one at the sixth. After winning their debut against Clark and James, the U.S. team were overwhelmed by the Rock of Italy.

Match 11
Loren Roberts and Peter Jacobsen (U.S.) defeated Ian Woosnam and Philip Walton (Europe), one up.

Comment: The must-have match for the Americans. Jacobsen wanted retribution after Friday's mental error at the seventh. He had a chance to be the hero by making the match-winning putt at the eighteenth and responded to give the U.S. team its only point of the morning.

Match 12

Bernhard Langer and Philip Walton (Europe) defeated Corey Pavin and Tom Lehman (U.S.), 4 and 3.

Comment: The U.S. team that had been so strong on Friday just didn't have it working. Gilford played as well with Langer as he did with Ballesteros. Langer made the big shot, chipping in at the twelfth.

Saturday-Morning Results
Europe 3, U.S. 1
Summary
Europe 6, U.S. 6

Saturday-Afternoon Four-Balls

Match 13

Fred Couples and Brad Faxon (U.S.) defeated Colin Montgomerie and Sam Torrance (Europe), 4 and 2.

Comment: Wadkins didn't play Couples and Love together, but it worked out here. Faxon made birdies at the tenth and eleventh, Couples did the same at the twelfth and the thirteenth, and the U.S. team closed out the match at the sixteenth. This dropped Monty's record to 1–3.

Match 14

Ian Woosnam and Costantino Rocca (Europe) defeated Davis Love III and Ben Crenshaw (U.S.), 3 and 2.

Comment: A flat pairing for Wadkins. Love made the team's only birdie. Crenshaw's putting problems continued. Rocca was spectacular once again, and Woosnam improved his four-balls record to 9-3-1.

Match 15

Jay Haas and Phil Mickelson (U.S.) defeated Seve Ballesteros and David Gilford (Europe), 3 and 2.

Comment: The magic finally rubbed off Gilford. Ballesteros was at his all-time Ryder Cup worst, spraying shots everywhere. Haas avoided going 0–3 with birdies at the second and third holes. Mickelson, the rookie, was 2–0.

Match 16

Corey Pavin and Loren Roberts (U.S.) defeated Nick Faldo and Bernhard Langer (Europe), one up.

Comment: Maybe the match of the week, certainly the most spectacular ending. Faldo and Langer had seven major championships between them, but they couldn't get past the Ryder Cup rookie (Roberts) and the Gritty Little Bruin (Pavin). It ended with Pavin chipping in for birdie at the eighteenth and Faldo missing a putt for the halve.

SATURDAY-AFTERNOON RESULTS
U.S. 3, EUROPE 1
SUMMARY
U.S. 9, EUROPE 7

SUNDAY SINGLES

Match 17

Tom Lehman (U.S.) defeated Seve Ballesteros (Europe), 4 and 3.

Comment: Wadkins needed Lehman to get a point early. The match is best remembered for Lehman not losing his cool when Ballesteros kept saving pars. At the twelfth green, Seve asked Tom to keep his ball marker down as a reference point, which led to a minor rules controversy. Not even that could fluster Lehman.

Match 18

Howard Clark (Europe) defeated Peter Jacobsen (U.S.), one up.

Comment: The first of five singles matches that would go to the eighteenth. Clark threw everything he had at Jacobsen, chipping in to save par at the second, making a hole in one at the eleventh, and finally sinking a downhill four-footer at eighteen to win the match. Jacobsen went one up four times, but Clark always came back to halve the match the next hole. It was Clark's first Ryder Cup singles match since Tom Kite spanked him 8 and 7 at the Belfry in 1989.

Match 19

Mark James (Europe) defeated Jeff Maggert (U.S.), 4 and 3.

Comment: Maggert won his first two matches on Friday, but didn't have it on the weekend. James had gone 1-4-1 in Ryder Cup singles, but spent all day Saturday practicing, and it paid off. He birdied the second, holed out from the sand for a birdie at the fourth, and was three up after five. Maggert could never climb out of that hole.

Match 20

Fred Couples (U.S.) halved Ian Woosnam (Europe).

Comment: They played a singles match at the Belfry in 1993, and Woosnam made a knee-knocker on the last green to halve the match. This time it was Couples put in that situation, and after putting poorly all day he birdied seventeen and saved par at eighteen to get a half point for the U.S.

Match 21

Davis Love III (U.S.) defeated Costantino Rocca (Europe), 3 and 2.

Comment: Another rematch from the Belfry, with the same result. After a disappointing Saturday, Love made five birdies in a nine-hole stretch. The Italian birdied the thirteenth and had a chance at the fifteenth, but when he missed a birdie putt at the par three, Rocca was dormie. Love's birdie putt at the sixteenth—his sixth of the day—closed Rocca out.

Match 22

David Gilford (Europe) defeated Brad Faxon (U.S.), one up.

Comment: One of the pivotal matches. Gilford took the lead with a par at the fourteenth, then made a four-footer at seventeen to stay one up going to the last. At eighteen, Gilford blew a 5-wood over the green, but Faxon pulled a 5-iron into the left front bunker. Gilford chunked his first chip, but made a twelve-footer to save bogey. Faxon, the last U.S. player to qualify for the team, almost holed from the sand, but missed a seven-footer coming back.

Match 23
Colin Montgomerie (Europe) defeated Ben Crenshaw (U.S.), 3 and 1.

Comment: Crenshaw, the Masters champion, could still not buy a putt, but was level through twelve. Montgomerie finished 3-3-3-3, going birdie, par, birdie, birdie starting at the fourteenth. It left Crenshaw 0–3 for the week and dropped his Ryder Cup record to 3-8-1.

Match 24
Nick Faldo (Europe) defeated Curtis Strange (U.S.), one up.

Comment: The backbreaker for the U.S. Strange could have won with a par at the sixteenth, but failed to hit the green with a 6-iron. The two-time U.S. Open champion finished bogey-bogey-bogey. Faldo pulled even with a par save at the seventeenth, then won the match with "a four to remember" at eighteen.

Match 25
Sam Torrance (Europe) defeated Loren Roberts (U.S.), 2 and 1.

Comment: This wasn't the same Loren Roberts that went 3–0 in his first three Ryder Cup matches. He turned in three-over 38 and was two down to Torrance, who had a spotty 1-3-3 Ryder Cup singles record. Roberts got it to one down, but a birdie at the sixteenth by Torrance put him away.

Match 26
Corey Pavin (U.S.) defeated Bernhard Langer (Europe), 3 and 2.

Comment: The fourth time Pavin and Langer met in this Ryder Cup. For the third time, it was Pavin getting the point. Langer birdied the ninth and was one down at the turn, but Pavin went back to two up with a curling birdie putt at the twelfth and closed it out with a par at the sixteenth.

Match 27

Philip Walton (Europe) defeated Jay Haas (U.S.), one up.

Comment: Haas was dormie, but holed out a sand shot at the sixteenth and scraped out a win at the seventeenth when Walton missed a short putt. With the honors on the eighteenth tee, Haas popped up his drive into the left trees, had to lay up, then spun a wedge shot back off the green. Walton never saw the fairway, but just had to two-putt for bogey to halve the hole, win the match, and clinch the Cup.

Match 28

Phil Mickelson (U.S.) defeated Per-Ulrik Johansson (Europe), 2 and 1.

Comment: Two rookies put in a situation where they could determine the outcome, but their match turned out to be meaningless. Johansson birdied the second, third, fourth, and sixth holes to go three up. Mickelson rallied and went one up with his third straight birdie at the twelfth. The match ended at the seventeenth when the news came from eighteen that Walton had won the Cup for Europe. The win made Mickelson only the thirteenth player in U.S. Ryder Cup history to go unbeaten and untied.

Sunday Singles Results
Europe 7½, U.S. 4½

Final Summary
Europe 14½, U.S. 13½

Hole	Par	Yardage	Hole	Par	Yardage
1	4	440	10	4	429
2	4	401	11	3	192
3	3	202	12	4	372
4	5	570	13	5	598
5	4	406	14	4	323
6	3	167	15	3	184
7	4	431	16	4	439
8	4	426	17	4	458
9	4	419	18	4	445
Out	**35**	**3,462**	**In**	**35**	**3,440**
			TOTAL	**70**	**6,902**